World History II

Robert Taggart

JWW472 v1.0

POWER BASICS®

Senior Author .... Robert Taggart

Editorial Director .... Susan Blair

Project Manager/Senior Production Editor .... Maggie Jones

Project Editor .... Erica Varney

Director of Marketing .... Jeff Taplin

Interior Design .... Mark Sayer

Cover Design .... Roman Laszok

Typesetting .... Sheila Russell
Mark Sayer
Ian Weidner

Editorial Staff .... Elizabeth Lynch
Richard Lynch
Holly Moirs
Kate O'Halloran
Mary Rich
Kathy Sammis

ISBN 978-0-8251-5688-5

J. Weston Walch, Publisher
10200 Jefferson Blvd. | Culver City, CA 90232
www.socialstudies.com/walch
Printed in the United States of America

Table of Contents

Table of Contents

To the Student

Welcome to *Power Basics® World History II.* This book will teach you about the key people, places, and events in the history of the world from the end of the Middle Ages to the late 1800s. You will also learn about how these elements of history continue to affect societies around the world today.

Unit 1: A Rebirth in Europe introduces the changes that marked the end of the medieval period in Europe and the start of the Renaissance. You will learn how changes in farming and the growth in trade led to new social systems, national structures, and approaches to religion. You will also learn about some of the great thinkers and artists of the Renaissance period.

Unit 2: Asia's Empires discusses the strong cultures that arose in Japan, China, and India. You will read about the Qing and Ming dynasties in China and the Mogul empire in India. You will also read about the feudal period in Japan under the shoguns and the closing of Japan to outsiders.

Unit 3: European Exploration and the New World discusses the meeting of East and West brought about by European interest in Asian spices and other goods. You will learn about the search for new trade routes that led Columbus to the Americas. And you will read about the European drive to explore, seize, and colonize these new lands.

Unit 4: Europe Colonizes the Globe discusses the results of European exploration, including the rise of European trading economies and the response of China and Japan to European attempts to trade with them. You will read about Britain's role in India after the fall of the Mogul Empire, and the effects of European expansion in Africa, including the slave trade.

Unit 5: New Ideas Lead to Revolution introduces the Enlightenment, a period of new ideas in many areas. You will read how these ideas helped inspire revolutions around the world, including in the American colonies, in France, and in Latin America. You will also learn about the governments that followed the revolutions.

To the Student, *continued*

Unit 6: The Industrial Revolution describes the series of developments that led to industrialization, first in Britain and then in other countries. It addresses the changes in society that came about as a result of industrialization.

Unit 7: Nationalism and Social Reform discusses two of the major movements of the nineteenth century. You will see how the social evils of the Industrial Revolution led to different approaches to helping workers achieve fair treatment. You will learn about the growing sense of national identity in Europe and the drive for expansion in the United States. You will also learn about the struggle to end slavery in the United States, and to give women the right to vote.

Unit 8: Imperialism discusses the way European powers built empires around the world, including in Africa and southern Asia. You will read about the different ways these powers used to take control of other countries and how the conquered nations responded to colonization. You will also read about Japan's reopening to the West.

Power Basics® World History II has many special features that make learning easier. "Tips" give you hints on ways to master the ideas and facts in the text. "In Real Life" sections give you examples of real-life events and people that will help you relate to the information you are learning. "Think About It" questions ask you to look at information in new ways. And the "Words to Know" section at the start of each lesson includes important new terms introduced in the lesson. The words are defined in the Glossary at the end of the book. Finally, the appendixes at the back of the book include further useful information.

As you move through *Power Basics® World History II,* you will become more informed about world history and you will understand its effects on the world we live in today. We hope that you enjoy this material as you learn.

UNIT 1

A Rebirth in Europe

LESSON 1: The Renaissance

GOAL: To explain how the Renaissance replaced the Middle Ages; to discuss key Renaissance ideas and individuals

WORDS TO KNOW

Book of Songs

ceiling of the Sistine Chapel

courtiers

courts

Dark Ages

David

The Decameron

feudalism

"the first humanists"

humanism

Italian Renaissance

The Last Supper

manorialism

Mona Lisa

notebooks

Renaissance

Roman Catholic Church

The School of Athens

theology

NAMES TO KNOW

Giovanni Boccaccio

Leonardo da Vinci

Donatello

Giotto

Lorenzo the Magnificent

Cosimo de' Medici

Giovanni de' Medici

Medicis

Michelangelo

Petrarch

Raphael

William Shakespeare

The Middle Ages

The Middle Ages in Europe lasted about 1,000 years, from about 500 C.E. to about 1500 C.E. The term "Middle Ages" also refers to what happened in Western Europe during this time.

It is important to remember four key things about the Middle Ages: feudalism, manorialism, the role of the church, and the lack of learning. Why are these four so important? As you read this book, you will see how each of these things changed. Let's review each of them now.

Feudalism was the system of government during most of the 1,000-year period of the Middle Ages. Nobles who were loyal to kings fought as knights. In exchange for their loyalty, they were given pieces of land called fiefs to rule.

Most fiefs included several manors, or large farms. On the manors, serfs, or poor peasants bound to the manor, lived short, hard lives. A typical manor included a large manor house where a noble lived. In contrast, the serfs lived in a tiny, rude village. Most of the rest of the manor consisted of farm fields and forest. Each manor was mostly self-sufficient. This economic system, based on the manor, was called **manorialism.**

For nobles and peasants alike, the Church played a central role in life during the Middle Ages. Virtually every European was a member of the **Roman Catholic Church.** The Church was therefore very powerful. During the Middle Ages, it had enormous social, financial, and even military influence.

The Middle Ages are sometimes called the **Dark Ages,** although this term mostly refers to the time between 500 and 1000 C.E. This is because life was hard and there was little learning. Very few people could read or write. Fewer still really understood the forces that were controlling their lives. There were few towns, and travel between them was dangerous. An epidemic called the Black Death (the bubonic plague) killed countless numbers of people. Bathing was often difficult. No one understood the value of sanitation. In short, for almost everyone in Europe, life in the Middle Ages was short, hard, dangerous, and filled with ignorance.

But, toward the end of the Middle Ages, things began to change. This was especially true of the systems of feudalism and manorialism. Trade, which had almost ceased to exist for much of the Middle Ages, began to increase. With the increase in trade, marketplaces and the cities built around them began to grow. As more people made their living in towns, manorialism became less common. Feudalism, which depended on manors and fiefs, also began to decline in importance. Where a patchwork of hundreds of small kingdoms once stood, a few larger kingdoms took over. The nations of England and France, for example, began to take their modern form.

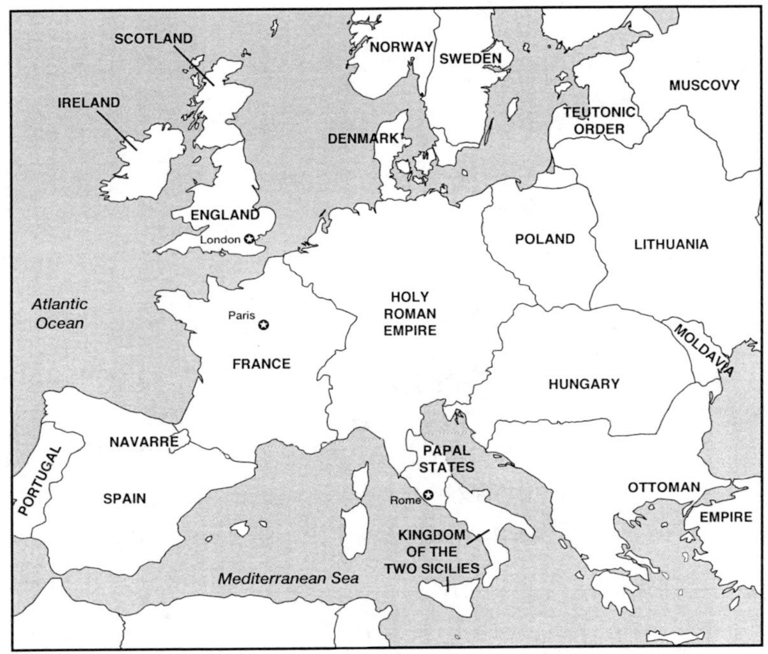

Europe in 1500

It is important to remember that these changes took place gradually. And, they took place in some areas before others. In some areas of Europe, the change from manorialism to a town-and-trade economy took hundreds of years. In other, smaller areas, the change occurred more quickly, even within one person's lifetime.

So, two things that marked the Middle Ages—feudalism and manorialism—slowly began to change. Eventually, life in Europe was completely different. At this point, we say that the Middle Ages were over. The Middle Ages ended in about 1500. A new era had begun. During this new era, the two other characteristics of the Middle Ages—the powerful role of the Church and widespread ignorance—began to change as well. In fact, there were so many important and interesting changes in European life after the Middle Ages that this entire unit is devoted to this new era.

■ PRACTICE 1: The Middle Ages

Check each statement below that is TRUE.

☐ **1.** Feudalism was a characteristic of the Middle Ages.

☐ **2.** During the Middle Ages, most people were well educated.

☐ **3.** The Roman Catholic Church was very powerful during the Middle Ages.

☐ **4.** The economic system of the Middle Ages was called manorialism.

The End of the Middle Ages

You have read that the Middle Ages in Europe ended in about 1500. Notice how the word *about* is used. This is important. It tells you that the Middle Ages did not end at a particular time. Remember, the ending of the Middle Ages was a gradual process. It slowly gave way to a new era over many years. You will begin to read about this new era shortly.

By about 1500, most of the things we associate with the Middle Ages, such as feudalism and manorialism, either had changed or were on their way toward ending. In some parts of Europe, the whole system had disappeared. In other parts, things were just beginning to change.

Of course, the people who lived in the Middle Ages didn't realize this. To begin with, not a single one of them thought, "I am living during the Middle Ages." They could have no idea that they were living in the "middle," between the ancient world and the modern world. The Middle Ages is just a name historians have given to the period. Likewise, the people who lived toward the end of the Middle Ages didn't know the world was changing forever. Remember, the change happened slowly.

Nevertheless, historians like things neat and orderly. To help you and other students of history, they have tried to give certain dates to signify the end of the Middle Ages.

One date that is used for the end of the Middle Ages is one you may already know: 1492. In that year, Christopher Columbus sailed to the "New World" of North America. Since this marked the beginning of many changes in European life, it is a good date for marking the end of the Middle Ages.

TIP

> You can't possibly remember every date and name you read in this book. But, there are some tricks that will help you remember many of them. For example, here's a rhyme that will help you remember the date 1492:
>
> *Columbus sailed the ocean blue*
>
> *in fourteen-hundred and ninety-two.*
>
> Try to make up little rhymes like this for other important dates. They will help jog your memory about a date and why that date is important.

Another date that historians use to mark the end of the Middle Ages is 1453. In 1453, the Muslim Ottoman Empire conquered the Christian Byzantine city of Constantinople. Constantinople was the great capital of the Byzantine Empire throughout the Middle Ages. So, its fall serves as a good symbol to mark the end of the Middle Ages.

A third date that some historians think marks the end of the Middle Ages is 1455. By 1455, a German, Johannes Gutenberg, had developed a new system for printing. This new system meant books could be printed much more quickly and easily. With this system of printing came the widespread communication of ideas—ideas that would change history. Remember how one of the marks that distinguish the Middle Ages was ignorance and a lack of learning? That began to change with the development of printing. This is why 1455 is considered by some to be the end of the Middle Ages.

None of these dates actually marks the end of the Middle Ages. The year 1492 marks a change in geography. The year 1453 marks a change in government. The year 1455 marks a change in learning. All of these changes, and many more, mark the end of the Middle Ages. So, remember the end of the Middle Ages as at about 1500.

PRACTICE 2: The End of the Middle Ages

Circle the letter of the correct answer to each of the following questions.

1. In what year did Columbus sail to North America?
   - a. 1492
   - b. 1453
   - c. 1455
   - d. 1500

2. In what year was Constantinople conquered by the Ottoman Empire?
   - a. 1492
   - b. 1453
   - c. 1455
   - d. 1500

3. In what year did Gutenberg finish developing a new system of printing?
   - a. 1492
   - b. 1453
   - c. 1455
   - d. 1500

The Renaissance

The era of European history that came after the Middle Ages is called the **Renaissance.**

Just as the Middle Ages ended gradually, the Renaissance developed gradually. In fact, the two periods overlapped. So, it is most proper to say that the Renaissance slowly replaced the Middle Ages instead of saying that the Middle Ages ended and the Renaissance began.

The Renaissance lasted for about 300 years. It began toward the end of the Middle Ages, around 1300, and continued until about 1600.

So, what exactly was the Renaissance? The answer lies in the name itself. The word *renaissance* comes from an old Latin word that means "to be reborn." During the Renaissance, educated people paid new attention to the great scholarly and artistic accomplishments of ancient Greece and

Rome. They wanted to recapture the greatness of the world before the Middle Ages. So, the Renaissance was a "rebirth," or revival, of ancient ideas.

These ideas were not just "reborn" and repeated. The European leaders of the Renaissance built their own ideas on the ancient ones. They studied these ideas and applied them to their own time, but they also modified and extended them. They made ancient ideas their own. And, they tried to correct ancient ideas that were wrong. Their hope was to create a new age by returning to the art, philosophy, literature, history, and science of the ancients. In doing so, they changed the face of Europe and much of the rest of the world. This is why the Renaissance is so important.

So, remember that the Renaissance was a great cultural movement, a great period of European history, and a great period of revival in learning.

IN REAL LIFE

If anyone ever calls you a "renaissance person," say thank you! Today, people use that term to refer to someone who is intelligent, educated, and—especially—talented in a wide range of fields. So, if you are good at math, fixing cars, child care, and drawing, for example, you can consider yourself a renaissance man or woman! Who else do you know who could be described as a Renaissance man or woman?

PRACTICE 3: The Renaissance

Decide if each statement below is true (**T**) or false (**F**). Write the correct letter on the line before each statement.

_____ **1.** The word *renaissance* means "Middle Ages."

_____ **2.** The Renaissance took place between about 1300 and 1600.

_____ **3.** The Renaissance was a great period of European history and a period of revival in learning.

Humanism

Remember that Christianity and the Roman Catholic Church dominated life in the Middle Ages. The Church touched the life of everyone in Europe at that time. It was a religious, a political, an economic, and a military force.

But, toward the end of the Middle Ages, some people began to question the authority of the Church. Scholars and artists began to look at life in a new way. Instead of concentrating on the Church and religion, they began to concentrate on people and the world. In the Middle Ages, most learned people focused on **theology**, or the study of God. During the Renaissance, more people focused on the study of humanity. Because their focus was on humanity, this outlook is called **humanism.**

Humanism was the most important development of the Renaissance. Humanists came from all areas of intellectual pursuit. Historians, religious leaders, philosophers, artists, political figures, authors—all became humanists. They all began to focus on the human world. They studied and worked in ways that they hoped would improve their understanding of human life and human problems.

TIP

You may come across some unfamiliar words in this book. Learning to take them apart may help you understand and remember them. For example, look at the word *humanism.* You can break this word into a root word, *human,* and a suffix, *-ism.* The suffix *-ism* means "a system of principles or beliefs." If you add the meaning of this suffix to the root word, *human,* you can see that humanism is a belief system focused on humans, or people. The suffix *-ism* is also part of two other words you learned earlier: *feudalism* and *manorialism.*

The great shift from theology to humanism can easily be seen in artwork. Most paintings of the Middle Ages represent ideas about religion. During the Renaissance, however, artists focused on human beings in the human world. These artists were humanists.

When you think about the change from the Middle Ages to the Renaissance, think about this change in artwork. It symbolizes the great change from religious thinking to humanism. This was the key development of the Renaissance.

■ PRACTICE 4: Humanism

Circle the letter of the correct answer to each of the following questions.

1. What is theology?
- **a.** a religion
- **b.** another term for humanism
- **c.** the study of God
- **d.** a style of painting

2. What is humanism?
- **a.** a religion
- **b.** an artistic or a scholarly focus on humanity
- **c.** the study of God
- **d.** a style of painting

3. What was the most important development of the Renaissance?
- **a.** humanism
- **b.** theology
- **c.** art
- **d.** feudalism

The Italian Renaissance

The Renaissance eventually spread throughout Europe, but it started in Italy in the 1300s. This early part of the Renaissance is often called the **Italian Renaissance.**

In the 1300s, Italy was not a single country as it is today. It was made up of about 250 separate city-states. Each city-state was ruled by a major city. Most of these cities were small, with populations of about 10,000 people each. A few were large. For example, the city of Milan had a population of about 100,000 people. Milan ruled the surrounding countryside.

In Italy in the 1300s, whoever controlled a city was very powerful. They ruled the people of the city and the surrounding area. Many cities were controlled by single families. These families built elaborate **courts,** or groups of people associated with their rule. These courts included scholars and artists whom the rulers supported.

In other cities, there was not just one ruling family. Instead, many wealthy and powerful families joined together to form a ruling class. These ruling families also supported artists and scholars.

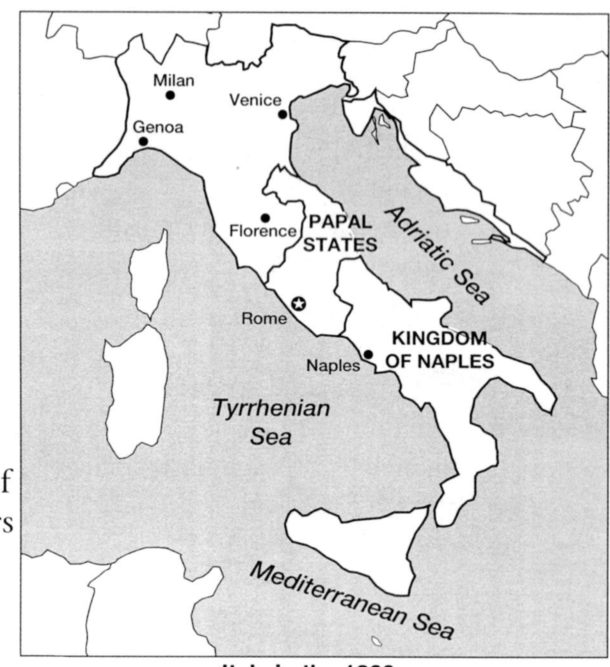

Italy in the 1300s

It was the artists and scholars supported by the rulers of Italy who became the first humanists. Many of the great artists and scholars you will read about were members of the courts in Italy. For this reason, they were called **courtiers.**

Three cities and their courts had special roles in the Italian Renaissance. They were Milan, Venice, and Florence. Of these, Florence is remembered as the greatest city of the Italian Renaissance. In fact, Florence during the Renaissance is thought of as one of the most magical places in history.

IN REAL LIFE

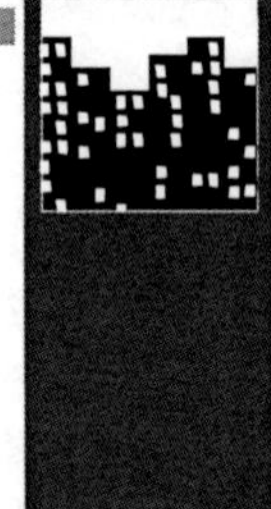

Today, Florence ranks as one of the top tourist destinations in Europe. It is a beautiful city, with many wonderful things to see and do. The main attractions in Florence are nearly 500 years old. What was going on in Florence so long ago? That's right—the Renaissance! People are still drawn to the beautiful art and architecture created during that magical time in history.

■ PRACTICE 5: The Italian Renaissance

Circle the letter of the correct answer to each of the following questions.

1. Where did the Renaissance begin?
   - **a.** Italy
   - **b.** France
   - **c.** Germany
   - **d.** the United States

2. What was the greatest city of the Renaissance?
   - **a.** Milan
   - **b.** Florence
   - **c.** Venice
   - **d.** Rome

3. Who supported the artists and thinkers of the Italian Renaissance?
   - **a.** courtiers
   - **b.** wealthy ruling families
   - **c.** the artists and thinkers themselves
   - **d.** the king of Italy

The Medicis

The Renaissance was a great cultural movement. It took place in such areas as literature, science, and art.

When you read history, you often read about such things as "kingdoms" and "wars." These things—whenever they take place—involve great numbers of people. The Renaissance was different. It involved relatively few of the people who were alive during the time. A few authors, scientists, artists, and others really stand out.

As you read about some of these people, think about how influential they were. It is a rare person who single-handedly changes the way great numbers of people look at their world. The outstanding individuals of the Renaissance accomplished just that.

Some of the most important individuals of the Renaissance all came from the same family. This was the Medici family. As you recall, many of the cities of Italy were ruled by powerful families. The **Medicis** were the most famous ruling family of the Italian Renaissance. The Medicis became prominent in the late 1300s. They ruled the great Renaissance city of Florence for almost 400 continuous years.

The Medicis were extremely wealthy and powerful. They used their influence to expand Florence and to control it. Most important, they used their wealth to support many great Renaissance thinkers and artists. For example, you might have heard of the great artist Michelangelo. Michelangelo was supported by the Medicis.

The first great Medici was **Giovanni de' Medici** (1360–1429). He was the first Medici to become very wealthy. His money, and the money of the rest of the Medicis, came primarily from banking, and also from trade.

Giovanni's son was **Cosimo de' Medici** (1389–1464). By 1434, Cosimo controlled the government of Florence. Even today, Cosimo de' Medici is called "the father of his country." This is because he gave great amounts of money to support the arts and was a strong ruler in Italy.

But the most famous Medici of all was Lorenzo de' Medici, or **Lorenzo the Magnificent** (1449–1492.) Lorenzo was a man of many talents. He was a poet as well as a politician. Under Lorenzo, Florence became the most powerful city-state in all of Italy. It also became one of the most beautiful cities in the world. Even today, many buildings built during Lorenzo's rule attract people to Florence from around the world.

The Medici Chapel in Florence, Italy

There were also other famous Medicis. Two Medici women became queens of France. Two other Medici men became popes.

But the Medicis are best remembered today for their support of the artists, writers, and others who promoted humanism. They were the most important ruling family of the Italian Renaissance.

■ PRACTICE 6: The Medicis

Match each description with a name from the list below. Write the letter of the correct name on the line before each description.

a. Giovanni de' Medici **b.** Cosimo de' Medici **c.** Lorenzo the Magnificent

_____ **1.** the most famous Medici

_____ **2.** the first powerful and wealthy Medici

_____ **3.** also called "the father of his country"

Petrarch and Boccaccio

As you recall, humanism was expressed through art and scholarly work. It was also expressed through literature. Two of the great humanist writers of the Italian Renaissance were **Petrarch** (1304–1374) and **Giovanni Boccaccio** (1313–1375).

Giovanni Boccaccio

Both men, like other humanists of the time, sought out the writings of ancient Rome and Greece. Petrarch rediscovered the works of the great Romans, Cicero and Livy. Their documents had been hidden away in monastery libraries. Without Petrarch's discovery of these documents, we might not know of them today.

Petrarch tried to copy the style of the ancient writings he discovered. His most famous writings are love poems written in a form of poetry called the sonnet. Collected in his ***Book of Songs,*** they speak of human love, and of love for God. These poems—still enjoyed today—inspired such later great writers as William Shakespeare.

Giovanni Boccaccio was a fellow writer and a friend of Petrarch. While Petrarch wrote poetry, Boccaccio wrote in prose. (Prose is the "ordinary" language people use when speaking and writing, as opposed to poetry.) In fact, Boccaccio is considered the first great prose writer of the modern era.

Boccaccio's most famous work is ***The Decameron.*** The word *decameron* comes from the Greek word meaning "ten." *The Decameron* is a collection of 100 stories told by characters over a period of 10 days. The stories give insight into life during this time. They express many ideas about love, conflict, and human personalities.

Petrarch and Boccaccio, together, are sometimes called **"the first humanists."** They stand as symbols of the Renaissance and of humanism. They searched for and read ancient works; they tried to copy them; and, in their own works, they focused on individual people and human problems.

■ PRACTICE 7: Petrarch and Boccaccio

Match each description with a name or term from the list below. Write the letter of the correct name or term on the line before each description.

a. "the first humanists" **b.** Boccaccio **c.** Petrarch

_____ **1.** author of the *Book of Songs*

_____ **2.** author of the *The Decameron*

_____ **3.** a term sometimes used to describe Petrarch and Boccaccio

Giotto and Donatello

Giotto (about 1267–1337) was a painter in Florence. Just as Petrarch and Boccaccio were the first humanist writers, Giotto was the first humanist painter.

As you may remember, painters of the Middle Ages did not paint nature realistically. Their paintings were designed to communicate ideas about God. With Giotto, this changed. He was the first painter of the Renaissance to paint nature as it really appeared.

The painters of the Middle Ages also did not paint human figures realistically. Again, their paintings represented religious ideas. But Giotto painted real, flesh-and-blood human beings. His figures show genuine human emotions. These realistic figures—in realistic natural settings—set a new tone in painting. Giotto's work influenced painters throughout the Renaissance.

Like Giotto, **Donatello** (1386–1466) tried to make his artwork realistic. Donatello was a sculptor. His sculptures portrayed the human body realistically. His most famous sculptures were of David, the hero in the Bible who killed Goliath. The David sculptures show a strong, nude, young man. They were the first nude sculptures made in Europe since before the Middle Ages.

■ PRACTICE 8: Giotto and Donatello

Decide if each statement below is true (**T**) or false (**F**). Write the correct letter on the line before each statement.

_____ **1.** Giotto is famous as the first humanist writer.

_____ **2.** The painters of the Middle Ages did not paint humans realistically.

_____ **3.** Donatello is famous for his realistic paintings.

_____ **4.** Donatello's most famous sculptures were of a biblical hero.

Raphael

Raphael was perhaps the most famous painter of the Renaissance. He lived from 1483 to 1520—just 38 years. But during his short life, he created masterpieces that would influence painters for centuries. His paintings still fill people with a sense of wonder today.

In 1508, the pope summoned Raphael to paint for him. During his time in Rome, Raphael painted his greatest works. He painted many scenes from history, classic Greek and Roman legends, and the Bible. His most famous works are his paintings of the Virgin Mary, such as his *Madonna of the Meadow.*

Raphael's *Madonna of the Meadow*

One painting in particular shows Raphael's humanism. In ***The School of Athens,*** Raphael created a beautiful scene of the leading Greek philosophers and scientists. Plato and Aristotle are at the center of the painting. This choice of subject marks Raphael as a humanist. The realistic portrayal of these figures is also a hallmark of humanist art. Also present in the painting are artists of Raphael's own time. This shows how the painters and other thinkers of the Renaissance were trying to connect the great minds of the ancient world with those of their own time.

■ PRACTICE 9: Raphael

Circle the letter of the correct answer to each of the following questions.

1. What are the subjects of Raphael's most famous paintings?
- **a.** battle scenes
- **b.** the Virgin Mary
- **c.** wealthy nobles
- **d.** Greek and Roman legends

2. How does *The School of Athens* show Raphael's humanism?
- **a.** through its subject (Greek thinkers) and their realistic portrayal
- **b.** through its use of human beings as subjects
- **c.** through its use of color
- **d.** through its portrayal of the Virgin Mary

Michelangelo

For many people, **Michelangelo** stands as the greatest artist of the Renaissance. And for many others, he stands as the greatest artist of all time. Michelangelo lived from 1475 to 1564. He is best remembered for his magnificent marble statues. But he was also an accomplished painter, architect, and even a poet.

Michelangelo studied under Donatello, and was supported by Lorenzo de' Medici. So, he lived and worked at the very heart of the Italian Renaissance.

A true humanist, Michelangelo celebrated the human body in his work. His statues of people are known for their power and grace. Michelangelo is also known for the grandeur of his work. His statues are large, and many of his paintings are huge, elaborate murals.

Michelangelo thought of himself as a sculptor, not a painter. When Pope Julius II asked him to paint the **ceiling of the Sistine Chapel** in the Vatican, he tried to turn down the job. The paintings on this ceiling took three years to complete. They show nine scenes from the Old Testament of the Bible. This ceiling is one of Michelangelo's best-known works.

Detail of "The Creation," on the Ceiling of the Sistine Chapel

Michelangelo's other most famous work is ***David,*** which portrays a character from the Bible. This sculpture still stands in Italy, attracting people from all over the world. It is a beautiful work, celebrating the strength and character of the biblical hero.

In painting and in sculpture, Michelangelo created works that have withstood the test of time. There can be little doubt that centuries from now Michelangelo's work will still fill people with the sense of awe and beauty they did during his lifetime.

■ PRACTICE 10: Michelangelo

Circle the letter of the correct answer to each of the following questions.

1. What are two of Michelangelo's most famous works?
   a. *The School of Athens* and *David*
   b. *David* and the ceiling of the Sistine Chapel
   c. the ceiling of the Sistine Chapel and a portrait of wealthy nobles
   d. *David* and a portrait of the Virgin Mary

2. Who was Michelangelo's teacher?
   a. Lorenzo de' Medici
   b. Raphael
   c. Donatello
   d. Giotto

3. Who supported Michelangelo?
   a. Lorenzo de' Medici
   b. Raphael
   c. Donatello
   d. Giotto

Leonardo da Vinci

Just as the name Michelangelo means "artist" to many people, the name **Leonardo da Vinci** means "genius."

Mona Lisa

You probably are already familiar with one of da Vinci's paintings: the ***Mona Lisa.*** It is perhaps the most famous painting in the world. In it, da Vinci displays the artistic talent that made him one of the greatest of the Renaissance painters. In his careful, realistic painting, he also displays the qualities of humanism.

Another of da Vinci's paintings is perhaps just as famous. This famous work is ***The Last Supper,*** which has been reproduced more than any other painting in history. When people, Christians and non-Christians alike, think about the Last Supper, they usually picture da Vinci's painting. The image captures the moment just after Jesus announced that one of his apostles, or close followers, would betray him. The figures are very human, and each of the apostles shows a different emotional reaction to Jesus's stunning announcement.

If da Vinci were just a great artist, he would still be celebrated as a genius. But his genius went beyond painting. Da Vinci's work influenced art, the study of anatomy, astronomy, warfare, botany (the study of plants), geology (the study of the earth), and engineering.

Da Vinci wrote about and sketched his ideas in his famous **notebooks.** They include countless thoughts, thousands of sketches, and hundreds of inventions. For example, da Vinci sketched flying machines, cranes, bridges, and even a parachute.

Artist, inventor, scientist, engineer—da Vinci did it all. It is no wonder, then, that he is recognized as one of the greatest geniuses who has ever lived.

THINK ABOUT IT

Da Vinci was an accomplished artist, engineer, scientist, . . . the list is endless. Is there anyone alive today who you think is a genius in many fields? If so, who is it and at what does he or she excel? If you can't think of anyone, what do you think this says about modern society? Write your answer on a separate sheet of paper.

PRACTICE 11: Leonardo da Vinci

Decide if each of the following statements is true (**T**) or false (**F**). Write the correct letter on the line before each statement.

_____ **1.** *The Last Supper* is a painting by da Vinci.

_____ **2.** *David* is a painting by da Vinci.

_____ **3.** The *Mona Lisa* is one of da Vinci's most famous paintings.

_____ **4.** Da Vinci worked in a great number of fields.

_____ **5.** Da Vinci kept all of his ideas in his head and never wrote any of them down.

The Spread of the Renaissance

All of the people you have been reading about—Petrarch, Donatello, Michelangelo, da Vinci, and the rest—lived in Italy in the 1300s, 1400s, and 1500s. As you remember, the Renaissance began in Italy. But, the Renaissance was to spread throughout Europe.

The Renaissance spread to Germany, England, France, Spain, and the other nations of Europe. The ideas of the Italian Renaissance were carried to these places by people who visited Italy and then returned home. These travelers included merchants, bankers, and traders.

The Renaissance was also spread, in a way, by warfare. Parts of Italy were invaded by armies from Spain, Germany, and France. The invading soldiers were stunned by what they found in Italy. When they returned to their homelands, they reported what they had seen.

But, above all, the ideas of the Renaissance were mostly spread by young people. They were students of the arts and scholarship. Hearing of the greatness of Italy, they traveled there from throughout Europe. During the Renaissance, it was thought that a true education could only be had in Italy.

The people of northern Europe adapted the ideas of the Renaissance to their own needs. The new ideas were especially popular in Germany and the Low Countries (present-day Luxembourg, Belgium, and the Netherlands). This became known as the Northern Renaissance.

Dutch writer and thinker Desiderius Erasmus used humor to make people think critically about their world. German painter Albrecht Dürer has been called "the da Vinci of the North." His work shows his interest in nature, anatomy, and perspective. Dutch painter Pieter Brueghel used Italian techniques to paint the peasants of his homeland.

In England, the finest works of the Renaissance appeared on the stage. Writers such as **William Shakespeare** used ideas from many sources, including history and fairy tales. Their plays dealt with human emotions—love, jealousy, anger, heroism. Many plays from this period are still performed today.

Within just a few generations, humanism had taken hold throughout Europe. A new era had begun. The Renaissance would touch all aspects of life in Europe. It would radically shape science, religion, and everyday life.

■ PRACTICE 12: The Spread of the Renaissance

Circle the letter of the correct answer to each of the following questions.

1. What was one of the ways the Renaissance spread from Italy to the rest of Europe?

- **a.** books and paintings
- **b.** people moving to Italy from the rest of Europe
- **c.** students of the arts and scholarship
- **d.** movies and television

2. How did war help spread the Renaissance?

- **a.** Soldiers who invaded Italy were impressed by what they saw there.
- **b.** Italy conquered other countries and introduced them to its ideas.
- **c.** Civilians fled war-torn Italy to other countries.
- **d.** Italy forced other parts of Europe to follow its lead.

3. What was the Renaissance in England known for?

- **a.** paintings in buildings
- **b.** outdoor sculptures
- **c.** plays on the stage
- **d.** story collections

LESSON 2: A New Science

GOAL: To identify and discuss the contributions of several important scientists of the Renaissance

WORDS TO KNOW

Copernican Revolution

Copernican system

ellipse

experiments

geocentric system

heliocentric system

Inquisition

laws of planetary motion

observation

Ptolemaic system

recorded

science

NAMES TO KNOW

Tycho Brahe

Nicolaus Copernicus

Galen

Galileo

Johannes Gutenberg

Johannes Kepler

Ptolemy

Andreas Vesalius

Understanding Science

As you have read, Europeans made great strides in literature and the arts during the Renaissance. But these were not the only fields important during this time. Another field—science—was changed forever during the Renaissance. In fact, the Renaissance saw the birth of modern science.

To appreciate what the scientists of the Renaissance accomplished, you first have to understand just what science is.

The word *science* comes from an old Latin word meaning "knowledge." This gives you a good clue as to what science is. People have always tried to gain knowledge about their world. So, in a way, there have always been scientists. But today, the term "science" doesn't mean just any kind of knowledge. Science is a particular way of gaining knowledge about the world in order to understand it.

Basically, **science** is a way of gaining knowledge by making careful observations, identifying and recording facts, and organizing these facts into a system. Scientists develop theories, or general rules, to explain the facts they observe. Theories attempt to explain why things happen. These theories must be tested, or confirmed, in experiments. As scientists learn more and more, old theories are discarded and replaced by new theories that explain the facts better. Scientists use the tools of mathematics and logic to help them learn and to express their ideas.

It was during the Renaissance that many of these ideas first took a real hold. During the Renaissance, careful observation and recording of those observations, the use of mathematics, and the testing of theories through experiments started to be established. The great revolution that would firmly establish modern science was beginning.

You will remember that the Roman Catholic Church had a profound influence on thought in the Middle Ages. During this time, most scholars were interested in theology, the study of God. There was some interest in science. But the people of the Middle Ages relied on what Greek and Roman writers, especially the Greek philosopher Aristotle, had said. There was little interest in new observations. The opinions of the ancients were accepted as fact. As a result, most people in the Middle Ages had completely misinformed and inaccurate ideas about how nature worked.

This changed with the rebirth of science during the Renaissance. And, much of the credit in the change goes to just a few individuals. You will read about them on the following pages.

IN REAL LIFE

Think about how important science is to life today, and to your life in particular. Science is used in virtually every field. Science helps farmers grow the foods you eat. Scientists help design everything from cars to buildings to clothing. Science, in other words, touches nearly every aspect of your life. So, understanding how science came to be is critical for you to understand your world.

■ PRACTICE 13: Understanding Science

Decide if each statement below is true (**T**) or false (**F**). Write the correct letter on the line before each statement.

_____ **1.** Identifying and recording facts is a characteristic of science.

_____ **2.** Testing theories in experiments is a characteristic of science.

_____ **3.** Recording the opinions of other people is a characteristic of science.

Nicolaus Copernicus

One of the ancients who very much influenced thought during the Middle Ages was the Greek thinker **Ptolemy**. Ptolemy recorded the ideas of Greek astronomy. Remember that for Europeans in the Middle Ages, the ideas of such thinkers went unchallenged. The major idea put forth by Ptolemy was that Earth was the center of the universe. All other heavenly bodies, he said, moved around Earth in very complex patterns.

The idea that Earth is at the center of the universe is called the **geocentric system.** (This comes from the Greek words *geo,* which means "Earth," and *centric,* which means "center.") The geocentric system is also sometimes called the **Ptolemaic system.**

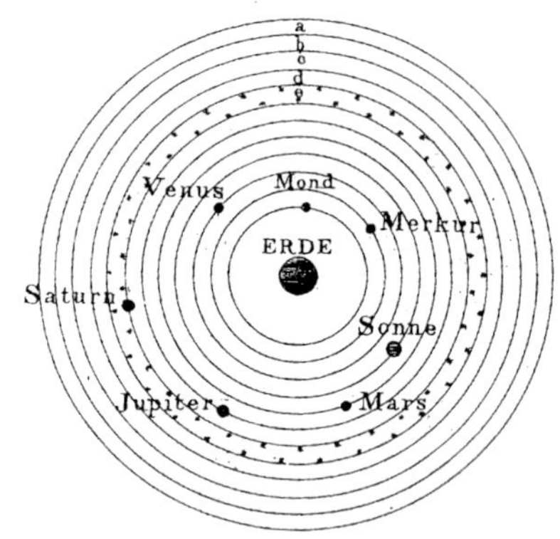

System of Ptolemy

■ **THINK ABOUT IT**

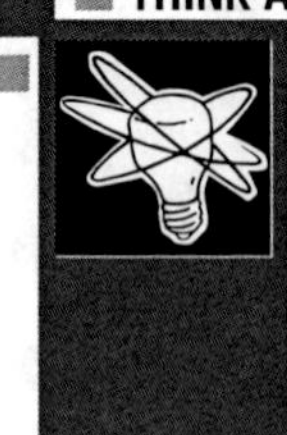

The geocentric system, as you have just read, has another name. It is the Ptolemaic system. Stop for a moment and think about this name. Why is it called that? What other things can you think of that get their names in a similar way? Write your answer on a separate sheet of paper.

Today, we know that the geocentric system does not explain our universe. But for nearly 1,400 years, it was accepted as an established fact. Ptolemy's work was accepted by the powerful Roman Catholic Church during the Middle Ages. This was because the geocentric system fit into the Church's ideas about human beings' place in the universe.

During the Renaissance, this way of thinking began to be challenged. You will remember that one of the basic characteristics of modern science is the observation of nature. One scientist who observed nature was **Nicolaus Copernicus**, a Polish astronomer who lived from 1473 to 1543. Copernicus challenged the Ptolemaic system. By doing so, he forever changed the way we look at the universe.

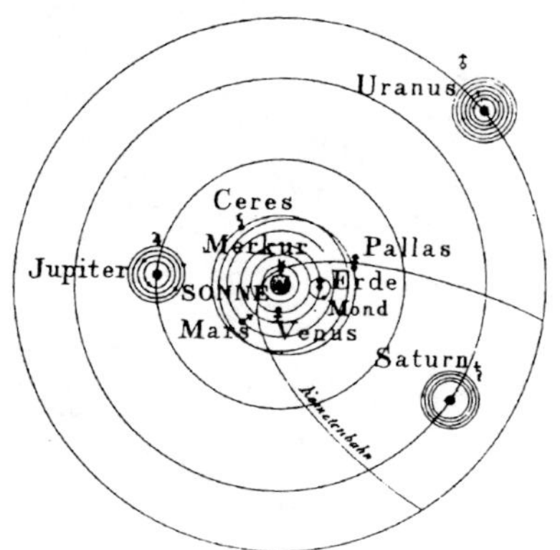

System of Copernicus

What Copernicus did was to carefully observe the movements of heavenly bodies. Then he described their movements in mathematical form. He decided that the movements of heavenly bodies would make more sense if the Sun were at the center, instead of Earth. If this were true, then the heavenly bodies wouldn't have to move in complex patterns to account for what people observed.

Simple circles, or orbits, around the Sun would explain what people saw. In other words, Copernicus's explanation was more systematic, simple, and elegant.

In 1453, Copernicus put forth his ideas in a book called *On the Revolution of the Celestial Spheres.* In it, he stated that the planets, including Earth, revolve around the Sun. He also stated that Earth rotates on its axis, and that the Moon orbits Earth. All of this is true.

In contrast to the geocentric system, Copernicus's idea is called the **heliocentric system** (*helios* is the Greek word that means "sun"). In honor of Copernicus, it is also called the **Copernican system.** The heliocentric system is so different from the geocentric system that this great change in our understanding is sometimes called the **Copernican Revolution.**

Copernicus did more than just put forth his idea. He supported it with logic, mathematics, and evidence. In other words, he put forth a true scientific theory—one that could be tested. As you remember, the ability to test theories is one of the hallmarks of modern science. In fact, many people view 1453 and the publication of Copernicus's work as the starting point of modern science.

■ PRACTICE 14: Nicolaus Copernicus

Circle the letter of the correct answer to each of the following questions.

1. What idea did Nicolaus Copernicus set forth?
- **a.** the heliocentric system
- **b.** that Earth orbits the Sun, and not vice versa
- **c.** the Copernican system
- **d.** all of the above

2. What centuries-old idea did Copernicus disprove?
- **a.** that the Sun orbits Earth
- **b.** the geocentric system
- **c.** the Ptolemaic system
- **d.** all of the above

Tycho Brahe and Johannes Kepler

Tycho Brahe was a Danish astronomer who lived from 1546 to 1601. He did not believe Copernicus. He thought, like most other people of his time, that Earth was the center of the universe.

As we now know, Copernicus was right and Brahe was wrong. However, Brahe made other important contributions to the advancement of science. Perhaps more than any other person of his time, he stressed the importance of **observation.** This is the process of carefully and objectively looking at a subject. Remember, observation is a hallmark of modern science. For years, Brahe made careful observations of the sky. He didn't use a telescope, because it hadn't been invented yet. But he watched carefully and used old-fashioned instruments to aid him. Just as important, he wrote down, or **recorded,** what he observed. In doing so, Brahe was acting like a modern scientist.

Brahe's careful observations detected errors in some earlier observations, which he was able to correct. These corrections helped later astronomers in their work. But his most important contribution was his legacy of observing carefully and recording what he observed.

One of the scientists who benefited from Brahe's work was **Johannes Kepler,** Brahe's assistant. Kepler was a German astronomer and mathematician. He lived from 1571 to 1630.

What Kepler did was try to map the orbits of the planets. He tried to map the orbit of Mars based on what Brahe had observed. Try as he might, he couldn't make what Brahe observed fit into a circle. You see, at this point, everyone thought that orbits went in circles. (Copernicus thought this, too.) In near desperation, Kepler tried to make the observed orbit of Mars fit into an **ellipse,** or oval, instead of into a circle. It worked perfectly.

So, Kepler put forth the idea that planets orbit the Sun in ellipses. He was correct. Today, this is known as one of Kepler's **laws of planetary motion.** His other two laws detail the speed and distance planets travel in elliptical orbits.

Kepler's laws overturned the 2,000-year-old idea of circular orbits. Again, observation and mathematics won out over tradition and belief. Like Copernicus, Kepler had changed our view of the universe. His work confirmed Copernicus's work. So, it makes sense that Kepler was also the first scientist to openly support Copernicus.

■ PRACTICE 15: Tycho Brahe and Johannes Kepler

Circle the letter of the correct answer to each of the following questions.

1. What was one of Brahe's most important contributions to science?
- **a.** discovering that Earth revolved around the Sun
- **b.** inventing the telescope
- **c.** observing and recording
- **d.** discovering that the Sun revolved around Earth

2. What was one of Kepler's most important contributions to science?
   a. discovering the laws of planetary motion
   b. discovering that the planets' orbits were circular
   c. inventing the telescope
   d. proving that the Sun moves in an elliptical orbit

Galileo Galilei

You may have heard of **Galileo.** You may even remember him as the man who invented the telescope. In fact, Galileo did not invent the telescope. But he did make the first one that was really useful for observing the sky. This was just one of his many important contributions.

Galileo Galilei (1564–1642) lived in Italy. As a teacher there, he was required to teach the Ptolemaic system. Over the years, however, he realized that the Copernican theory was really the correct one.

Galileo

In 1609, Galileo built his first telescope. When he turned it to the heavens, he made a series of remarkable discoveries. He saw that the Moon was covered with craters and mountains. Before, people had accepted the ancient Greek view that it was smooth. Galileo also discovered the rings around Saturn. In an important discovery, he saw moons around Jupiter. Here was the first real proof that heavenly bodies could orbit one another. Looking at Venus, he saw that the Sun shone on it in different ways at different times. This helped prove the Copernican theory that the planets orbit the Sun.

THINK ABOUT IT

Galileo was the first to see the moons around Jupiter. He named these moons the "Medicean Planets." Why do you think he chose this name? Here is a hint: During the Renaissance, scientists relied on the financial support of rich and powerful families. To gain this support, scientists did what they could to honor and show respect to these families. Write your answer on a separate sheet of paper.

Galileo was more than an astronomer. He also made important discoveries in the science we now call physics. For example, he discovered rules about falling bodies, inertia, and levers. These were important discoveries. But even more important was the way he discovered them.

Galileo was the first person to really use **experiments** to test ideas, or theories, about how nature worked. He conducted a series of logical experiments, recorded the results, expressed them in mathematical form, and deduced a theory. This is just like the "science" you read about on page 25. In fact, Galileo is sometimes referred to as "the father of experimental science." Scientists around the world use methods pioneered by Galileo.

You might think that Galileo was richly rewarded for his work. In fact, Galileo was punished. Remember that the most powerful force in Europe during this time was the Roman Catholic Church. The Church did not approve of humanism or the new science. This was because the humanists and new scientists were discovering things about humankind and nature that went against the Church's teachings. In particular, Galileo's support of the Copernican idea that the planets orbit the Sun, and not Earth, got him into trouble. For the Church, this idea challenged certain ideas in the Bible.

The **Inquisition**, an arm of the Church set up to investigate people who contradicted the Church, put Galileo on trial. Under threat of torture, he was forced to take back his support of Copernicus's ideas.

Galileo's trial before the Inquisition is a famous event in history. It symbolizes the two great worldviews that were coming into conflict during the Renaissance. On one side stood tradition, theology, and the power of the Roman Catholic Church. On the other side stood science, humanism, and the power of free thought. The conflict between these two worldviews—and the eventual triumph of Galileo's—lies at the heart of the Renaissance.

IN REAL LIFE

In 1992, 350 years after Galileo's death, Pope John Paul II gave an address. He admitted that the Church had made errors. Pope John Paul II said that Galileo was not guilty of heresy, or opinions that went against Church teachings.

■ PRACTICE 16: Galileo Galilei

Decide if each statement below is true (**T**) or false (**F**). Write the correct letter on the line before each statement.

_____ **1.** Galileo invented the telescope.

_____ **2.** The Roman Catholic Church supported Galileo's work.

_____ **3.** Galileo used experiments to test his ideas.

Andreas Vesalius

The men you have been reading about—Copernicus, Brahe, Kepler, and Galileo—were all astronomers. But other areas of science also advanced during the Renaissance. One great advance occurred in 1543. In this year, the Belgian anatomist **Andreas Vesalius** (1514–1564) wrote a book called *On the Fabric of the Human Body.* Vesalius's book gave a very detailed description of everything that was known about the human body. He based his book on careful observations he had made while dissecting human corpses.

What made Vesalius's work so significant is that it was based on careful, objective observation of the real world. It wasn't based on legend or what people believed to be true. Until then, physicians had relied on the ancient and often incorrect writings of the Greek physician **Galen.** But now, true to the spirit of the Renaissance, knowledge about the human body was being gained by observation. Just as the astronomers communicated their new scientific knowledge about the sky, Vesalius communicated new scientific knowledge about the body.

■ PRACTICE 17: Andreas Vesalius

Circle the letter of the correct answer to each of the following questions.

1. What was the title of Vesalius's book?

- **a.** *On the Revolution of the Heavenly Spheres*
- **b.** *Dialogue Concerning the Two Chief World Systems*
- **c.** *On the Fabric of the Human Body*

2. How did Vesalius learn about the human body?
    a. He made observations while dissecting human corpses.
    b. He studied drawings made by Leonardo da Vinci.
    c. He studied the writings of the Greek physician Galen.

Johannes Gutenberg

In the Middle Ages, there were very few books. And they weren't even printed. Books were slowly copied by hand by monks in monasteries. Very few people could read. All of this began to change during the Renaissance. Much of this change was due to the work of a German named **Johannes Gutenberg** (1400–1468).

Gutenberg is sometimes called "the father of printing and publishing." But Gutenberg didn't invent the printing press. What he did was combine movable type, molds for the type, oil-based ink, and a special printing press into a complete, efficient printing system—the first of its kind in history.

Gutenberg's Printing Press

Virtually all of the books printed for the next 500 years, well into the twentieth century, used the basic methods that Gutenberg developed. The Gutenberg Bible, which Gutenberg and his associates printed in 1455, is perhaps the most famous book in the world.

Gutenberg printed about 180 copies of the Bible. Only 48 copies still exist today. Most of those copies include only part of the Bible. In all, there are now just 16 complete copies of the Gutenberg Bible.

IN REAL LIFE

Gutenberg introduced printing with movable type in Europe. However, this kind of printing had been used in China for 400 years. Chinese movable type was made of wood or clay. Gutenberg developed a way to make type from metal.

Gutenberg died in 1468. Within just 50 years of his death, at least 250 cities in Europe had printing presses. Gutenberg died poor. He never knew that his work would be instrumental in changing the world.

TIP

You are reading about Johannes Gutenberg—"the father of printing and publishing." This nickname will help you remember Gutenberg's contribution to human life. In fact, whenever you read about a nickname given to a historical figure, try to remember it. Nicknames in history—just like nicknames in real life—are a good way to help you remember something important about the individual.

PRACTICE 18: Johannes Gutenberg

Circle the letter of the correct answer to each of the following questions.

1. What is Gutenberg known for?
   a. his scientific work
   b. translating the Bible
   c. developing a method of printing
   d. making discoveries about Earth and the Sun

2. What is Gutenberg sometimes called?
   a. "the father of printing and publishing"
   b. "the first humanist"
   c. "the first writer"
   d. "the father of modern science"

3. About how many copies of the Bible did Gutenberg print?
   a. 250
   b. 48
   c. 16
   d. 180

LESSON 3: The Reformation

GOAL: To explain the reasons for the Reformation and its results

WORDS TO KNOW

Anglicanism
excommunicate
middle class
Ninety-five Theses
Protestant ethic
Protestants
Puritans
Reformation
sale of indulgences
urbanization

NAMES TO KNOW

John Calvin
Martin Luther

Urbanization and the Rise of a Middle Class

During the Middle Ages, there was little trade and almost no industry. Most people were poor peasants who worked on manor farms. The towns were small, few, and far between. Mostly, they were tiny villages. Europe was, as a rule, a very poor place. Slowly, over centuries, all of this changed. The main reason for the change was that the economy in Europe slowly improved.

Toward the end of the Middle Ages, trade began to increase. This was largely the result of the contacts Europeans made with the outside world. Trade routes developed between Europe and Asia.

As trade grew, a need arose for a place to conduct trade. At first, trade was conducted in small village markets. Over time, these markets grew, and trade fairs were held throughout Europe. As trade and trade fairs grew, so did towns. Throughout history, as trade has increased, so has the size of towns. This is because people who make their living from trade—traders and merchants—don't need to live on farms.

The growth of towns and cities is called **urbanization**. Slowly but surely, Europe became urbanized. The people who lived in towns were different from their country cousins. They tended to be more sophisticated, educated, and wealthier. During the Middle Ages, there were only two main economic classes in Europe: the very rich nobles and the very poor peasants. With the rise of trade and towns, a new economic class of people emerged. This was the **middle class.** The middle class was wealthier than the poor but not as wealthy as the rich. Middle-class people were mostly traders and merchants. They had nowhere near as much wealth as nobles. But they were much better off than the peasants. As their numbers grew, so did their influence on European life.

■ PRACTICE 19: Urbanization and the Rise of a Middle Class

Circle the letter of the correct answer to each of the following questions.

1. What is urbanization?
- **a.** the movement of people from cities to the suburbs
- **b.** the desire to live on farms
- **c.** the growth of cities and towns
- **d.** the growth of farms

2. What is the middle class?
- **a.** an economic class of people that is wealthier than the poor but not as wealthy as the rich
- **b.** the largest class of people in any society
- **c.** the most powerful class of people in any society
- **d.** a class of people bound to nobles as part of the feudal system

The Roman Catholic Church

By the Middle Ages, the Christian religion had spread throughout western Europe. The Church touched the life of almost everyone in Europe during the Middle Ages. From baptism at birth, to a wedding ceremony, to last rites, the Church was a central part of most people's lives.

"The Church" was the Roman Catholic Church, headquartered in Rome. It was the only church in Europe. The Church was headed by the pope. Archbishops answered to the pope, and bishops answered to the archbishops. In turn, local priests answered to the bishops. In this way, the authority of the Church filtered down to nearly everyone in Europe.

As you can see, the Church was highly organized, much like a government. In fact, the Church at this time had many powers that governments today have. The Church established laws for the people in the lands it held. It settled disputes. At times, the Church even raised armies and went to battle.

Moreover, the Church was extremely wealthy. The Church became the largest landholder during the Middle Ages. As a result, the Church grew rich and powerful. The Church also held power because Church officials could **excommunicate** people, or cut them off entirely from the Church. Excommunication was a powerful weapon. This was because the Church was so important to the people of Europe. Scientists who supported Copernicus, for example, were threatened with excommunication.

The Church ruled for centuries. Then, during the Renaissance, it was challenged. The challenge to the power of the Roman Catholic Church would result in one of the greatest religious upheavals in history. The upheaval continues to touch the lives of people around the world to this very day.

■ PRACTICE 20: The Roman Catholic Church

Circle the letter of the correct answer to each of the following questions.

1. What was the most powerful religious and social force during the Middle Ages?

- **a.** the Church
- **b.** the Roman Catholic Church
- **c.** both *a* and *b*, since they refer to the same thing
- **d.** the Medici family

2. What is excommunication?

- **a.** the act of challenging the authority of the Roman Catholic Church
- **b.** the act of entering the Roman Catholic Church
- **c.** a religious upheaval
- **d.** the act of cutting someone off from the Roman Catholic Church

The Reformation

The great challenge to the Roman Catholic Church would come to be called the **Reformation.** The Reformation was a religious movement that took place during the 1500s. Before the Reformation, the Roman Catholic Church was the only church in Europe. After the Reformation, half of Europe belonged to different churches.

The Reformation is so called because it resulted in a *reform* of religious life in Europe. There were many causes of the Reformation. Perhaps the chief cause was the abuse of power by the Roman Catholic Church. This abuse of power took many forms.

One abuse had to do with the way the Church obtained money. The vast network of the Church and its many officials needed money to function. To get it, the Church sometimes sold positions within the Church. Many poor people resented this.

Church leaders also abused their positions to personally benefit from the wealth of the Church. Many bishops and other Church officials lived like kings. They had huge, lavish homes built for themselves. Many people felt that monks and nuns no longer led lives of poverty. It seemed that Church leaders thought more about money than about faith. Again, this caused widespread resentment.

The Church also engaged in a practice called the **sale of indulgences.** Indulgences were pardons from sin. Under this practice, people could be pardoned for their sins by giving money to the Church.

These practices began to appall many people throughout Europe—including members of the Church itself. To them, the Church was neglecting spiritual leadership in favor of worldly wealth and power. Moreover, as more people became educated, they began to question the Church's interpretation of the Bible. Also, the new middle class no longer needed the protection of feudal and manor lords, who were often also bishops of the Church. So, they felt free to question the Church. All of these factors combined to create a great revolution against the Church. The greatest leader of this revolution, or Reformation, was **Martin Luther.** You will learn more about Martin Luther in the next section.

THINK ABOUT IT

You are reading about how people in Europe were growing increasingly dissatisfied with the Roman Catholic Church. You have just heard about a Church practice called the "sale of indulgences." In this practice, people who paid money to the Church were forgiven for their sins. Why would such a practice cause resentment? Write your answer on a separate sheet of paper.

PRACTICE 21: The Reformation

Decide if each statement below is true (**T**) or false (**F**). Write the correct letter on the line before each statement.

_____ **1.** As people became more educated, they flocked to join the Church.

_____ **2.** The sale of indulgences contributed to people's dissatisfaction with the Church.

_____ **3.** Most Church leaders were poor and humble.

_____ **4.** The Reformation affected the Roman Catholic Church.

Martin Luther

Martin Luther (1483–1546) was the leader of the Reformation. He was a Catholic monk. In 1512, at the age of 29, he earned his Doctorate of Theology at the University of Wittenberg in Germany. Luther then became a member of the faculty there.

Martin Luther

Luther was appalled by the sale of indulgences. Moreover, during a trip to Rome, he was shocked by the wealth, worldliness, and corruption of the Church leaders. In protest, he nailed a document to the door of the church in Wittenberg, where he lived. The date was October 31, 1517. The document was Luther's **Ninety-five Theses,** or ninety-five statements. In this document, he denounced the corruption of the Church, especially the sale of indulgences. The Ninety-five Theses were printed and widely distributed. (Remember, Gutenberg had developed printing about 50 years earlier.) People were amazed that someone had spoken out so boldly against the Church. And many people agreed with what Luther had said.

Soon, Luther spoke out in even stronger terms against the Church. He came to deny the authority of the Church and the pope completely. He argued that people did not need the Church to attain salvation. Luther said that people had a direct relationship with God. They only needed their Bibles, their minds, and their souls to achieve God's grace. Faith, to Luther, was more important than doing good works. Buying indulgences, Luther said, would do nothing to help sinners.

Of course, such ideas made Church leaders very angry. They struck at the heart of the Church's power and authority. If people followed Luther's ideas, they wouldn't need the Church at all! In the past, anyone who said such things would have been tried by the Inquisition. They would have been tortured, and may have even been put to death. But people in Luther's Germany, including some powerful nobles, agreed with Luther. His ideas were supported by the common people, and he was protected by the nobles.

Luther wrote many pieces in support of his ideas. But one of his most important works was a new translation of the Bible. He translated it into German, instead of Latin. As a result, anyone who could read could study the Bible firsthand. People didn't need the Church to interpret it for them. Of course, this further undermined the power of the Church.

■ PRACTICE 22: Martin Luther

Circle the letter of the correct answer to each of the following questions.

1. What were the Ninety-five Theses about?

- **a.** Luther's belief that there was no God
- **b.** Luther's protest of corruption and the sale of indulgences
- **c.** Luther's respect for the Roman Catholic Church
- **d.** all of the above

2. Which of the following statements is TRUE?
   a. Luther believed that people did not need the Roman Catholic Church to attain salvation.
   b. The Roman Catholic Church welcomed Luther's ideas.
   c. The Roman Catholic Church tortured Luther and put him to death.
   d. all of the above

Protestantism

Martin Luther's actions set off a chain reaction of protests throughout Europe. The Reformation was under way. People who broke from the Roman Catholic Church came to be called **Protestants** because they protested against the Church. Protestantism took hold in northern Europe. Catholicism remained strong in southern Europe.

The Protestants of northern Europe formed many different denominations, or sects. Each denomination was organized differently and had some differences in beliefs. All of them believed, in sharp contrast to the Catholics, that they didn't need the Roman Catholic Church to receive God's grace.

In Switzerland, a priest named **John Calvin** (1509–1564) became influential. Calvin thought that God decided the fate of every person. He directed efforts that would lead to the firm establishment of Protestantism in Switzerland, France, and other countries throughout northern and western Europe.

In England, Queen Elizabeth I created an official form of Protestantism that was called **Anglicanism** in 1563. It combined some Catholic elements with Protestant ideas. Anglicanism was a moderate form of Protestantism. But many people in England didn't support Anglicanism. They objected to the presence and powers of bishops in the Anglican church. They preferred the Congregational system of John Calvin. These people became known as **Puritans,** because they followed a more "pure" version of Protestantism. Within a century, the Puritans, fleeing religious persecution, would come to America.

PRACTICE 23: Protestantism

Circle the letter of the correct answer to each of the following questions.

1. What were people who broke from the Roman Catholic Church called?
   - **a.** disciples
   - **b.** Protestants
   - **c.** peasants
   - **d.** nobles

2. Who directed efforts that would spread Protestantism throughout northern and western Europe?
   - **a.** Martin Luther
   - **b.** the Roman Catholic Church
   - **c.** John Calvin
   - **d.** Galileo Galilei

The Results of the Reformation

The Reformation was one of the greatest and most influential events in the history of Europe. Before the Reformation, there was only the Roman Catholic Church. After the Reformation, Europe was divided. In the north, Protestant countries were home to many different versions of Protestantism. In southern Europe, the Roman Catholic Church remained strong. Even today, religious life in Europe follows these general lines.

Some historians think the growth of Protestantism led to the growth of what is called the **Protestant ethic,** or way of life. The Protestant ethic stresses the importance of home and family and the role of the individual in community life. Hard work and thrift are celebrated. Such ideas are directly linked to Luther's and other Protestants' ideas about life in the world as related to God, without the intervention of a church. The ideas of the Protestant ethic have transferred over into other spheres of life, such as business and the government.

But, the most important result of the Reformation was simply the establishment of Protestantism. Today, about one third of the two billion Christians in the world are Protestants.

■ PRACTICE 24: The Results of the Reformation

Decide if each statement below is true (**T**) or false (**F**). Write the correct letter on the line before each statement.

_____ **1.** After the Reformation, there was only one major church in Europe.

_____ **2.** The Reformation marked the end of Catholicism.

_____ **3.** The Roman Catholic Church remained strongest in southern Europe.

_____ **4.** The Protestant ethic stresses hard work and thrift.

UNIT 1 REVIEW

Circle the letter of the correct answer to each of the following questions.

1. What idea was the intellectual core of the Renaissance?
- **a.** humanism
- **b.** artwork
- **c.** theology
- **d.** courtiers

2. Who were the Medicis?
- **a.** a powerful ruling family
- **b.** the first humanists
- **c.** a group of artists
- **d.** important writers

3. Along with Petrarch, who is considered one of the first humanists?
- **a.** Donatello
- **b.** Michelangelo
- **c.** Boccaccio
- **d.** da Vinci

4. What idea did Nicolaus Copernicus put forth?
   a. the Ptolemaic system
   b. the heliocentric system
   c. the geocentric system
   d. all of the above

5. Who put forth the idea that planets orbit the Sun in ellipses?
   a. Johannes Kepler
   b. Tycho Brahe
   c. Nicolaus Copernicus
   d. Galileo Galilei

6. What is Gutenberg known for?
   a. his scientific work
   b. translating the Bible
   c. developing a method of printing
   d. being tried by the Inquisition

7. What happened to towns and cities toward the end of the Middle Ages?
   a. They disappeared.
   b. They grew in size and number.
   c. They shrank.
   d. They were captured by the Roman Catholic Church.

8. What did the phrase "the Church" usually refer to in Europe during the Middle Ages?
   a. the Roman Catholic Church
   b. the Protestant Church
   c. the church in Wittenberg
   d. all of the above

9. What religion or religious faith was a result of the Reformation?
   a. Christianity
   b. Hinduism
   c. Roman Catholicism
   d. Protestantism

10. Which was a result of the Reformation?

a. the establishment of a variety of new religious faiths
b. the establishment of Protestantism
c. the growth of the Protestant ethic
d. all of the above

UNIT 1 APPLICATION ACTIVITY

Effects of the Reformation

Before the Reformation, the Roman Catholic Church dominated Europe. All Christian Europeans were Catholics. After the Reformation, a full half of all Europeans attended Protestant churches. Since then, Protestantism, Anglicanism, and other forms of Christianity have spread throughout the world.

To see how dramatic this change was, chart the numbers of Roman Catholics, Protestants, Anglicans, and other Christians in the world today. You can find this information in any world almanac. Write each number on the lines below.

- Roman Catholics: ________________________
- Anglicans: ________________________
- Protestants: ________________________
- Other Christians: ________________________

Now, enter this information in the bar graph that follows. Once you have finished, this graph will help show you the relationships between the different religious groups.

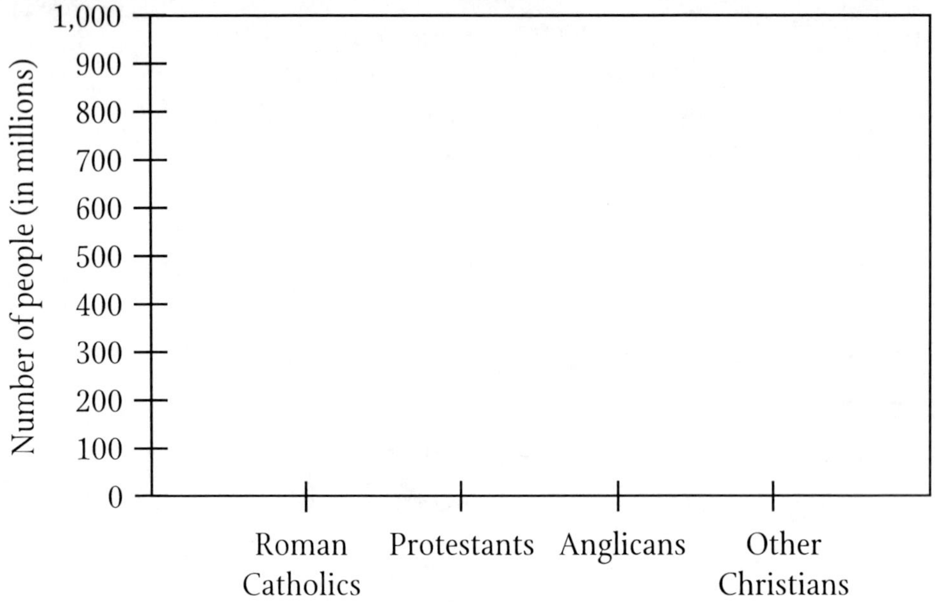

When you have finished creating your bar graph, answer the question below.

- How would your graph have been different if the Reformation had never happened?

UNIT 2

Asia's Empires

LESSON 4: China Enters the Modern Age

GOAL: To describe and discuss major developments in the history and culture of China during the Ming and Qing dynasties

WORDS TO KNOW

dynasty
Manchus
Qing dynasty
foot binding
Ming dynasty
queue
Great Wall of China

NAMES TO KNOW

Emperor Kangxi
Nurhachi

PLACES TO KNOW

Beijing
Manchuria

The Ming Dynasty

From 1368 to 1644, China was ruled by the **Ming dynasty**. (A **dynasty** is a series of rulers from the same family or group of people.) The Ming dynasty had replaced the Yuan dynasty. The Yuan dynasty was a foreign dynasty. It was created by the Mongols, who invaded and ruled China under Genghis Khan and Kublai Khan. China had been ruled harshly under the Yuan dynasty. By the mid-1300s, rebels throughout China fought to overthrow the Yuan dynasty. Eventually, they succeeded. With the Mongols gone, the Chinese again established a Chinese dynasty. This was the Ming dynasty.

Ming Vase

The Ming dynasty was a period of wealth and stability in China. The porcelain produced during this time is recognized among the great artworks in the history of the world.

During the Ming dynasty, the Chinese tried to return things to the way they had been before the Mongols came. For example, the Mongols had done away with the Chinese civil-service examinations. Under the

Ming dynasty, these exams were put back in place. The Ming dynasty ruled China in a way consistent with the teachings of Confucius, a Chinese philosopher.

Remembering the rule of the Mongols, the Chinese began to hate foreigners. They considered foreign peoples and ideas inferior to Chinese people and ideas. Instead of concentrating on overseas trade, they focused on keeping the Chinese heartland safe from invaders.

The Mongols had come from the north. Throughout the Ming dynasty, the Chinese were concerned about another possible invasion. They took several steps to prevent it, including improvements to the **Great Wall of China.** This wall had been built centuries earlier to keep invaders from the north out of China. Under the Ming dynasty, the Great Wall was strengthened with more watchtowers. (Interestingly, the Great Wall was not built to keep people out of China—soldiers could easily climb it with ladders. But the wall kept soldiers from bringing their horses with them. Without their horses, armies were much less effective.)

In addition, the Chinese moved their capital city. They didn't move it farther away to protect it. Instead, they moved it north, to **Beijing.** This way, Chinese rulers could keep a closer watch on the northern frontier.

The Great Wall of China

All along the northern frontier, Chinese armies stood at the ready. Occasionally, small bands of nomads from the north would raid China. Mostly, though, there was peace. This is because the Mings worked out an arrangement with the nomads of the north. The Ming goal was to keep the many tribes separated, so they would not gather too much strength. The Chinese gave gifts of money and honor to nomad chiefs. In exchange, these tribes promised not to invade China and to pay China a yearly tribute.

All of these steps kept China safe for nearly 300 years. But soon, another threat arose north of the Great Wall, as you will see.

■ PRACTICE 25: The Ming Dynasty

Circle the letter of the correct answer to each of the following questions.

1. What steps did the Ming dynasty take to protect China from northern invaders?
   - **a.** They strengthened the Great Wall.
   - **b.** They stationed armies in the north.
   - **c.** They made arrangements with nomads of the north.
   - **d.** all of the above

2. Where did the Ming dynasty move their capital city?
   - **a.** north
   - **b.** south
   - **c.** east
   - **d.** west

The Manchus

The region to the northeast of China is called **Manchuria**. Like the rest of the area north of China, Manchuria was home to many different tribes of nomads. Individually, they were no real threat to China and the Ming dynasty. But united, they could become a powerful force.

In the early 1600s, a chief named **Nurhachi** (1559–1626) united the many tribes of Manchuria under his rule. Where there had been many peoples, there was now a single people. They were called the **Manchus,** after Manchuria. Like the Mongols under Genghis Khan, the Manchus under Nurhachi were fierce, excellent horse soldiers. They were also committed to getting the wealth of China for themselves.

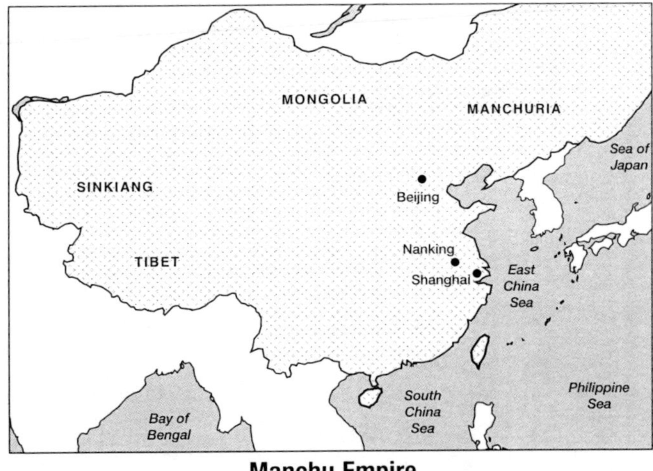

Manchu Empire

First, the Manchus conquered the Korean Peninsula to the southeast and areas to the west. They then struck south, into China. Within just a few years, by 1644, they conquered the Chinese capital of Beijing.

Once, before the Ming dynasty, China had been ruled by foreigners—the Mongols of the Yuan dynasty. Now, the Chinese had been conquered by foreigners again. The Manchus, like the Mongol conquerors before them, set up a new dynasty in China. This was the **Qing dynasty.** It lasted for almost 300 years, until 1911.

TIP

When you read, it may be tempting to pass over any maps. But spending a few minutes studying a map will actually make it easier for you to read quickly. Why? Because maps give you a mental picture, a setting, in which you can imagine the events you read about. For example, by looking at the map on page 51, you can imagine Manchu horsemen riding from Manchuria into China and capturing Beijing.

PRACTICE 26: The Manchus

Circle the letter of the correct answer to each of the following questions.

1. Where is Manchuria located?

- **a.** southeast of China
- **b.** northeast of China
- **c.** west of China
- **d.** in what is now Tibet

2. Who united the tribes of Manchuria?

- **a.** Beijing
- **b.** the Ming dynasty
- **c.** Nurhachi
- **d.** Genghis Khan

3. When did the Manchus conquer Beijing?
   a. 1600
   b. 1644
   c. 1911
   d. 1500

The Qing Dynasty

With the founding of the Qing dynasty, China again came under foreign rule. The Manchus, after all, were not Chinese. To reinforce the differences between themselves and the Chinese they ruled, the Manchus introduced several rules.

During the Qing dynasty, the Manchus required all Chinese men to wear their hair in a single braid of hair, called a **queue.** It made the differences between Chinese and Manchurian men more distinct. And it served as a symbol of submission to the power of the Manchus.

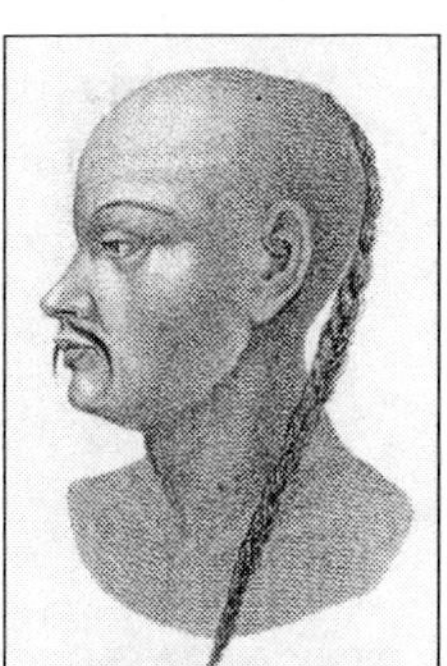
Man Wearing a Queue

But the queue was only the most obvious difference. The Manchus worked hard to maintain the differences between themselves and their Chinese subjects. All Manchu men were required to speak the Manchu language. They also had to maintain Manchu cultural traditions. Moreover, Manchus and Chinese were forbidden to marry each other. Chinese people were not allowed to travel to and settle in Manchuria. It was reserved for Manchus only.

■ PRACTICE 27: The Qing Dynasty

Circle the letter of the correct answer to each of the following questions.

1. Which statement about the Qing dynasty is FALSE?
   a. Manchus had to speak Chinese.
   b. Manchus and Chinese could not marry.
   c. Manchuria was reserved for Manchus.
   d. Manchus were the ruling class.

2. What is a queue?
   a. a language
   b. a Chinese man
   c. a hairstyle
   d. a ponytail

Qing Rule

As you have read, the Manchus took several steps to separate themselves from the Chinese. So, it might surprise you to learn the Qing dynasty was a very "Chinese" dynasty in many ways.

What this means is that the Manchus adopted many Chinese practices. Even before they invaded China, the people of Manchuria had adopted much of Chinese culture. As you know, this often happens when groups of people live close to one another. So, the Manchu rulers of the Qing dynasty were not as "foreign" as the Mongol rulers had been. The Manchus adopted even more of the Chinese culture once they ruled China.

Moreover, the Manchus of the Qing dynasty used traditional Chinese methods of government. That is, China was ruled by an emperor and a dynasty. Confucianism was supported. The Chinese civil-service examinations remained in place. Strong local families supported the government by collecting taxes to send to the capital and by overseeing public projects, such as road building. (In return, they got to keep some of the tax money.)

All of this was familiar to the Chinese. So, although the Manchus were foreign, they were enough like the Chinese in culture, and in the way they ruled, to make many Chinese comfortable with their rule.

Of course, most Chinese were poor peasants who lived on farms. To them, life was the same whoever was in charge. They still had to work hard and pay taxes to the government. But the elite Chinese of the cities who might have challenged Manchu rule did not. This was partly because they were not powerful enough to do so. It was also because the Manchus seemed very "Chinese" in their culture and actions.

■ PRACTICE 28: Qing Rule

Decide if each statement below is true (**T**) or false (**F**). Write the correct letter on the line before each statement.

____ **1.** The Manchus were not Chinese.

____ **2.** The Manchus adopted much of Chinese culture.

____ **3.** The Manchus forced their culture on the Chinese.

____ **4.** The Manchus ruled China in traditional Chinese ways.

Emperor Kangxi

One of the most successful of the Qing, or Manchu, emperors of China was **Emperor Kangxi.** He ruled China from 1661—less than 20 years after the Manchus conquered Beijing—until 1722.

Kangxi was a well-educated man. More important, he was educated in Chinese culture. For example, he knew all of the classic Chinese works, such as the teachings of Confucius.

Kangxi tried to follow the teachings of Confucius during his rule. He wholeheartedly supported the civil-service system, which required applicants to know the teachings of Confucius. In this way, Kangxi's rule reinforced traditional Chinese teachings and government.

Kangxi is remembered as a "good" emperor. This is largely because of his work on behalf of the Chinese people. For example, he ordered the construction of levees to help control flooding along China's rivers. Such floods had devastated Chinese villages for centuries. Emperor Kangxi also directed the construction of storehouses for grain. By ordering farmers to stockpile grain, he made sure they would have food during years of poor harvests.

Emperor Kangxi ruled until 1722. His reign lasted a remarkable 61 years. His legacy was one of strong Manchu rule coupled with strong support of the Chinese people and their culture.

THINK ABOUT IT

Emperor Kangxi was supported by the Chinese people, even though he was not Chinese. Do you think it is important for a ruler to be a native citizen of the country he or she rules? Why or why not? Write your answer on a separate sheet of paper.

PRACTICE 29: Emperor Kangxi

Circle the letter of the correct answer to each of the following questions.

1. When did Emperor Kangxi rule?
- **a.** the 1400s and 1500s
- **b.** the 1500s and 1600s
- **c.** the 1600s and 1700s
- **d.** the 1700s and 1800s

2. Which statement about Emperor Kangxi is FALSE?
- **a.** Emperor Kangxi was a Manchu.
- **b.** Emperor Kangxi did little to help poor Chinese farmers.
- **c.** Emperor Kangxi ruled according to Chinese and Confucian tradition.
- **d.** Emperor Kangxi directed efforts to control floods.

Life During the Qing Dynasty

The Qing dynasty lasted for nearly 300 years. For most Chinese people during this time, life changed little. The Qing dynasty, like the Chinese Ming dynasty before it, did not promote change. Instead, it promoted tradition.

Of course, China did change during this long period of time. During the Qing dynasty, the population of China nearly doubled, to about 300 million people (more people than live in the United States today).

Another change occurred regarding the places most people lived. For centuries, most Chinese people had been farmers who lived in small villages. This continued to be true during the Qing dynasty. But urbanization, or the growth of towns and cities, was occurring. Urbanization had begun before the Qing period. It continued throughout this dynasty.

It was the growth of trade that led to urbanization. Over the centuries, more and more people became traders and merchants. China is a very large country, and different parts of China produced different things. In many regions, grain and other crops were the chief farm products. Traders and merchants brought goods from various parts of the country to other parts and to the cities.

China also traded with other nations, as it had for centuries. However, this trade was not on a large scale. Caravans carried teas, silk, and other goods across Asia to the west. Some sea trade continued in the south.

Certain goods brought from abroad did, however, influence Chinese life. Primarily, these were new crops, introduced by Europeans. These crops included peanuts and tobacco. The sweet potato, another import, was widely grown in areas where rice would not grow.

TIP

As you continue to read about Chinese history, you will come across many Chinese names. You may be tempted to skim over these names if they seem difficult to pronounce. But, if you can say the names to yourself, you are more likely to remember them. Here are two tips to help you pronounce words with a *q* or *x* : The letter *q* should be pronounced "ch," as in ***ch**ain*. The letter *x* should be pronounced "ks," as in the end-sound of ducks. So, the Qing dynasty can be pronounced "Ching" dynasty. And the Emperor Kangxi can be pronounced "Kangksi." You can use these tips to pronounce many Chinese names.

■ PRACTICE 30: Life During the Qing Dynasty

Decide if each statement below is true (**T**) or false (**F**). Write the correct letter on the line before each statement.

_____ **1.** The population of China increased during the Qing dynasty.

_____ **2.** Trade within China increased during the Qing dynasty.

_____ **3.** Urbanization within China increased during the Qing dynasty.

Qing Culture

During the Qing dynasty, from the early 1600s to the early 1700s, trade, cities, and the population of China grew. With these changes came slow changes in Chinese culture.

Remember, most Chinese people continued to be poor, uneducated farmers. But the growth of cities led to changes in the way many people lived.

During the Qing dynasty, city people enjoyed a new level of culture. Two cultural activities stand out. One was reading. More and more people learned to read. Literacy rates may have been as high as 40 percent for men and 10 percent for women. Books were being written in common, everyday language. Just as today, novels were very popular. Many of these novels told ancient folktales. Others told realistic stories about life in China. Plays, another type of cultural activity, were also widely enjoyed.

The Chinese had long valued learning, and scholarship was well supported during Qing rule. Many scholars of this period wrote about the history of China and the ideas of Confucius. Handbooks and encyclopedias were also painstakingly assembled by Chinese authors. Emperor Kangxi arranged to have 15,000 titles published. Book collectors built up private libraries.

PRACTICE 31: Qing Culture

Circle the letter of the correct answer to each of the following questions.

1. What cultural activity became popular in the cities during the Qing dynasty?

- **a.** reading novels
- **b.** attending the theater
- **c.** sports
- **d.** both *a* and *b*

2. What kind of scholarship was well supported during Qing rule?

- **a.** histories of China
- **b.** writings about Confucius's ideas
- **c.** encyclopedias
- **d.** all of the above

Women During the Qing Dynasty

As you just learned, the growth of trade during the Qing dynasty led to urbanization. In the cities, people enjoyed activities, such as reading and attending the theater, that were not available to poor country people.

Another difference between the culture of rural and urban Qing China had to do with women. In the country, women were valued as contributing members of the family. Although they had a lower status than men, they were needed to run the farms and bear children. Without women, the rural Chinese family could not survive.

However, it was different in the city. Families owed their survival to the work of the husbands and fathers. They worked as traders, merchants, or craftsmen. Women were not needed to contribute to the economy of the family. Over time, women were regarded as less and less important. Today, we would say that they were discriminated against.

Perhaps the most dramatic example of this discrimination was the practice of **foot binding.** Little girls, starting at about age five, had their feet tightly bound with cloth. They were required to keep their feet bound for several years. Over time, the pressure from the cloth would bend and eventually break the arch of each foot.

As you can imagine, foot binding was very painful. It resulted in feet that were curved under and about half the size of normal feet. Women who had had their feet bound, of course, found it difficult even to walk.

Foot binding was a status symbol for the Chinese of this time. By crippling the women in his family, or by marrying a woman already crippled, a man proved that he did not need "his" women to work.

Foot binding had been practiced before, but it reached its peak during the Qing dynasty. Despite government efforts to prevent it, the practice was widespread.

THINK ABOUT IT

Throughout history, people in every culture have done painful things to their bodies to identify with a certain group or image. This continues to happen today, even in modern American culture. Some examples are tattoos, body piercing, and high-heeled shoes for women. Can you think of any other examples? Have you ever done something like this to fit in? Write your answers on a separate sheet of paper.

PRACTICE 32: Women During the Qing Dynasty

Circle the letter of the correct answer to each of the following questions.

1. What was foot binding?
   - **a.** the practice of binding and breaking girls' feet
   - **b.** a style of footwear
   - **c.** a way to prepare a man's feet for battle
   - **d.** none of the above

2. What word describes the way urban women were treated during the Qing dynasty?
   - **a.** disrespectfully
   - **b.** equally
   - **c.** fairly
   - **d.** respectfully

The Decline of the Qing Dynasty

The Qing dynasty was established in 1644. It lasted until 1911. Many factors led to the decline of the Qing. One was China's increased population. The growing numbers of people were difficult for the Qing rulers to govern effectively. There were fewer and fewer government officials in relation to the number of people. Many officials became corrupt and accepted bribes. They used public moneys to line their own pockets instead of to help the people.

As the population increased, so did taxes. Tired of high taxes and corrupt officials, the Chinese people grew increasingly unhappy with Qing rule. Eventually, in the 1700s, there was a rebellion.

Meanwhile, China's northern frontier—from which the Manchus originally came—was being threatened. The Chinese armies had grown weaker, since there hadn't been a war in generations. Armies of the northern tribes began to increase their raids on China.

All of these factors led to the decline of the Qing dynasty. The final fall of the Qing, however, resulted from European influence in China. You will learn about this in a later lesson.

■ PRACTICE 33: The Decline of the Qing Dynasty

Circle the letter of the correct answer to each of the following questions.

1. Which of the following factors contributed to the fall of the Qing dynasty?
- **a.** an increasing population
- **b.** corrupt government officials
- **c.** raids from northern tribes
- **d.** all of the above

2. Which of the following was the MOST important factor in the fall of the Qing dynasty?
- **a.** an increasing population
- **b.** corrupt government officials
- **c.** high taxes
- **d.** the role of the Europeans

LESSON 5: India Under Mogul Rule

GOAL: To explain the origins, development, and decline of the Mogul Empire in India

WORDS TO KNOW

Age of Invasions	**Hindu**	**Mogul Empire**
castes	**Islam**	**Moguls**
gurus	**Marathas**	**Sikhism**

NAMES TO KNOW

Akbar	**Babur the Tiger**	**Shah Jahan**
Aurangzeb	**Nanak**	

PLACES TO KNOW

Golden Temple	**Taj Mahal**	**India**

The Age of Invasions

The great Gupta Empire ruled **India** from about 300 to about 500. This time is remembered as a golden age in India. In 535, though, the Gupta Empire was conquered. For nearly a century before that, many peoples had begun to invade India. India suffered from these invasions for another thousand years. There were so many invasions that the period of Indian history from about 500 to about 1500 is sometimes called the **Age of Invasions.**

Two Huns

The first to invade the Gupta Empire were the Huns. They came from the north and conquered all of northern India. Within a century, the Huns were defeated. But, northern India had been split into smaller kingdoms. In 612, the leader of one of these kingdoms, Harsha, conquered the others. He then ruled what had once been the Gupta Empire. After his death, India once again split into small kingdoms.

In the early 700s, the Muslims entered India. By about 1200, they had conquered the land. At this time, the Muslims ruled a great empire that stretched across much of Asia, Africa, and Europe. The Muslims treated the Hindu peoples of India harshly. They killed countless Hindus and took all that they had. Still, the Muslims brought many important ideas to India. They introduced things such as paper and gunpowder. They also took many Indian ideas, such as Arabic numerals, and spread them throughout their empire.

Eventually, the Muslims, too, were conquered. A new empire in India arose. You will read about this empire below and on the following pages.

■ PRACTICE 34: The Age of Invasions

Circle the letter of the correct answer to each of the following questions.

1. When was the Age of Invasions?
- **a.** about 300 to about 500
- **b.** about 500 to about 1500
- **c.** about 700 to about 1200
- **d.** about 400 to about 500

2. Who conquered India around 1200?
- **a.** the Huns
- **b.** the Hindus
- **c.** the Muslims
- **d.** the Chinese

The Mogul Empire

Babur the Tiger was a fierce warrior, a Muslim, and the ruler of a small kingdom in central Asia. After losing his kingdom, he led his people on a conquest. In 1526, at the Battle of Panipat, he defeated the Muslims who had been ruling India. Babur set himself up as emperor, and the **Mogul Empire** began.

The name *Mogul* is really just a different version of the name *Mongol.* The Mongols were the nomadic tribes of central Asia who were united under Genghis Khan. In fact, Babur was related to Genghis Khan, who had lived three centuries before. The descendants of the Mongols who ruled in India are called the **Moguls.** This is why the empire Babur founded is called the Mogul Empire.

Babur the Tiger died in 1530, just four years after his rule began. By that time, the empire covered north central India, or about one fourth of the area that is India today. Within 200 years, however, the empire stretched across almost all of India. The map to the right shows the Mogul Empire at its peak, in the early 1700s.

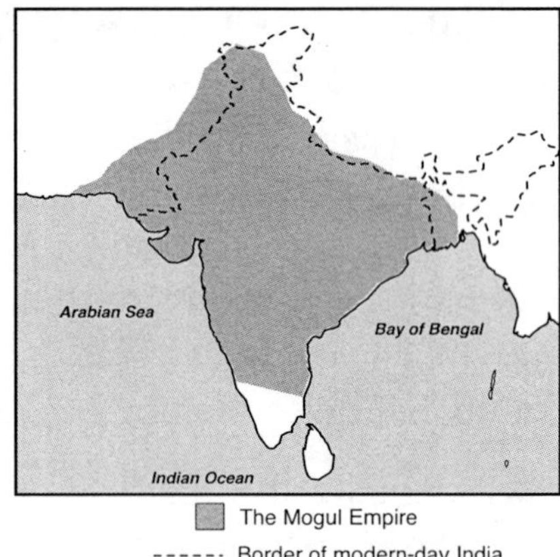

The Mogul Empire in the Early 1700s

PRACTICE 35: The Mogul Empire

Circle the letter of the correct answer to each of the following questions.

1. Who founded the Mogul Empire?

- **a.** Genghis Khan
- **b.** Babur the Tiger
- **c.** Kublai Khan
- **d.** none of the above

2. Where was the Mogul Empire located?

- **a.** central Asia
- **b.** India
- **c.** Panipat
- **d.** China

3. About how much of the area that is India today was ruled by the Moguls under Babur the Tiger?

- **a.** about one fourth
- **b.** about one half
- **c.** about three fourths
- **d.** nearly all

4. About how much of India was under Mogul rule by the early 1700s?
    a. about one fourth
    b. about one half
    c. about three fourths
    d. nearly all

Hindus and Muslims in the Mogul Empire

Babur the Tiger, who founded the Mogul Empire, was a Muslim. This means that he was a follower of the religion of **Islam.** He captured northern India from other Muslim rulers. At this time, most of the people of India were not Muslim. Nearly everyone in India followed the **Hindu** religion.

The Hindu and Muslim religions are very different. For example, the Muslims believe in one god. The Hindus worship many gods. Muslims believe in the fundamental equality of all people. In Hindu society, there is a rigid system of division into classes, called **castes.** At the time, Muslims believed a man could have many wives. Hindus did not. These are just a few of the many important differences that separated the mass of Indian people from their Muslim rulers.

Differences in religion often lead to conflict. When Muslims invaded India, around 1000 C.E., they killed countless numbers of Hindus. Later, they were less harsh. And many Hindus converted to Islam to avoid persecution or to escape from the caste system.

Still, Muslims treated Hindus as second-class citizens at best. The Hindus, along with other non-Muslims, were even forced to pay a special tax.

One man who helped change the fate of Hindus in India was a Muslim named **Akbar.** Akbar was the greatest of the Mogul emperors. He ruled for nearly 50 years, from 1556 to his death in 1605. He was the grandson of Babur, who had founded the empire.

Akbar knew that peace and prosperity depended on harmony among the different religions in India. To promote such harmony, he repealed the special tax that non-Muslims had been forced to pay. To symbolize the new spirit of tolerance, he even married a Hindu woman. Akbar's tolerance and support of the Hindu religion won him the loyalty of the Hindus under his rule. Moreover, Akbar had an interest in all religions. He invited members of many religions to discuss and debate religious ideas with and before him. Akbar's promotion of religious tolerance has been called one of his great contributions to India.

Akbar was also known for strengthening the empire. He expanded Mogul rule east, west, and south. Akbar also strengthened the Mogul system of government and set up new systems of money and taxation.

PRACTICE 36: Hindus and Muslims in the Mogul Empire

Circle the letter of the correct answer to each of the following questions.

1. What religion was Akbar?

- **a.** Hindu
- **b.** Muslim
- **c.** Christian
- **d.** none of the above

2. How did Akbar show tolerance for Hindus in India?

- **a.** by marrying a Hindu woman
- **b.** by repealing the special tax on non-Muslims
- **c.** by holding debates on religious ideas
- **d.** all of the above

Shah Jahan and the Taj Mahal

Shah Jahan followed Akbar as the next great ruler of the Mogul Empire. He ruled from 1628 to 1658. Like Akbar's rule, Shah Jahan's rule is well remembered as a time of peace and prosperity.

But Shah Jahan is best remembered for building the **Taj Mahal.** The Taj Mahal is universally recognized as one of the most beautiful buildings in the world. Shah Jahan ordered it built as a tomb for one of his wives, Mumtaz Mahal.

The Taj Mahal has many elements of both Muslim and Hindu design. Shah Jahan invited designers, artists, architects, and engineers from far and wide to help design it. Today, the Taj Mahal is one of the most recognized buildings in the world.

The Taj Mahal

It took 20,000 workers about 20 years to build the Taj Mahal. They worked from 1632 to 1653. The square central structure measures 186 feet on each side. Its dome is 120 feet tall. Each of the four towers, or minarets, that surround the main building stands 133 feet tall. The entire building is built of white marble. Teams of elephants dragged huge blocks of marble from as far away as 100 miles.

After his death, Shah Jahan was laid to rest in the Taj Mahal.

THINK ABOUT IT

You might think the Taj Mahal was named after Shah Jahan's wife, Mumtaz Mahal. In fact, however, the word *mahal* means "building." The word *taj* means "crown." The Taj Mahal's name means "crown of buildings." Why do you think it is called that? Write your answer on a separate sheet of paper.

PRACTICE 37: Shah Jahan and the Taj Mahal

Circle the letter of the correct answer to each of the following questions.

1. What is the Taj Mahal?
   a. a palace
   b. a tomb
   c. a fort
   d. a temple

2. Who built the Taj Mahal?
   a. Shah Jahan
   b. Akbar
   c. Mumtaz Mahal
   d. Babur the Tiger

3. What is the Taj Mahal made of?
   a. brick
   b. marble
   c. wood
   d. granite

Nanak and Sikhism

Nanak was not an emperor of the Mogul Empire. But he was a powerful force in the empire. Nanak was born a Hindu in the late 1400s. As a young man, he became a prophet and a mystic. His goal was to unite the two great faiths in India at the time—Hinduism and Islam—into one religion. In his teachings, he adopted some of the elements from both faiths. For example, he adopted the Muslim belief in one god and the Hindu belief in reincarnation.

Nanak's teachings and those of his followers gave birth to a new religion: **Sikhism**. Sikhs believe that Nanak and nine other Sikh **gurus,** or teachers, spoke the word of God. The most holy site of Sikhism is the **Golden Temple**. This is a beautiful building built in 1577 by the fourth of the ten Sikh gurus, Ram Das.

A Sikh Today

Nanak taught, among many other things, that people should be peaceful. But many Muslims persecuted the Sikhs. In response, the Sikhs became militant. By 1699, the Sikhs had organized a powerful army. For centuries, they fought for their own homeland in India. Today, the Indian state of Punjab is largely controlled by India's 15 million or so Sikhs. But battles between Sikhs and the Indian government continue to flare up.

■ PRACTICE 38: Nanak and Sikhism

Circle the letter of the correct answer to each of the following questions.

1. What religion did Nanak begin?
- **a.** Hinduism
- **b.** Islam
- **c.** Sikhism
- **d.** Nanakism

2. What is a guru?
- **a.** a teacher
- **b.** a holy site
- **c.** an emperor
- **d.** a Muslim

3. What is the holiest shrine for Sikhs?
- **a.** the Taj Mahal
- **b.** Punjab
- **c.** the Golden Temple
- **d.** Mecca

Aurangzeb and the Decline of the Mogul Empire

Aurangzeb was Shah Jahan's son. Aurangzeb's older brother, Dara Shikoh, was to succeed their father on the throne. But Aurangzeb wanted to become shah. He threw his father in prison. To seize control of the empire, Aurangzeb then fought his brothers and executed two of them. These cruel acts were just some of many that would be the hallmark of Aurangzeb's rule. He declared himself emperor of the Mogul Empire in 1658. Aurangzeb took the title "Alamgir," which means "world conqueror."

In the years that followed, Aurangzeb worked to become the "world conqueror" of his title. He tried to bring the whole subcontinent of India under his rule. Aurangzeb's forces succeeded in taking Assam to the northeast and Kashmir to the north. After years of fighting, he took the Deccan region from the **Marathas,** a warlike group of tribes. Under Aurangzeb, the empire reached its greatest size.

Aurangzeb's rule was marked by violence. However, the emperor was driven by religious faith. Unlike the rulers before him, he lived a very simple life. He believed that Islam did not allow anyone to listen to music. He sent away all the musicians, singers, and dancers at the court. Because Islam does not allow images of living beings, Mogul artists could no longer include people in their paintings.

Aurangzeb also said that Muslim law should be followed in India. He forbade drinking and gambling. He did away with all taxes that were not part of Islamic law or tradition. When this hurt the economy, he brought back the tax on non-Muslims.

In fact, he was harsh with non-Muslims in many ways. Some historians think his aim was to convert all non-Muslims in India to Islam. Most people in India at that time were Hindus. Under Aurangzeb, they had to obey Muslim law, not Hindu law. Some Hindu customs were made illegal. Hindu religious fairs were outlawed. No new Hindu temples could be built, and some existing temples were destroyed. Hindus had to pay the special tax that Muslims did not have to pay.

The Sikhs were also treated harshly. Sikhs had supported Aurangzeb's brother Dara. As a result, Aurangzeb was severe with the Sikhs. He tried to convert the ninth Sikh master, Guru Tegh Bahadur Ji, to Islam. When Bahadur Ji refused, Aurangzeb had him executed. Bahadur Ji's successor wanted the Sikhs to be able to defend their faith. More and more, the Sikhs became a militant group. They were willing and ready to take up arms for their faith.

Aurangzeb's harsh treatment of non-Muslims caused a great deal of resentment. At the same time, the years of war on the northern, eastern, and southern borders had drained the economy. The Marathas in the Deccan had never stopped fighting. They continued to rule within the Deccan. Also, the expanded empire was too large to rule efficiently. Individual states rebelled and declared themselves independent.

Even before Aurangzeb died in 1707, the empire was falling apart. In the years after his death, it collapsed. The Sikhs set up an independent state in the Punjab. The Marathas regained control of the Deccan. By 1740, the Marathas had more territory than the Moguls.

IN REAL LIFE

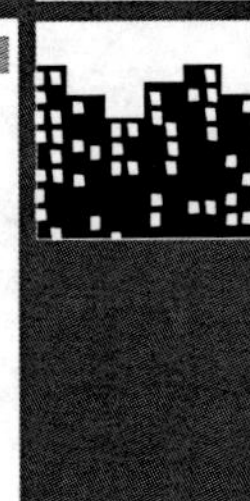

Have you ever heard a company executive called a *mogul*? This English word means "a powerful person." It comes from the rulers of the Mogul Empire. Other nations saw these rulers as very powerful and important. Can you think of anyone in your life who has been referred to as a mogul? Brainstorm a list with classmates.

Within 50 years, Mogul rulers could not hold the empire together. Traders from Europe soon came to control much of the divided land. The great Mogul Empire was no more.

PRACTICE 39: Aurangzeb and the Decline of the Mogul Empire

Circle the letter of the correct answer to each of the following questions.

1. What religion was Aurangzeb?
- **a.** Hindu
- **b.** Sikh
- **c.** Muslim
- **d.** Christian

2. What was Aurangzeb's policy toward Hindus and Sikhs?
- **a.** He tolerated them.
- **b.** He encouraged them.
- **c.** He tried to get rid of them.
- **d.** He ignored them.

3. What was the result of this policy?
- **a.** The Mogul Empire was strengthened.
- **b.** The Mogul Empire fell apart.
- **c.** There was little change.
- **d.** The Sikhs took over the empire.

LESSON 6: The Feudal State of Japan

GOAL: To describe Japanese government and life under Japanese feudalism and the shogunates

WORDS TO KNOW

Ashikaga shogunate

Bushido

closing of Japan

daimyo

domains

firearms

Great Peace of the Tokugawas

hara-kiri

Japanese feudalism

Minamoto shogunate

samurai

seppuku

shogun

shogunate

Tokugawa shogunate

NAMES TO KNOW

Ashikaga Takauji

Minamoto

Minamoto Yoritomo

Tokugawa Ieyasu

PLACES TO KNOW

Edo

Tokyo

Feudalism and the Shogunate

Early Japan was ruled by wealthy, powerful families. Each family controlled a large estate of land. The lord of each estate was called a **daimyo.** The majority of Japanese people—poor farmers—were ruled by the daimyos. This system of government is known as **Japanese feudalism.**

Early Japan did have an emperor, but his power was limited. He was usually just a figurehead. The real control was held by the powerful families. By the late 1100s, the family who ruled Japan was the **Minamoto** family.

The head of the Minamoto family was **Minamoto Yoritomo** (1147–1199).

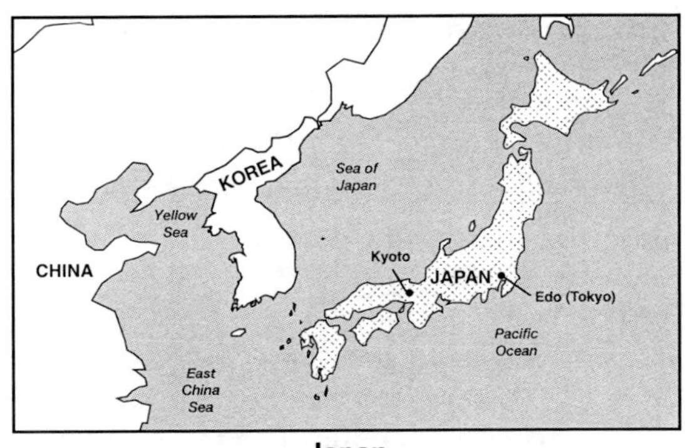

Japan

In 1192, Yoritomo was named the first **shogun,** or general, of Japan. The daimyos came under the control of the shogun. In theory, the emperor ruled Japan. But the real power was held by the shogun and his family. After 1192, the goal of every powerful family in Japan was to provide the shogun. The Japanese government under the shogun was called the **shogunate.** The period during which the Minamotos controlled the shogunate is called the **Minamoto shogunate.**

The shogunate lasted in Japan from 1192 to 1867. You will read more about the shogunate on the following pages.

TIP

Notice how some of the boldface words in the text above are related. For example, the name **Minamoto** and the word **shogun** both appear in the name of the period, **Minamoto shogunate.** Historical periods are often named for the most important people who lived during the period, or for the time's most important events.

PRACTICE 40: Feudalism and the Shogunate

Decide if each statement below is true (**T**) or false (**F**). Write the correct letter on the line before each statement.

_____ **1.** Under Japanese feudalism, most of the people were shoguns.

_____ **2.** The first shogun of Japan was Minamoto Yoritomo.

_____ **3.** The first shogun of Japan was a member of the Minamoto family.

_____ **4.** During the shogunate, Japan's emperor was the most powerful person in the land.

The Shogun

As you have learned, the first shogun of Japan was Yoritomo of the Minamoto family. Over the centuries, two other ruling families—the Ashikaga and the Tokugawa—would also provide shoguns. You will read about these families later.

The word *shogun* means "great general" in Japanese. The shogun was the chief military officer of Japan.

The shogun was supposed to serve the emperor. In reality, he was the leader of Japan. But even the shogun was not an independent ruler. Each shogun worked to advance the powerful family of which he was a member. Thus, while Yoritomo was shogun, he shared power with other members of his family, the Minamoto. This was in keeping with Japanese tradition, in which rule rested within strong families.

The shogun—and the family he supported—had enormous power. The shogun was the chief military officer of Japan. The shogun also controlled all appointments to the government, the law of the entire country, the finances of the government and the country, and even the courts. It is hard to imagine the power that each shogun wielded.

From the moment the shogunate began, the goal of every powerful family in Japan was to gain control of it. As a result, the period of the shogunate was marked by many civil wars.

■ PRACTICE 41: The Shogun

Circle the letter of the correct answer to each of the following questions.

1. What does *shogun* mean?

a. "great general"
b. "family"
c. "emperor"
d. "high priest"

2. What did the shogun control?
   a. all appointments to the government
   b. the law of the country
   c. the finances of the government and the country
   d. all of the above

3. Who was the first shogun?
   a. Ashikaga
   b. Tokugawa
   c. Yoritomo
   d. Yamaha

The Samurai

The shogun was the most powerful person in Japan. But he could not control everything on the local level. At this level, the daimyos held power. The daimyos were military lords who ruled the various regions of Japan.

The warriors who worked for the daimyos were the famous **samurai.** Actually, most daimyos were samurai themselves. The word *samurai* refers both to these individual warriors and to the group, or class, to which they belonged. At the height of the shogunate period, about five percent of all Japanese people, or 1 in 20, were members of the samurai.

Most samurais were land-owning daimyos who held power over the poor peasants on their land. Samurai lived according to a strict code of bravery and honor, called **Bushido.** To a samurai, dishonor was worse than death. To avoid it, he would commit **seppuku,** or **hara-kiri.** Both terms refer to a ritual form of suicide in which the samurai killed himself by cutting open his abdomen with a sword.

TIP

Understanding the origin of a term can sometimes help you remember its meaning. The word *hara-kiri* comes from two Japanese words: *hara,* meaning "belly," and kiri, meaning "cutting." You may even hear this word used in modern English to mean "suicide."

The samurai are legendary for their bravery. A true samurai was supposed to be able to withstand incredible pain and hardship without complaint. Samurais were also expected to put loyalty above all else. Bushido called for absolute loyalty to one's family and daimyo, no matter what the cost.

A samurai wore a special headdress and carried two swords. Samurai were among the greatest swordsmen in history. Their swords were works of art, made by a special, ritualistic process that made them as strong as the warriors who wielded them.

PRACTICE 42: The Samurai

Circle the letter of the correct answer to each of the following questions.

1. What was a samurai?

- **a.** a code of conduct
- **b.** a warrior
- **c.** a kind of suicide
- **d.** a sword

2. What was Bushido?

- **a.** a code of conduct
- **b.** a warrior
- **c.** a kind of suicide
- **d.** a sword

The Ashikaga Shogunate

As you have read, the first shogun was Yoritomo of the Minamoto family. After Yoritomo died, other shoguns from the Minamoto family took his place.

Over time, the Minamoto shogunate began to lose control of Japan. Remember, rival families often warred to try to become the leaders of Japan. In 1336, armies loyal to the Ashikaga family captured the important city of Kyoto. The Ashikagas quickly gained power, and in 1338, **Ashikaga Takauji** (1305–1358) became shogun of Japan. His shogunate was based in Kyoto.

The Ashikaga family controlled Japan for more than 200 years. This period is called the **Ashikaga shogunate.** During this time, each new shogun came from this family. But like the Minamotos before them, the Ashikagas gradually lost control. During at least half of their rule, the country was in a state of civil war. Samurais loyal to different families fought battle after battle. Each was trying to control the shogunate.

Eventually, one family would win out. During their rule, Japan would enjoy a great period of peace and prosperity.

■ PRACTICE 43: The Ashikaga Shogunate

Circle the letter of the correct answer to each of the following questions.

1. What shogunate did the Ashikaga shogunate replace?

a. the Minamoto shogunate
b. the Kyoto shogunate
c. the Tokugawa shogunate
d. the samurai shogunate

2. Who was the first Ashikaga shogun?

a. Kyoto
b. Yoritomo Minamoto
c. Ashikaga Takauji
d. Bushido

The Tokugawa Shogunate

Toward the end of the Ashikagas' rule, civil war racked Japan. During the late 1500s, three rival daimyos came to power in quick succession. The first, Oda Nobunaga, ended the Ashikagas' rule. He was soon killed. Toyotomi Hideyoshi then came to power. An ambitious man, he tried, but failed, to conquer Korea.

The third daimyo who came to power during this period was **Tokugawa Ieyasu** (1543–1616). He became shogun in 1603. When he became shogun, Tokugawa Ieyasu established his capital at **Edo.** Later, Edo would be renamed Tokyo. **Tokyo** is still the capital of Japan.

Tokugawa Ieyasu wanted a unified Japan without civil war. He divided Japan into 250 **domains,** or regions. Each domain was ruled by a daimyo loyal to the Tokugawa shogunate. These daimyos swore allegiance to Tokugawa Ieyasu and the other Tokugawa shoguns who followed him.

The **Tokugawa shogunate** controlled Japan for the next 250 years. The Tokugawa shogunate lasted until the end of the shogunate period in 1867. During most of this time, there was no civil war or rebellion in the country. Thus, the period from about 1603 to 1867 is called the **Great Peace of the Tokugawas.**

■ PRACTICE 44: The Tokugawa Shogunate

Circle the letter of the correct answer to each of the following questions.

1. What city did Edo later become?
- **a.** Tokugawa
- **b.** Nagasaki
- **c.** Tokyo
- **d.** Hiroshima

2. Which statement about the Tokugawa shogunate is FALSE?
- **a.** Tokugawa Ieyasu became shogun in 1603.
- **b.** The Tokugawa shogunate ruled Japan for the next 250 years.
- **c.** The Tokugawa shogunate was the last shogunate in Japan.
- **d.** During the Tokugawa shogunate, there were many civil wars.

Life During the Great Peace of the Tokugawas

Life in Japan changed during the Tokugawa shogunate. This stands to reason, since the Tokugawas ruled Japan for about 265 years.

One of the major changes was in the way the country was governed. The Tokugawa took steps to create a stable government and a stable Japan.

To help create a stable government, the Tokugawas reduced the power of the daimyos. They prohibited daimyos from entering into alliances with each other. They also prohibited daimyos from building new castles. The Tokugawas even went as far as holding the families of the daimyos hostage. The families had to live in the capital, and the daimyos themselves were required to spend every other year there.

The Tokugawa shogunate also launched a campaign to disarm the peasants. They were not allowed to own swords or any other weapons. Thus, the Tokugawas eliminated the chance of a peasant uprising.

To help create a stable society, the Tokugawas instituted a new system of social classes. It was based on the social class system in China. At the top of this class system were the warriors. Next in importance were workers and peasant farmers. Merchants ranked at the bottom of the class system. These classes were hereditary, which means that they were determined by birth. A person could not advance to a higher class. And, only members of the warrior class were allowed to be government officials.

Some other changes that took place during the Tokugawa period were, of course, beyond that family's control. During this time, trade within Japan increased. As more people made their living by trade, the number and size of cities grew. As you recall, this process is called urbanization.

All of these changes meant that modern Japan was slowly taking shape.

THINK ABOUT IT

By reducing the power of the daimyos, disarming the peasants, and starting a class system, the Tokugawas did everything they could to stabilize Japanese society. Why do you think this was so important to them? Write your answer on a separate sheet of paper.

PRACTICE 45: Life During the Great Peace of the Tokugawas

Circle the letter of the correct answer to each of the following questions.

1. What did the Tokugawa shogunate do to control the daimyos?

- **a.** prohibited daimyos from entering into alliances with each other
- **b.** prohibited daimyos from building new castles
- **c.** held families hostage
- **d.** all of the above

2. What happened to trade and urbanization in Japan during the Tokugawa shogunate?
    a. Both increased.
    b. Both decreased.
    c. Both stayed the same.
    d. Trade decreased, but urbanization increased.

Foreign Contacts and the Closing of Japan

Japan is an island nation. In the days before modern ships, aircraft, and electronic communications, it was very isolated from the rest of the world.

As you may know, the Japanese did have extensive contact with the Chinese earlier in their history. Under Toyotomi Hideyoshi, Japan tried to invade Korea. But for the most part, Japan remained isolated.

Japan's isolation began to change in the mid-1500s. Portuguese sailors, seeking new trading partners, arrived in Japan. They traded with the Japanese.

In a pattern that was often repeated, the traders were followed by Christian missionaries. These were people trying to spread the Christian faith. The missionaries, mainly Jesuits, concentrated on converting daimyos. Then newly Christian daimyos encouraged the people they led to adopt the religion. The tactic worked well. Hundreds of thousands of Japanese converted to Christianity.

This did not sit well with the Tokugawas. As you might imagine, they viewed any change, especially one so widespread, as a threat to their rule. Moreover, the Tokugawas felt that the foreign traders corrupted Japanese culture in other ways. For example, the traders introduced **firearms** (guns) into the country. Here was a weapon that could easily defeat the samurai.

The Tokugawa shogunate responded to these threats by simply closing the borders of Japan. Under new rules, no foreigner was allowed into Japan. The policy was aimed at eliminating threats to the Tokugawa shogunate. This policy is known as the **closing of Japan**.

The policy was successful. Traders and missionaries were no longer allowed in Japan. Even shipwrecked sailors who struggled to the Japanese shore were often killed.

This policy of isolation went both ways. Not only were foreigners not allowed into Japan, but Japanese were not allowed to leave Japan. Foreign travel was prohibited. So, too, was the construction of any ships that could cross the ocean.

This policy eventually changed. But for 200 years, it worked incredibly well. Japan had effectively sealed itself off from outside influence. The Tokugawas and other Japanese concentrated on improving Japan from within. The result was one of the most unusual cultures in history.

IN REAL LIFE

The closing of Japan may seem like an incredible page from history, and something that could never happen again. But, in fact, this type of policy was in place in Europe as recently as the 1980s.

After World War II, many countries in Eastern Europe came under the control of the Soviet Union's Communist party. The borders of these countries were "closed" to prevent people from having any contact with Westerners.

The most dramatic example of this policy was the Berlin Wall. Berlin is a city in Germany. After the war, the eastern half of the city (and the country) came under Communist control. In 1961, the East German government put up a wall to separate East Berlin from West Berlin. By 1980, the Berlin Wall was 10 feet high. It extended for 75 miles. Many East Germans who tried to cross the wall to get to West Berlin were shot and killed.

In 1989, the Communist government in East Germany collapsed. The whole world watched as the Berlin Wall was torn down, and the city was reunited.

■ PRACTICE 46: Foreign Contacts and the Closing of Japan

Circle the letter of the correct answer to each of the following questions.

1. Which European nation first began to trade with Japan?
   a. England
   b. France
   c. Portugal
   d. Spain

2. Why did the Tokugawas object to firearms?
   a. Firearms were dangerous.
   b. Firearms could defeat the samurai.
   c. Firearms were expensive.
   d. Firearms were already in Japan.

3. What did the missionaries do?
   a. traded with the Japanese
   b. studied Japanese religion
   c. converted the Japanese to Christianity
   d. attacked the Japanese

4. How did the Tokugawas react to the threats of foreign contact?
   a. They closed the borders of Japan.
   b. They killed all of the missionaries.
   c. They allowed Japanese to travel freely.
   d. They allowed only shipwrecked sailors to stay in Japan.

5. Which of the following was prohibited after the closing of Japan?
   a. travel to foreign countries
   b. construction of ships that could cross the ocean
   c. trade with foreign countries
   d. all of the above

UNIT 2 REVIEW

Circle the letter of the correct answer to each of the following questions.

1. What did Nurhachi do?
   a. unite the peoples of Manchuria
   b. bind the feet of women
   c. create cities throughout China
   d. do away with the Chinese civil-service exams

2. Why was foot binding practiced?
   a. as a form of art
   b. to prevent disease
   c. as a status symbol
   d. all of the above

3. What led to the decline of the Qing dynasty?
   a. high taxes
   b. corrupt officials
   c. a growing population
   d. all of the above

4. What faith did the rulers of the Mogul Empire follow?
   a. Hinduism
   b. Islam
   c. Christianity
   d. Sikhism

5. What faith did most of the people of the Mogul Empire follow?
   a. Hinduism
   b. Islam
   c. Christianity
   d. Sikhism

6. Which emperor treated non-Muslims harshly?
   a. Aurangzeb
   b. Babur the Tiger
   c. Shah Jahan
   d. Akbar

7. What was a daimyo?
    a. a feudal lord
    b. the general of Japan
    c. someone who spread Christianity
    d. a period of peace

8. What was a shogun?
    a. a feudal lord
    b. the general of Japan
    c. someone who spread Christianity
    d. a period of peace

9. What European nation was first to trade with Japan?
    a. England
    b. France
    c. Portugal
    d. Spain

10. Why did the Japanese rulers object to contact with the Europeans?
    a. The Europeans brought firearms.
    b. The Europeans brought Christianity.
    c. The Europeans corrupted Japanese culture.
    d. all of the above

UNIT 2 APPLICATION ACTIVITY
Lessons From History

The events and developments of the Mogul Empire may seem like ancient history, far removed from your own life. But you may be surprised at how similar those issues are to those we face today.

In the chart on the next page, the first column lists some events and developments of the Mogul Empire. The second column shows you the general issue that was the basis for each event. For example, the persecution of non-Muslims was really an issue of cultural prejudice.

For each general issue, think of an example of this same issue in our world today. Write your examples in the third column. If you need help thinking of examples, talk with your neighbors and family members. You might also scan your local newspaper.

Event and / or development of the Mogul Empire	General issue	Example from today's world
Non-Muslims faced persecution.	cultural prejudice	
Members of a new religion, Sikhism, were treated poorly.	religious persecution	
Peoples whom the Moguls conquered, such as the Maratha, came to resent Mogul rule.	resentment of government	
Cruel policies of a harsh leader, Aurangzeb, caused widespread discontent.	unfair government policies	

UNIT 3
European Exploration and the New World

LESSON 7: The Need for New Trade Routes

GOAL: To identify the factors that led to the Age of Exploration; to discuss the voyages of early Portuguese explorers

WORDS TO KNOW

Age of Exploration

caravel

cog

demand

discoverers

explorers

forecastle

frame and plank construction

full-rigged ship

lateen sail

missionaries

Ottoman Empire

rudder

scurvy

sea route

sterncastle

trade

trade routes

NAMES TO KNOW

Vasco da Gama **Bartholomeu Dias** **Henry the Navigator**

PLACES TO KNOW

Calicut, India **Cape of Good Hope** **Indies**

The Age of Exploration

In this unit, you will learn about the **Age of Exploration.** The Age of Exploration has other names, too, like the Age of Discovery and the Great Age of European Exploration.

The Age of Exploration lasted from about 1400 to 1600. During this time, European sailors explored many parts of the world, especially North America. We call these sailors **explorers** and **discoverers.** We say that they "discovered" the places they sailed to, but of course they did not. The peoples who already lived there had "discovered" these areas thousands of years earlier. But these regions were new to the Europeans. To *discover* means to "uncover," and the Europeans did "uncover" these areas for themselves.

Many of the most famous people in history, such as Christopher Columbus, achieved greatness during the Age of Exploration. The results of the many explorations changed European life forever. They also changed life in the new areas the Europeans explored. In fact, many historians view the Age of Exploration as the greatest period of change in history.

■ PRACTICE 47: The Age of Exploration

Circle the letter of the correct answer to each of the following questions.

1. What is another name for the Age of Exploration?
   a. the Age of Discovery
   b. the Great Age of European Exploration
   c. the Golden Age
   d. both *a* and *b*

2. When was the Age of Exploration?
   a. about 1100 to about 1400
   b. about 1400 to about 1600
   c. about 1600 to about 1900
   d. about 900 to about 1000

Trade with Asia

What started Europeans exploring? There are many reasons, and different explorers had different reasons for their voyages. But one reason stands out above all others: **trade.**

Europeans had traded with Asians for centuries. Traveling mostly overland along the Silk Road, Europeans wanted spices (especially pepper, cinnamon, and cloves), silks, jewels, porcelain, and other items from Asia. In return, Asians earned money from this trade.

By the end of the Middle Ages, though, a change occurred. The **Ottoman Empire** gained control of the trading routes between Europe and Asia. The Ottomans could set the price on Asian goods. This empire grew rich as a "middleman" between Europe and Asia.

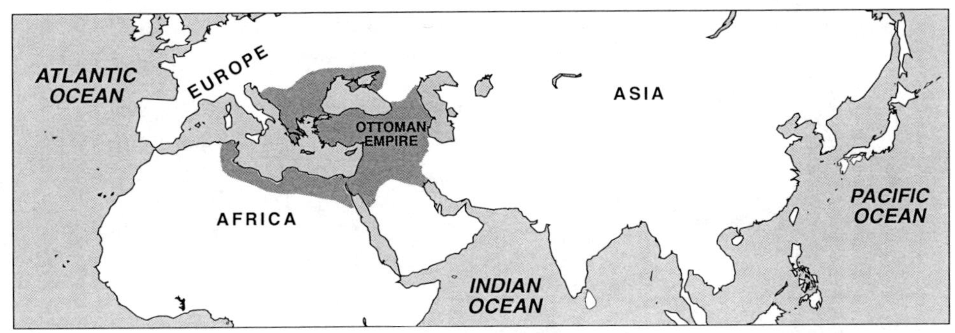

The Ottoman Empire

The Ottomans were able to increase prices constantly because the **demand,** or desire, for the products of Asia was growing in Europe. Whenever demand increases, prices increase as well. The European demand for Asian goods increased largely because the European economy was improving. Europeans had more money. They wanted to spend it on Asian goods. Also, during the Crusades, many more Europeans became aware of Asian goods. Finally, many Europeans made money as merchants and traders. They imported goods from Asia, increased the items' prices, and sold them to customers at a profit.

The Europeans soon realized that they could save money by importing goods *directly* from Asia, rather than going through the Ottoman Empire. To do this, they needed to establish direct **trade routes** with Asia. Since the overland route was blocked by the Ottoman Empire, they needed a **sea route.** Europeans set off exploring to find a sea route to Asia. The Age of Exploration had begun.

The Europeans searched for a sea route to the Indies. The **Indies** is what Europeans called the eastern parts of Asia (India, China, Japan, and the islands of the southwest Pacific). It might surprise you to learn that most of the great explorers you will read about never reached the Indies. But their expeditions uncovered many other parts of the world that were new to the Europeans.

TIP

History isn't just the story of what happened in the past. It is also the story of why these things happened. Think about the Age of Exploration. This was one of the most important periods in history. It changed the face of the globe and even led to the formation of the United States. All of this didn't just happen by chance. The reason it all started, as you have just read, is because the Europeans wanted direct sea trade with Asia. Whenever you read history, look for the "why." It will give you a complete picture of the events you are reading about.

PRACTICE 48: Trade with Asia

Circle the letter of the correct answer to each of the following questions.

1. With what area of the world was Europe interested in trading at this time?

- **a.** the Americas
- **b.** the Indies
- **c.** the Ottoman Empire
- **d.** Africa

2. What is another name for the Indies?

- **a.** eastern Asia
- **b.** India
- **c.** the Silk Road
- **d.** the Caribbean

3. How did the Europeans want to reach the Indies?

- **a.** by land
- **b.** by sea
- **c.** through the Ottoman Empire
- **d.** by air

Missionaries

Christianity was an important factor during the Age of Exploration. Most Europeans of this time were Christian. They believed that theirs was the only true religion. Non-Christians were often persecuted and even killed. Christians wanted to convert everyone to their religion.

This desire followed the explorers overseas. Most of them were motivated, at least in part, by their desire to spread Christianity. For instance, Christopher Columbus believed God had chosen him to spread the Christian religion. The people who supported expeditions often felt the same way.

Wherever the explorers went, missionaries followed. **Missionaries** are people who are sent out to teach about and convert others to a religion. Sometimes, missionaries even went with the explorers on their journeys. In a pattern that was repeated over and over, missionaries tried to convert the peoples in the lands the explorers "discovered."

There were two main causes of the Age of Exploration. First, Europeans wanted to find a sea route to Asia. And second, they wanted to spread Christianity.

IN REAL LIFE

Today, most people of the Americas and about one third of the people in the entire world are Christians. This is largely the result of the work missionaries began during the Age of Exploration.

PRACTICE 49: Missionaries

Decide if each statement below is true (**T**) or false (**F**). Write the correct letter on the line before each statement.

_____ **1.** Missionaries followed many explorers.

_____ **2.** Explorers followed many missionaries.

_____ **3.** Missionaries wanted to spread the Christian religion.

A New Kind of Ship

So far, you have read about two important factors that helped bring about the Age of Exploration: the desire to establish new trade routes and the desire to spread Christianity. Of the two, the desire to open trade routes was the more important.

A third factor that helped European explorers sail far and wide was the development of a new kind of ship.

By about 1200, northern European shipbuilders had developed a kind of sailing ship called the cog. A **cog** had a large hull (frame or body), so it could carry a lot of trade goods. The hull was also strong and able to take the pounding of ocean waves. The cog had a single mast that carried a large, square sail. At the front (bow) and back (stern) of the ship, structures called castles were built. The front castle, or **forecastle,** was used for storage and as a place from which sailors could fight. The back castle, or **sterncastle,** was where the captain and important passengers stayed.

One important feature of the cog was that it was steered by a **rudder**. Before, ships had been steered by oars that came out of the side near the stern. The rudder was stronger and let sailors steer the ship better.

Meanwhile, another important development was taking place in southern Europe, around the Mediterranean. Centuries earlier, Arabs had invented the lateen sail. The **lateen sail** is triangular instead of square. Ships with lateen sails sailed better, especially when they were headed into the wind. Shipbuilders in southern Europe began to use the lateen sail more frequently. They attached lateen sails to ships that were built a new way, with **frame and plank construction.** This construction made ships light and strong.

So, in northern Europe, sturdy cogs steered by rudders were developed. In southern Europe, lateen sails were being used more often, and frame and plank construction had been developed. By the mid-1400s, European shipbuilders had developed a new kind of ship. It combined the advantages of the northern European cog and the southern European lateen ships. This new kind of ship was called the **full-rigged ship**.

Full-rigged ship

The full-rigged ship had three masts. The mast in the stern carried a lateen sail. The full-rigged ship had a forecastle and a stern castle. The ship was steered by a rudder. It had the roomy, sturdy hull of a cog, built with frame and plank construction. In short, the full-rigged ship was the best ship Europe had ever seen.

The development of the full-rigged ship helped lead to the Age of Exploration. During the entire period, it was the kind of ship European explorers used to discover the rest of the world.

The Europeans had already wanted to sail in uncharted seas. Now, they had the ships that could do it. A few outstanding individuals would soon sail into history.

THINK ABOUT IT

The development of the full-rigged vessel was a critical factor in the Age of Exploration. How do you think history might have been different if the Europeans had not developed such a ship? What technological developments of your own time do you think are changing history? Write your answers on a separate sheet of paper.

PRACTICE 50: A New Kind of Ship

Circle the letter of the correct answer to each of the following questions.

1. Where was the cog developed?
- **a.** northern Europe
- **b.** southern Europe
- **c.** Africa
- **d.** Asia

2. What shape is a lateen sail?
- **a.** square
- **b.** wide at the top
- **c.** circular
- **d.** triangular

3. What kind of ships did most explorers use?
   a. cogs
   b. full-rigged
   c. lateen
   d. galleys

Henry the Navigator

In the beginning of the Age of Exploration, one man stands out as especially important. He is Prince Henry of Portugal. He is known as **Henry the Navigator.**

Henry lived from 1394 to 1460. He was a prince, the son of a king and queen. Henry wanted to expand Portugal's limited trade with northern Africa. He also wanted to find African gold, which was being exported to Europe. Henry thought that if Portuguese ships could reach the source of this gold directly by sea, then he and Portugal would be greatly enriched.

It might surprise you to learn that Henry wasn't really a navigator or even a sailor. Rather, he raised money and organized expeditions. Henry invited the finest mapmakers and navigators of his time to help him. But, he never actually went on any of his expeditions.

Henry was governor in southern Portugal. There, on the rocky coast at Sagres, Henry began to gather together people with knowledge of the sea. They included sailors, mapmakers, shipbuilders, and instrument-makers. In Sagres, more accurate maps were created. Instruments for finding the way at sea were improved. A new type of ship, the **caravel,** was developed. It combined space for cargo with ease of handling and seaworthiness. With maps, ships, and instruments, Henry's sailors were well prepared for exploration.

Henry directed more than 50 expeditions. Almost all of them explored southward, down the western coast of Africa. Each expedition brought back word of more lands farther to the south. By the time Henry died, sailors under his direction had reached almost halfway down the African coast, to where the continent curves to the east. These were new lands to the Europeans. More important, Prince Henry and his men discovered new methods of navigation that would help the later explorers such as Bartholomeu Dias and Vasco da Gama.

PRACTICE 51: Henry the Navigator

Circle the letter of the correct answer to each of the following questions.

1. On how many voyages of exploration did Henry the Navigator go?
   - **a.** none
   - **b.** one
   - **c.** two
   - **d.** three

2. Where did the expeditions organized by Henry travel to?
   - **a.** to Portugal
   - **b.** to the Indies
   - **c.** down the west coast of Africa
   - **d.** up the east coast of Africa

Bartholomeu Dias

The voyages made under the direction of Prince Henry the Navigator inspired the Portuguese. They thought that if they kept pushing south, they would reach the tip of Africa. Then, they hoped, they could sail around Africa to the Indies and establish the long-desired trade route.

Bartholomeu Dias (about 1450–1500) was determined to do just that. In 1487, he set out from Portugal to try to sail around Africa to the Indies. He was sailing under the orders of King John II of Portugal.

Sailing far south along the coast of Africa, Dias and his crew were hopeful. Then a terrible storm blew their ships far out to sea. Lost, they were blown south. They did not see land for almost two weeks.

When the storm cleared, Dias realized that they had sailed far south, beyond the tip of Africa. He led his ships north, and sailed along the southeastern African coast. For the first time, Europeans had sailed beyond the tip of Africa.

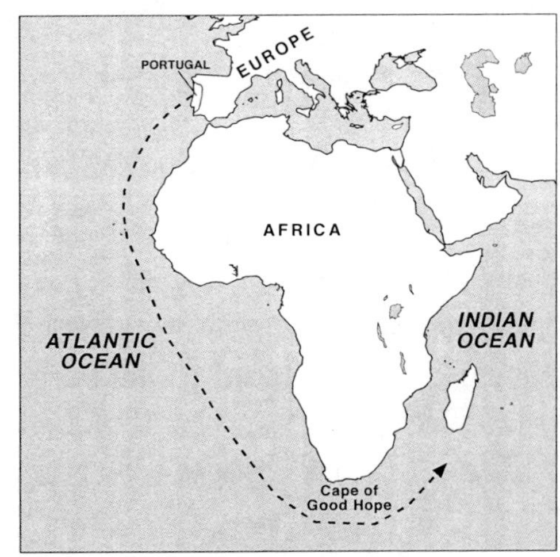

Dias's Route

Dias wanted to continue on to Asia. But his men were exhausted, and their supplies were low. Turning back toward Europe, Dias saw the tip of Africa as he sailed past. He named it the Cape of Storms, after the great storms that had first blown him past it. Later, the king of Portugal changed the name. He called it the **Cape of Good Hope.**

TIP

Learning about history can help you understand the names you read on a map. For example, you just read that the king of Portugal called the southern tip of Africa the Cape of Good Hope. Why did he name it so? Because now the Portuguese had "good hope" of finding a sea route to Asia. Their hope would soon be fulfilled.

PRACTICE 52: Bartholomeu Dias

Circle the letter of the correct answer to each of the following questions.

1. Which nation did Dias sail for?
- **a.** Spain
- **b.** England
- **c.** Portugal
- **d.** Italy

2. Where is the Cape of Good Hope?
- **a.** northern Africa
- **b.** Portugal
- **c.** the southern tip of Africa
- **d.** the tip of South America

Vasco da Gama

Ten years after Dias's journey, the Portuguese tried again to reach Asia by sea. In 1497, King Manuel I of Portugal ordered **Vasco da Gama** (about 1460–1524) to follow Dias's route. His orders were to sail around the tip of Africa to Asia.

Da Gama led an expedition of four ships. It took them nearly five months of hardship just to reach the Cape of Good Hope. Their voyage was plagued by bad weather and short supplies. Worse, about 100 of the 170 men died from scurvy. **Scurvy** is a disease caused by a lack of vitamin C in the diet. Until a cure for scurvy was found in 1753, the disease killed many sailors of this period.

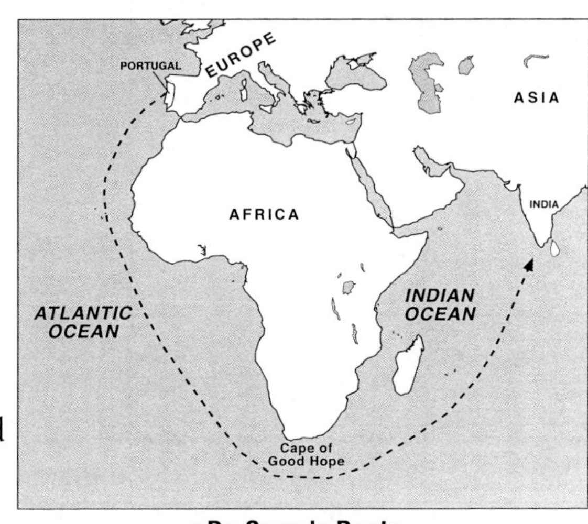

Da Gama's Route

Rounding the Cape of Good Hope, da Gama sailed up the eastern coast of Africa. There, he stopped at the great African city-states of Mombasa and Mozambique. At another port, Malindi, da Gama hired an Arab trader to lead his fleet across the Indian Ocean to India.

Da Gama reached **Calicut, India,** on May 20, 1498. The Portuguese had finally established a sea route to Asia.

But da Gama was not welcomed in India. The Muslim merchants there did not want to have to compete with Europeans in trade. Da Gama and his men were harassed and threatened. They returned to Portugal in 1499, two years after their departure. Out of the 170 men who had sailed with da Gama, only 55 survived.

Da Gama's expedition was a failure as a trading expedition. But, it was successful in establishing a sea route to Asia. Within three years, da Gama returned to India with 15 ships, ready to trade. Along with trade goods came soldiers who attacked and killed any Muslim traders or Indians who would not trade. From then on, Portugal was a major trading nation in India.

Then Da Gama returned home. But in his later years, he became the Portuguese viceroy, or ruler, of India. He died there in 1524, knowing that his voyages had opened up a sea route from Europe to Asia for the first time.

■ PRACTICE 53: Vasco da Gama

Circle the letter of the correct answer to each of the following questions.

1. Which nation did da Gama sail for?

- **a.** Italy
- **b.** Spain
- **c.** England
- **d.** Portugal

2. What did King Manuel order da Gama to do?

- **a.** follow the route of Prince Henry
- **b.** follow the route of Columbus
- **c.** follow the route of Dias
- **d.** follow the route of the Crusades

3. What is scurvy?

- **a.** vitamin C
- **b.** a disease
- **c.** bad weather
- **d.** a small ship

4. Where in Asia did da Gama land?

- **a.** Calicut
- **b.** Mombasa
- **c.** Mozambique
- **d.** Mali

5. What was da Gama's main accomplishment?

- **a.** discovering a sea route to Africa
- **b.** discovering the Americas
- **c.** discovering a sea route to Asia
- **d.** discovering a land route to China

LESSON 8: Columbus Finds a "New World"

GOAL: To describe the voyages of Columbus and the Columbian Exchange

WORDS TO KNOW

Admiral of the Ocean Sea

Columbian Exchange

fourth voyage

Indians

Niña

Pinta

Santa Maria

second voyage

third voyage

NAMES TO KNOW

Christopher Columbus

Queen Isabella I

PLACES TO KNOW

America

Cuba

Hispaniola

Isabella

New World

San Salvador

West Indies

A Western Route

Bartholomeu Dias and Vasco da Gama were both Portuguese explorers who searched for a sea route to the Indies. As you just learned, Dias never made it. But da Gama, sailing to India, did. Both expeditions headed south around Africa so they could sail east to the Indies. Most people thought that this was the shortest and most direct sea route from Europe to the Indies.

A few other people, however, thought that sailing west would get them to the Indies more quickly. As you know, Earth is a sphere, or ball. You can get to any spot on Earth by heading either east or west. Depending on your destination, one way is shorter than the other. At the beginning of the Age of Exploration, most Europeans were convinced that the eastward route was shorter.

You may have heard that people at this time thought the world was flat. This is not true. All educated Europeans knew that the world was round. They agreed about the shape of Earth, but they disagreed about its size. The people who thought the world was larger believed that the eastward route was shorter. Those who thought the world was smaller believed the westward route—which no one had yet sailed—would be shorter.

One of these people was a sailor named Christopher Columbus.

■ PRACTICE 54: A Western Route

Circle the letter of the correct answer to each of the following questions.

1. In which direction did Dias and da Gama sail when they traveled from Europe toward the Indies?

a. west
b. east
c. north
d. south

2. Which of the following statements is TRUE?

a. Europeans who favored an eastern route thought that the world was larger than did those who favored a western route.
b. Europeans who favored an eastern route thought that the world was flat and that sailors heading west would fall off the edge of the world.
c. Europeans thought that since the world was round, it didn't matter whether sailors headed west or east.
d. both *a* and *b*

Christopher Columbus

Christopher Columbus (1451–1506) was the son of an Italian wool weaver. Columbus had dreamed of going to sea since he was a boy. His dream came true at 19. For the rest of his life he would be a sailor.

Christopher Columbus

When he was in his mid-20s, Columbus lived in the city of Lisbon, Portugal. His brother, Bartholomew, was a merchant there who sold charts to sailors. Columbus had been a sailor for seven years. He studied his brother's charts. He read all he could about seafaring. He was intrigued by the idea that the Indies lay about 2,500 miles west of Portugal. Columbus thought he could lead a voyage west to the Indies. If he succeeded, he would achieve wealth and greatness.

Columbus proposed his idea to King John II of Portugal in 1482. This was the same king who had supported Dias. But the king turned him down. His advisers explained that the trip was too risky. Unlike Columbus, they believed that the Indies were actually much farther west than 2,500 miles. (Today, we know the distance is about 12,000 miles.) The king's advisers thought that Portugal should look for a way to reach Asia by sailing around Africa. Portuguese explorers continued to sail east, not west.

Columbus did not give up on his idea. His brother Bartholomew traveled to England to try to convince the king and queen there to fund, or pay for, the expedition. Columbus went to Spain to do the same.

In Spain, Columbus appeared before **Queen Isabella I**. Queen Isabella thought Columbus's idea was good. If he were successful, Spain would be greatly enriched. But Isabella's advisers—like those of King John II in Portugal—thought Columbus's plan was risky. They, too, thought the Indies were too far away to reach by heading west. Besides, Spain was busy fighting a war and didn't have the money to fund the expedition.

In one of the most famous moments in history, Columbus left Isabella, sadly riding away on a mule. But the queen changed her mind. She sent a messenger to overtake Columbus. This messenger told Columbus what he had long dreamed of hearing. He would get the support he wanted: three ships, men, a share of the trade, and the title of **Admiral of the Ocean Sea**. It was the greatest support yet given to any European explorer.

■ PRACTICE 55: Christopher Columbus

Circle the letter of the correct answer to each of the following questions.

1. In which direction did Columbus want to sail to go from Europe toward the Indies?
   - **a.** west
   - **b.** east
   - **c.** north
   - **d.** south

2. Which country sponsored Columbus's journey?
   - **a.** Italy
   - **b.** Spain
   - **c.** Portugal
   - **d.** England

3. Which statement about Columbus is TRUE?
   - **a.** Columbus wanted to prove that the world was round.
   - **b.** Columbus wanted to sail to the Indies.
   - **c.** Columbus wanted to discover a new continent.
   - **d.** Columbus knew about how far to the west the Indies were.

Columbus's First Voyage

Columbus set sail from Spain on August 3, 1492. The three ships under his command were the ***Niña,*** the ***Pinta,*** and the ***Santa Maria.*** All told, 90 men set sail on the three ships.

Columbus led his little fleet southwest to the Canary Islands, off the coast of Africa. There, the ships were repaired and supplies were taken on board. On September 6, they left the Canaries and headed due west. Three days later, they passed the last of the Canary Islands. They were sailing into the unknown, and into history.

Columbus was blessed with good weather and favorable winds during his voyage west. For three weeks, he and his men sailed, never spotting land. None of them had ever sailed as far out to sea before.

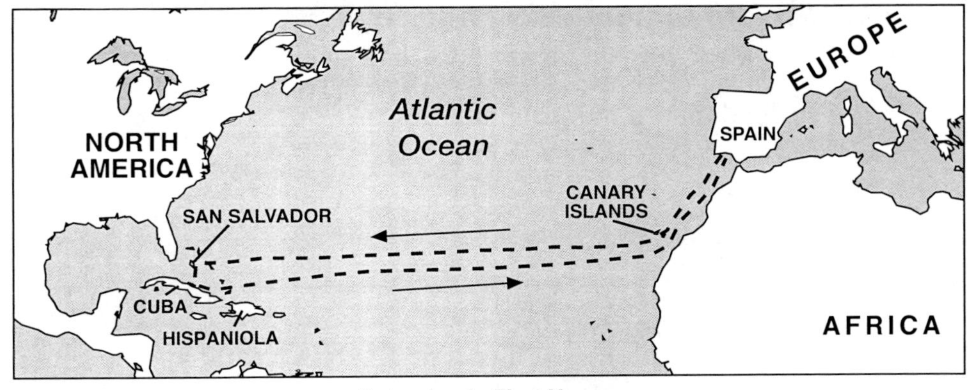

Columbus's First Voyage

The sailors began to feel uneasy. They were frightened that they would never return to Spain against the winds that were blowing them west. But Columbus was convinced of his mission and encouraged the men. On October 10, he told them that if they did not spot land in three days, they would head back.

Then, at 2:00 A.M. on October 12, 1492, a lookout spotted land by moonlight. Soon after sunrise, Columbus went ashore. They had landed on a little island, which Columbus called **San Salvador**.

When Columbus landed on San Salvador, he thought he was near the Indies. He thought that San Salvador was an island off the coast of Japan or China. Of course, he was nowhere near the Indies. He was actually in what we now call the Bahamas, off the coast of North America. Without knowing it, Columbus had stumbled onto a whole new world.

Columbus stayed on San Salvador for a few days. He then sailed south and found the island of **Cuba**. He sailed along the coast of Cuba, and then along the coast of another large island, **Hispaniola**. The *Santa Maria* was wrecked off the coast of Hispaniola on Christmas Day. Columbus directed his men to build a fort on Hispaniola. Then he left 40 men there to search for gold.

On January 16, 1493, he led his surviving two ships and the rest of his men on the voyage home. Also on board were several Tainos, native people of Hispaniola. The return voyage was difficult. At last, on March 15, 1493, Columbus and his two ships reached Spain.

■ PRACTICE 56: Columbus's First Voyage

Circle the letter of the correct answer to each of the following questions.

1. Which island did Columbus first land on?
   - **a.** Cuba
   - **b.** Hispaniola
   - **c.** San Salvador
   - **d.** Santa Maria

2. In what year did Columbus "discover" the New World?
   - **a.** 1490
   - **b.** 1491
   - **c.** 1492
   - **d.** 1493

3. Which statement about Columbus's first voyage is TRUE?
   - **a.** Columbus brought all of his sailors back to Spain.
   - **b.** None of Columbus's men survived the voyage.
   - **c.** Forty men were left on Hispaniola to search for gold.
   - **d.** Columbus discovered a new route to the Indies.

■ THINK ABOUT IT

Columbus discovered the Americas by mistake. He was aiming for the Indies. He had no idea that two giant continents—North and South America—stood between him and his goal. He had seriously miscalculated the size of Earth. Have you ever thought about how this great accident changed history? Can you think of any mistakes, miscalculations, or misinterpretations that had a major impact on your own life? Write your answers on a separate sheet of paper.

Columbus's Other Voyages

Most people think that Columbus just made one voyage to America. Actually, Columbus went on to make three more trips to America.

On his **second voyage,** Columbus commanded 17 ships and 1,000 men—a far cry from the little fleet that had made the first voyage. Columbus returned to the fort on Hispaniola that he had built on his first voyage. The men he had left there were all dead—killed by inhabitants of the island.

Soon after, Columbus founded the settlement of **Isabella** on the same island. Isabella was the first European colony in America. After further explorations of Cuba and Hispaniola, Columbus returned to Isabella. There, he led a fight against the Indians, and then returned to Spain.

Columbus's **third voyage** left Spain on May 30, 1498. This time, Columbus sailed farther to the south. On August 5, he landed in South America. He was the first European to set foot in South America, and the first since the time of the Vikings to visit either of the American continents. He referred to South America as an "other world" and called it "a great continent."

Columbus's **fourth voyage,** from 1502 to 1504, was his last. His goal was to find a passage through the "great continent" of South America that he had found on his third voyage. He still hoped to reach the Indies. Without knowing it, Columbus did come close to reaching the Pacific Ocean. In what is today Panama, Columbus was told of a great ocean that was just a few days' march away. Had he made that march, he would have reached the Pacific Ocean.

Columbus died just two years after returning from his last voyage. From the poor son of a weaver, he had risen to be Admiral of the Ocean Sea and one of the most famous people of all time.

■ PRACTICE 57: Columbus's Other Voyages

Circle the letter of the correct answer to each of the following questions.

1. How many voyages did Columbus make to the New World?

- **a.** one
- **b.** two
- **c.** three
- **d.** four

2. What was the name of the first European colony in the Americas?
   a. Isabella
   b. Hispaniola
   c. Panama
   d. Cuba

3. What happened to the men Columbus left on Hispaniola?
   a. They started a colony.
   b. They sailed back to Spain.
   c. They were killed by islanders.
   d. They found gold.

The Importance of Columbus

Christopher Columbus is one of the most famous people in history. Even now, 500 years after his adventures, many people in the United States celebrate Columbus Day in his honor. Columbus is remembered as "the man who discovered America." However, this is only partly true.

First, remember that Columbus never intended to reach America. No one in Europe at the time even knew that it existed. Columbus was trying to reach the Indies.

Second, Columbus only "discovered" America for the Europeans. People had lived in America for thousands of years before Columbus arrived.

Third, Columbus was not the first European to sail to America. The Vikings had sailed to North America 500 years before, and had even established colonies. But it was Columbus's "discovery" that led to lasting contact between Europe and America. This is why we think of Columbus as the man who "discovered" America.

These lasting contacts changed history forever. Columbus's voyages led directly to centuries of European exploration and colonization, and to the eventual conquest of America.

Soon after Columbus's voyages, a movement of individuals, peoples, cultures, ideas, tools, goods, plants, animals, diseases, and other things began to take place between the Americas and Europe. This is called the **Columbian Exchange,** after Columbus. It is called an exchange because all of these things were exchanged, or swapped, between the two continents. For example, while some animals that had never been in the Americas (such as the horse) came from Europe, other animals that had never been in Europe (such as the turkey) came from the Americas.

The Columbian Exchange changed the lives of people and the environment in both the Americas and Europe. For example, the diseases Europeans carried with them to the Americas, such as smallpox, measles, and influenza, killed millions of Native Americans, destroying entire cultures.

Of course, much of what was exchanged was not harmful. For example, Europeans brought back from the Americas important food crops, such as maize (corn) and the tomato.

The Columbian Exchange has not ended. Today, people, goods, and ideas are constantly traveling back and forth between the Americas and Europe. They are all part of the Columbian Exchange, which started with Christopher Columbus.

■ PRACTICE 58: The Importance of Columbus

Circle the letter of the correct answer to each of the following questions.

1. Which statement about Columbus's discovery of America is TRUE?

- **a.** He had never intended to reach America.
- **b.** Other people had been living in America for thousands of years before he arrived.
- **c.** Columbus was not the first European to sail to America.
- **d.** all of the above

2. Which of the following was brought to America from Europe as part of the Columbian Exchange?

- **a.** corn
- **b.** the tomato
- **c.** measles
- **d.** all of the above

"Indians," "America," and the "New World"

The voyages of Columbus and the Columbian Exchange had a lasting impact on the world. Some of the most interesting results are words you may already know.

The Europeans called Native Americans—the original inhabitants of the Americas—**Indians.** Actually, none of the many different Indian peoples had any word like *Indian.* Each culture had its own name for itself. The name *Indians* came from Christopher Columbus. Since he thought he was in the Indies, he called the people he found there Indians.

Another term from this period is the name ***West Indies.*** West Indies is the name given to the islands that separate the Atlantic Ocean from the Caribbean Sea. Columbus explored many of these islands. He thought they were in the Indies. Later, people realized his mistake. So, they called these islands the West Indies to distinguish them from the Indies in Asia, which were then called the East Indies.

Another important term is the name ***New World.*** The Americas are still sometimes called the New World. They were called this because the Americas represented a new world to the people of Europe. Of course, it was hardly new to the people who already lived here.

One of the first to use the term *New World* was an Italian explorer named Amerigo Vespucci. You will read about his voyages later. After his voyages, a German mapmaker thought that the New World should be named in honor of Amerigo. The name he came up with? ***America.***

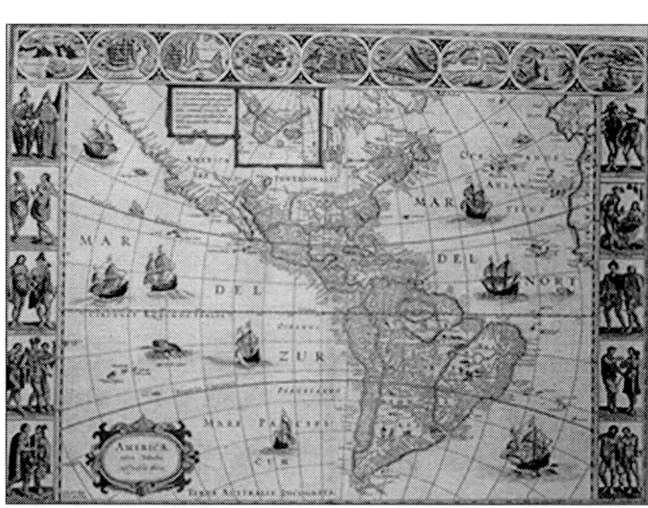

An Early Map of the Americas

IN REAL LIFE

Have you ever heard of Columbus, Ohio? What about Columbus, Georgia? Or, any of the other dozens of "Columbuses" in the United States? All are named for Christopher Columbus. That's also where the space shuttle *Columbia* got its name. A whole country in South America—Colombia—is named for him.

PRACTICE 59: "Indians," "America," and the "New World"

Circle the letter of the correct answer to each of the following questions.

1. Why did Europeans call Native Americans "Indians"?

- **a.** because they lived in the West Indies
- **b.** because that's what they called themselves
- **c.** because Columbus thought they lived in the Indies
- **d.** because each culture had its own name for itself

2. Why were the Americas called the "New World"?

- **a.** because Columbus was from the New World
- **b.** because the Americas were a "new world" to Europeans
- **c.** because that's what Native Americans called their land
- **d.** because it was another name for the Indies

3. Who was "America" named after?

- **a.** Amerigo Vespucci, an Italian explorer
- **b.** the Indians
- **c.** Christopher Columbus
- **d.** the Vikings

LESSON 9: Europeans Explore the Americas

GOAL: To identify the names, nationalities, and achievements of major explorers of the Age of Exploration

WORDS TO KNOW

circumnavigate

circumnavigation

Fountain of Youth

Mundus Novus

Northwest Passage

South Sea

Strait of Magellan

NAMES TO KNOW

Vasco Núñez de Balboa

John Cabot

Juan Sebastián del Cano

Jacques Cartier

Hernando de Soto

Sir Francis Drake

Martin Frobisher

Ferdinand Magellan

Juan Ponce de León

Giovanni da Verrazano

Amerigo Vespucci

Exploration Fever

Can you imagine how excited everyone would be if we discovered life on another planet? That's the feeling that swept over Europe following Columbus's great discovery. Here was an entirely new world. It was of unknown size, but obviously huge. It was inhabited by people who were unknown to the Europeans. There were new plants and animals. It contained unknown riches. The discovery of America was a sensation that electrified Europe.

The Europeans were eager to exploit whatever the Americas had to offer. They sent explorer after explorer to the New World. The nations that had the money to do so—Spain, Portugal, and England—all organized expeditions. Throughout the 1500s, hardly a year went by without an explorer on his way to, in, or coming back from the New World. You are about to read about several of these exciting adventures.

■ PRACTICE 60: Exploration Fever

Circle the letter of the correct answer to each of the following questions.

1. Which of the following European nations sent explorers to the New World?
   a. Spain
   b. Portugal
   c. England
   d. all of the above

2. How did Europe react to the discovery of the New World?
   a. People were amazed.
   b. People were eager to exploit the Americas.
   c. Nations organized expeditions.
   d. all of the above

Amerigo Vespucci and the Cabots

You have already learned that America is named for the Italian explorer **Amerigo Vespucci** (1454–1512). Between 1499 and 1504, Vespucci made three voyages to South America.

Amerigo Vespucci told of his travels in a kind of travel log. He called it ***Mundus Novus,*** which means "New World." *Mundus Novus* became extremely popular in Europe. It established Vespucci's reputation as a great explorer and, at the time, as the man who discovered the New World. This is why the German mapmaker thought that Vespucci, not Columbus, was the discoverer of the New World.

Like Vespucci, **John Cabot** (around 1450 to around 1499) was also an Italian explorer. But his trips were funded by England, not by Italy. Cabot convinced King Henry VII of England that he could reach the Indies—which he thought Columbus had reached—by a much shorter route. The king funded his voyage, and Cabot set sail from England in 1497. Cabot sailed across the North Atlantic, far to the north of the route Columbus had taken. He reached what is now Canada, leading the first English ships to reach the New World, and returned to England. Cabot was the first European to reach North America since the Vikings.

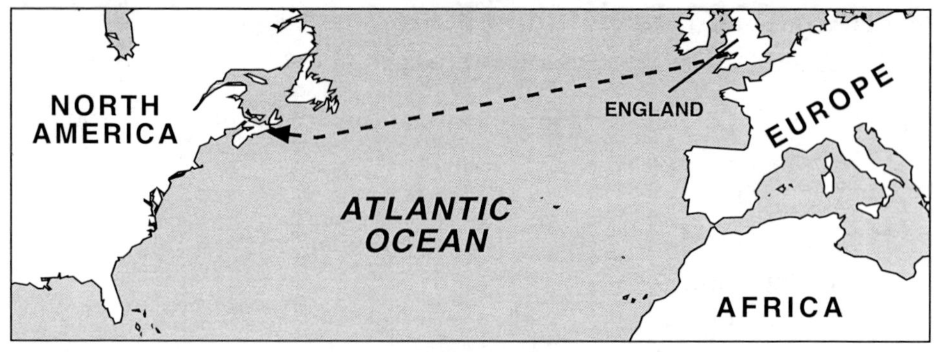

John Cabot's Route

Ten years later, England sent John Cabot's son, Sebastian Cabot, on a voyage to the same area. The younger Cabot's goal was to find a strait or other water passage through North America. Such a passage would let English explorers sail beyond America and reach the East Indies. The passage for which Cabot unsuccessfully searched became known as the **Northwest Passage.** Many other explorers would search, in vain, for such a passage through the Americas.

IN REAL LIFE

Have you ever heard of the Panama Canal? The Panama Canal is a waterway that was built so that ships could go from the Atlantic to the Pacific. The Panama Canal is a narrow waterway that runs through the country of Panama, in Central America. It was completed in 1914, and is considered one of the greatest engineering and strategic feats of the world. The Canal allows ships sailing between the Atlantic Ocean and Pacific Ocean to shorten their trips by thousands of miles. Because the Panama Canal is so important, there were many disputes over which country would control it. In accordance with the Panama Canal Treaty of 1977, the United States controlled it until the year 2000. After that, Panama took complete control of the Canal.

■ PRACTICE 61: Amerigo Vespucci and the Cabots

Circle the letter of the correct answer to each of the following questions.

1. Where did Amerigo Vespucci explore?
   - **a.** North America
   - **b.** South America
   - **c.** Italy
   - **d.** Germany

2. What was the Northwest Passage?
   - **a.** a hoped-for water passage through North America
   - **b.** a passage to the New World
   - **c.** a passage around South America
   - **d.** a passage around North America

Vasco Núñez de Balboa

Vasco Núñez de Balboa (1475–1519) was a rough, adventurous man. Today, he is remembered as a great explorer. But during his own time, he was a borderline criminal.

Balboa grew up poor in a port city in Spain. There, he heard many amazing tales from sailors returning from the New World. When he was in his mid-20s, he joined an expedition that explored the northern coast of South America. The expedition then sailed on to the island of Hispaniola, which Columbus had first explored about ten years before. By now, Hispaniola had become the Spanish base in the New World. In Hispaniola, Balboa fell into debt as he tried to make a living as a pig farmer.

After seven hard years, Balboa saw a new opportunity. The Spanish at Hispaniola had planned to sail back to South America to establish a settlement there. Balboa, though, was refused permission to join the expedition because of his debts. So, in 1510, he stowed away in a barrel on a ship that was carrying supplies to the new settlement.

Upon arriving in South America, the passengers of the supply ship found that the settlement had been abandoned. At this point, Balboa took charge. He knew the region from his earlier trip, and he was a forceful man. He led the Spaniards to a new site where they established a town called Darién. Darién was located near what is now the border between Venezuela and Peru.

From Darién, Balboa led expeditions into the surrounding countryside. From the Indians he learned of a great ocean that lay nearby. After three weeks of searching, Balboa spotted the huge ocean from a mountaintop. It was September 25, 1513. Four days later, Balboa waded into the ocean and claimed it for Spain. The Spanish called this new ocean the **South Sea**, because it lay to the south of the land where Balboa stood. Today, we know it by a different name: Balboa was standing on the eastern shore of the Pacific Ocean.

From poor boy, pig farmer, and stowaway, Balboa had become a great discoverer. But Balboa also made enemies. Spain appointed a new governor to Darién who accused Balboa of crimes. He had Balboa beheaded in Darién in 1519 when Balboa was about 44 years old.

TIP

As you read about the many explorers of the Age of Exploration, you may find yourself confused over who discovered what. One way to help you is to make a list that links each explorer with his discovery and his nationality. For example, you might write "Balboa—Spanish—discovered the Pacific" on your list. Add to this list each time you read about a new explorer. When you are finished, you will have a convenient study guide.

PRACTICE 62: Vasco Núñez de Balboa

Circle the letter of the correct answer to each of the following questions.

1. What is Balboa famous for discovering?
   - **a.** Hispaniola
   - **b.** the Pacific Ocean
   - **c.** Darién
   - **d.** the Americas

2. What do we call the South Sea today?
   a. the South Seas
   b. the Pacific Ocean
   c. the Atlantic Ocean
   d. the Indian Ocean

Ferdinand Magellan

The ocean that Balboa claimed for Spain—the Pacific—was at first called the South Sea. It was given the name *pacific,* which means "peaceful," by another great explorer, **Ferdinand Magellan** (about 1480–1521).

Magellan was a Portuguese explorer who had heard about Balboa's discovery. He thought it was possible to reach the South Sea by sailing south around the tip of South America. No one had ever gone this way before. Magellan hoped that by finding a water passage around South America, he could sail on to Asia.

Ferdinand Magellan

Magellan achieved what he set out to do, and more. His expedition was the first to **circumnavigate,** or sail all the way around, the world. We say that Magellan's trip was the first **circumnavigation** of the world.

Magellan left Spain in 1519 with five ships and 250 men. They sailed to South America, and then southward along the South American coast. Near the southern tip of the continent, they camped for about six months, waiting out the winter. When they set sail again, they passed through a strait into the Pacific Ocean. Today, this passage is still called the **Strait of Magellan.**

Only three of Magellan's five ships made it through the treacherous strait. Of the other two, one was wrecked, and the other turned back to Spain. The three that made it sailed out across the vast Pacific.

The three ships sailed for three months without sighting any land except for a couple of deserted islands. No one had ever gone on such a long sea voyage before. Finally, the ships reached the island of Guam. Magellan took on supplies from the natives there and continued his voyage. He next reached the Philippines. But Magellan never left these islands. He was killed by people who lived there.

The expedition continued under the leadership of **Juan Sebastián del Cano.** His ship sailed across the Indian Ocean and around the Cape of Good Hope, limping back to Spain in 1522—more than three years after it had departed. Fewer than 20 men had survived the lengthy, grueling expedition.

Magellan's voyage made history. It was the first clear proof that the world was round. And it proved that it was possible to sail around the world. For the first time in history, it seemed possible to conquer the world.

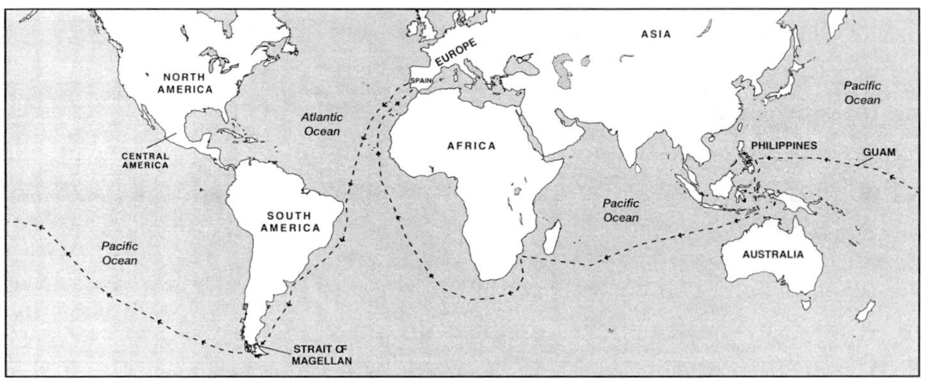

Magellan's Route

PRACTICE 63: Ferdinand Magellan

Circle the letter of the correct answer to each of the following questions.

1. What does *pacific* mean?
- **a.** stormy
- **b.** huge
- **c.** peaceful
- **d.** Spanish

2. How did Magellan reach the Pacific Ocean?
- **a.** by sailing around the Cape of Good Hope
- **b.** by sailing through the Northwest Passage
- **c.** by sailing through the Strait of Magellan
- **d.** by sailing around North America

3. What are Magellan and del Cano famous for?
   a. circumnavigating the globe
   b. circumnavigating the Pacific
   c. circumnavigating South America
   d. circumnavigating the Indies

Juan Ponce de León and Hernando de Soto

Have you ever heard of the **Fountain of Youth**? It is a mythical pool whose water gives eternal, or everlasting, youth. Of course, the Fountain of Youth does not really exist. But one Spanish explorer, **Juan Ponce de León** (1460–1521), thought it was real.

THINK ABOUT IT

Think about the time in which Ponce de León lived. Why do you think Ponce de León believed he might find the Fountain of Youth in the New World? Write your answer on a separate sheet of paper.

Ponce de León first came to the New World on Columbus's second voyage. He was a soldier who led the Spanish in Hispaniola in fights against the islanders. In 1508, he explored and conquered Puerto Rico.

In 1513, Ponce de León set off to find the island of Bimini, where the Fountain of Youth was supposedly located. He explored many islands in the Bahamas and landed in what is now Florida. In Spanish, *florida* means "full of flowers."

Ponce de León sailed almost all the way down Florida's eastern coast, around the tip, and up the western coast. He then sailed on to Mexico before returning home.

Another Spanish explorer, **Hernando de Soto** (1500–1542), explored farther north. In 1539, he led 600 soldiers north from Cuba and landed on the western coast of Florida. From there, he marched hundreds of miles through what would someday be the southern United States. The expedition marched through what would become Georgia, North and South Carolina, Tennessee, Alabama, Mississippi, Louisiana, Arkansas, and Oklahoma.

De Soto was looking for gold. He never did find any. But he did encounter, for the first time, many Native American peoples. As a rule, de Soto treated them cruelly. He killed many and enslaved others. Native American slaves carrying the Spaniards' gear made up a large part of de Soto's group that pushed through the wilderness. With 600 soldiers, 200 or so horses, and thousands of pigs, the expedition was an awesome sight. These were the first Europeans to see the Mississippi River. De Soto died of fever along its banks. His survivors built rafts and floated down the Mississippi.

Half of de Soto's men and an unknown number of Native Americans died during the four-year expedition. It was a cruel affair, but it was the most extensive exploration of North America ever made.

THINK ABOUT IT

All of the explorers you are reading about were hoping to find fame and fortune through their explorations. Some of them, such as Magellan and de Soto, found death. Do you think it was worth taking such a risk? Would you be willing to? Write your answers on a separate sheet of paper.

PRACTICE 64: Juan Ponce de León and Hernando de Soto

Circle the letter of the correct answer to each of the following questions.

1. Who searched for the Fountain of Youth?
- **a.** Juan Ponce de León
- **b.** Hernando de Soto
- **c.** Christopher Columbus
- **d.** both *a* and *b*

2. Which of the following explored a larger part of North America?
- **a.** Juan Ponce de León
- **b.** Hernando de Soto
- **c.** Vasco Núñez de Balboa
- **d.** both *a* and *b*

The Northwest Passage

As you recall, Europeans began searching for a Northwest Passage soon after they discovered the Americas. The Northwest Passage was a water route through the Americas that would enable the Europeans to sail on to the Indies.

Sebastian Cabot, sailing for England, failed to find it in the early 1500s. But he was not the last to try—and fail.

After Magellan's expedition had circumnavigated the globe, Europeans knew they could reach the Indies by sailing west. But Magellan's route around the tip of South America was very long. European traders hoped that a Northwest Passage would be a shorter route.

One explorer who searched for the Northwest Passage was an Italian named **Giovanni da Verrazano** (1485–1528). In 1524, he set off, funded by France. He never found the Northwest Passage. But he did explore much of the eastern coast of North America, from what is now South Carolina on up into Canada. Verrazano's ships were the first French ships to reach the New World.

IN REAL LIFE

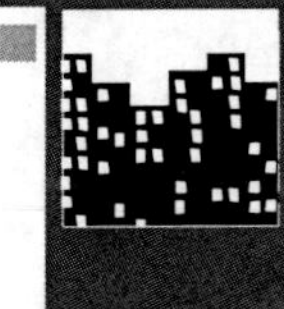

If you live near New York City, you may know Verrazano's name. A beautiful bridge crosses the Verrazano Narrows, joining Staten Island and Brooklyn. It is called the Verrazano-Narrows Bridge.

Jacques Cartier (1491–1557) was a Frenchman who explored Canada in the 1530s. He sailed up the St. Lawrence River, which he named, in hopes of finding the Northwest Passage. He also hoped to find gold. All told, Cartier made three trips to Canada and claimed the land for France. His claim led to the colonization of the region by France and the creation of a French empire in North America.

Jacques Cartier

The English also searched for the Northwest Passage. **Martin Frobisher** (1535–1594) was unsuccessful. **Sir Francis Drake** (about 1540–1596) tried it from the west coast. Drake also failed, but he did explore much of the western coast of North America.

No one succeeded. But the picture of the Americas was becoming clearer. Soon, Europeans would begin to colonize the New World.

IN REAL LIFE

In 1850, the Northwest Passage was finally found by explorer Robert McClure. However, it was a long time before McClure could share his discovery. His ship was caught in the ice until spring, 1851. When he tried to double-check what he had found, he was again trapped. The ship that came to rescue him met the same fate. Finally, in 1854, McClure was able to leave the Arctic and return to England. The British Parliament gave McClure and his crew a reward for finding the Northwest Passage. Still, it was 55 more years before anyone was able to sail through the passage without being trapped by the ice. Even today, most ships using this route are accompanied by another ship known as an icebreaker—just in case.

PRACTICE 65: The Northwest Passage

Check each statement below that is TRUE.

☐ **1.** Europeans searched for a Northwest Passage before they discovered the Americas.

☐ **2.** Giovanni da Verrazano sailed for France.

☐ **3.** Jacques Cartier sailed for Italy.

☐ **4.** Sir Francis Drake sailed for England.

☐ **5.** Sir Francis Drake found the Northwest Passage.

LESSON 10: European Conquest and Colonization

GOAL: To explain the motivations of conquistadors in the New World; to identify the countries that established colonies there

WORDS TO KNOW

Aztec Empire | **colony** | **Inca Empire**

colonization | **conquistadors** | **Quetzalcoatl**

NAMES TO KNOW

Atahualpa | **Montezuma II**

Hernando Cortés | **Francisco Pizarro**

PLACES TO KNOW

Jamestown | **Peru**

Lima | **Tenochtitlán**

Gold

As you learned in Lesson 7, the European explorers at the beginning of the Age of Discovery were motivated by their desire for a sea route to the Indies and to spread the Christian religion. Both of these desires remained strong throughout the Age of Discovery. But a third motivation appeared after the Europeans stumbled on the Americas.

Before 1492, the Europeans had no idea that the Americas even existed. Within 50 years, however, they had explored large parts of the huge landmass. So, while continuing to hope for an easy sea route to the Indies, they also wanted to see what the New World had to offer.

The early explorers were amazed by the natural beauty and abundant natural resources of the New World, which far surpassed anything in Europe. Here were incredibly tall trees, new plants and animals, and scenic splendors that stunned them. Surely, they thought, such a rich land would contain another natural wonder: gold.

The Europeans were hungry for gold. And they would stop at nothing to get it. Already, they had seen Indians wearing gold jewelry. They wanted to find the source of these riches themselves. So, many of the explorers who traveled inland, like de Soto, were motivated by this search for gold.

■ PRACTICE 66: Gold

Circle the letter of the correct answer to each of the following questions.

1. What were the principal motivations of European explorers at the beginning of the Age of Discovery?
   a. to establish trade routes to Asia
   b. to spread Christianity
   c. to find gold
   d. both *a* and *b*

2. What were the principal motivations of European explorers after the Americas were discovered?
   a. to establish trade routes to Asia
   b. to spread Christianity
   c. to exploit the New World
   d. all of the above

Hernando Cortés and Francisco Pizarro

One man who wanted gold was a Spaniard named **Hernando Cortés** (1485–1547). In 1519, Cortés sailed with 600 soldiers from Cuba to what is now Mexico. He had heard the Cuban Indians tell of a great empire that was rich in gold. Cortés was determined to find it.

Hernando Cortés

From the coast, Cortés led his men overland. He reached the great city of **Tenochtitlán,** which was the capital of the great **Aztec Empire.** The sight of Tenochtitlán awed the Spanish. It was larger than any European city at the time.

IN REAL LIFE

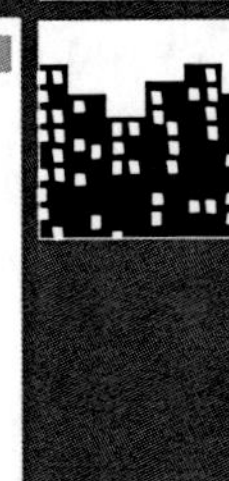

If you look at a Mexican flag, you will see a picture of an eagle, perched on a cactus, eating a snake. According to Aztec legend, the first Aztecs founded Tenochtitlán where they saw this very sight. Tenochtitlán remains one of the largest cities in Mexico and the world. Today, it is called Mexico City.

Even though he had just 600 men, Cortés managed to conquer the Aztecs. One reason for his success was an incredible stroke of luck (for Cortés, anyway). The Aztecs had a legend that said their chief god, **Quetzalcoatl**, had long ago sailed away and would someday return. The Aztec emperor, **Montezuma II** (1466–1520), may have thought that Cortés was Quetzalcoatl. This could have been due to Cortés's strange appearance and language.

Montezuma welcomed Cortés. But Cortés soon took him hostage. The Aztecs revered their leader and paid huge ransoms in gold for his safety.

Within a year, the Aztecs rebelled and forced the Spaniards from Tenochtitlán. But Cortés regrouped and conquered the city. He took control of the huge Aztec Empire.

Cortés's defeat of the Aztecs had a great impact on history. It was the foothold that eventually led to Spain conquering all of Central and South America.

Just as Cortés conquered the Aztec Empire, another Spaniard, **Francisco Pizarro** (1475–1541), conquered the **Inca Empire.** In 1513, Pizarro was a wealthy and powerful man. He lived in the Spanish settlement of Panama City in Central America. The Spaniards there heard tales of a great, wealthy Indian empire to the south. Pizarro led several expeditions in search of it. After three years of searching, he finally reached it in 1527. It was located in what is today **Peru.**

Pizarro then returned to Spain, where he received support for further expeditions. In 1531, he returned to the northern area of the Inca Empire and began his conquest. Over the next two years, Pizarro slowly but steadily headed south, into the heart of the Inca Empire. In a surprise attack, the Spaniards killed thousands of Incas and captured their ruler,

Atahualpa (about 1502–1533). As Cortés had done with Montezuma, Pizarro held Atahualpa hostage. The Incas, rich in gold and silver, paid a huge ransom. But the Spaniards killed him anyway and continued their rampage. They conquered the Inca capital in 1533.

Two years later, Pizarro founded the city of **Lima,** which is today the capital of Peru. Lima became the base from which Spain conquered most of South America.

Cortés and Pizarro were not so much explorers as ruthless conquerors, intent on wealth and fame. They, like other Spanish conquerors in the new world, are called **conquistadors.** This term comes from the Spanish word for conquerors.

IN REAL LIFE

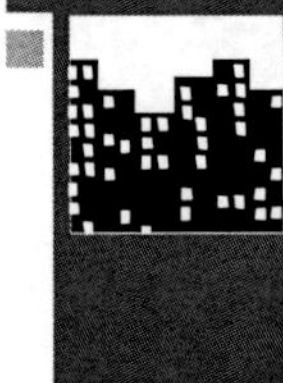

If you have ever traveled to Mexico, you may have been warned not to drink the tap water there. This is because bacteria in the water can give many foreigners stomach viruses. This illness is often called "Montezuma's revenge." The term refers to the Aztec emperor, Montezuma, whose empire was conquered by Cortés. As the legend goes, Montezuma is seeking to avenge his destroyed empire on any foreigner who comes to Mexico.

PRACTICE 67: Hernando Cortés and Francisco Pizarro

Circle the letter of the correct answer to each of the following questions.

1. Who conquered the Aztecs?

- **a.** Hernando Cortés
- **b.** Francisco Pizarro
- **c.** Montezuma II
- **d.** Vasco da Gama

2. Who conquered the Incas?

- **a.** Hernando Cortés
- **b.** Francisco Pizarro
- **c.** Ponce de León
- **d.** Montezuma II

3. Who founded Lima?
   a. Atahualpa
   b. Hernando de Soto
   c. Francisco Pizarro
   d. Montezuma

Colonization

As you have read, many explorers from France, England, and Spain came to the New World. Seeking gold and new lands and spreading Christianity, they slowly but surely explored the Americas.

Of course, the Europeans didn't just visit the Americas. They settled there. Their colonization started almost as soon as they discovered the Americas. **Colonization** is the practice of forming colonies, or settlements, in other lands. Remember, the first permanent European **colony** in America, Isabella, was founded by the first European to discover America, Christopher Columbus.

By the end of the Age of Exploration, there were many European colonies in the Americas. The first permanent English colony, **Jamestown,** was established in 1607. By this time, Spain had many colonies in America and was soon to control almost all of Mexico, Central America, and South America. Meanwhile, the French were colonizing Canada and large parts of what would be the central United States. The Netherlands and Portugal also established colonies along the eastern coast of South America.

All of these countries—England, France, Spain, the Netherlands, and Portugal—wanted the land and riches that America had to offer. Later, they would fight each other to win the Americas.

The Europeans who fought for the Americas were much different from Europeans of earlier generations. Just a few centuries earlier, no one in Europe even knew America existed. But by the end of the Age of Exploration, Europeans were settling in America in great numbers. Soon, they would completely conquer a great land that had been unknown to them just a few generations before.

There is, of course, one sad and final fact about the Europeans in the Americas. They took terrible advantage of Native Americans. Within just a few years of Columbus's arrival, approximately 1.5 million Native Americans had been killed by European attack or by the diseases the Europeans brought with them. Millions more deaths would follow. Tragically, whole cultures and civilizations were destroyed by the Europeans in their thirst for exploration and conquest.

THINK ABOUT IT

The area that was to become the United States was largely colonized by the English. How might life in the United States be different if it had been colonized by the Spanish instead? Write your answer on a separate sheet of paper.

PRACTICE 68: Colonization

Match each description with a term from the list below. Write the letter of the correct term on the line before each description.

a. France	**c.** new land	**e.** colonization
b. Isabella	**d.** Jamestown	**f.** Christopher Columbus

_____ **1.** This was the first European colony in the New World.

_____ **2.** This was the first permanent English colony in the New World.

_____ **3.** This was one of the things the explorers were seeking.

_____ **4.** This European country colonized much of Canada.

_____ **5.** This was the first European to discover America.

_____ **6.** This was the practice of forming settlements.

UNIT 3 REVIEW

Circle the letter of the correct answer to each of the following questions.

1. What motivated European explorers?

a. the desire to trade with Asia
b. the desire to spread Christianity
c. both *a* and *b*
d. neither *a* nor *b*

2. Which nation did Henry the Navigator, Bartholomeu Dias, and Vasco da Gama all come from?

a. Portugal
b. France
c. India
d. England

3. What country supported Columbus's expedition across the Atlantic?

a. Spain
b. Italy
c. Portugal
d. England

4. When Columbus landed on San Salvador, where did he think he was?

a. near Spain
b. in the Indies
c. near North America
d. in South America

5. Which of the following passed between Europe and America during the Columbian Exchange?

a. plants
b. animals
c. diseases
d. all of the above

6. Which nation did NOT send explorers to the New World?
   a. Portugal
   b. England
   c. Spain
   d. Italy

7. Which European explorer "discovered" the Pacific?
   a. Magellan
   b. Balboa
   c. Vespucci
   d. de Soto

8. What did Magellan's voyage prove beyond doubt?
   a. The world was flat.
   b. The world was safe.
   c. The world was round.
   d. Sailing around the world was impossible.

9. Which European countries colonized the Americas?
   a. Spain
   b. England
   c. France
   d. all of the above

10. Which European country controlled most of Central and South America?
   a. Spain
   b. England
   c. France
   d. Portugal

UNIT 3 APPLICATION ACTIVITY
A Letter Home

Suppose you were a member of an expedition during the Age of Exploration. What would the voyage be like? What sorts of things would you describe in a letter home to your family?

To begin this activity, choose one of the explorers from the list below. This is the explorer whose expedition you will join.

Bartholomeu Dias	Vasco Núñez de Balboa	Juan Ponce de León
Vasco da Gama	Ferdinand Magellan	Hernando de Soto
Christopher Columbus		

Now, find out as much as you can about the explorer you chose and his most famous expedition. You can find this information in your library and/or on the Internet. Once you have gathered information, write a letter home describing the voyage and your experiences. In the letter, try to answer as many of the questions below as you can.

- When did the expedition leave home?
- What was the goal of the expedition?
- What happened during the voyage?
- What were the conditions of the voyage?
- What type of leader/man was the explorer?
- What types of lands/people/animals were encountered on the voyage?
- How long did the voyage last?
- Did the expedition reach its destination? If so, what happened when it got there?
- Was the voyage successful?

Take notes and write your letter on a separate sheet of paper.

UNIT 4

Europe Colonizes the Globe

LESSON 11: A New Global Age

GOAL: To identify the major European trading nations of the 1500s, 1600s, and 1700s, and to discuss what and where they traded

WORDS TO KNOW

British East India Company

cultural exchange

Dutch

Dutch East India Company

Dutch West India Company

East Indiaman

ethnocentrism

First Global Age

galleon

mercantilism

missions

racism

sea dogs

trading nations of Europe

viceroys

NAME TO KNOW

Robert de La Salle

PLACE TO KNOW

Amsterdam

The Age of Exploration

You have learned that the period from about 1400 to 1600 is often called the Age of Exploration. It was during this period that Europeans really started to explore overseas. Christopher Columbus discovered the New World—the Americas—for Europeans. Vasco Núñez de Balboa saw the Pacific Ocean. Ferdinand Magellan and Juan Sebastián del Cano circumnavigated, or sailed all the way around, the entire world. Many other explorers traveled deep into North America. Spanish conquistadors conquered great Indian empires in Central and South America.

European exploration was motivated largely by the Europeans' desire to find a sea route to Asia. They wanted to begin a sea trade with "the Indies," as they called India, China, Japan, and other lands in the region. They accomplished this, as you will see. But the discovery of the New World also provided a new, undreamed-of opportunity for colonization. Colonization is the practice of forming colonies, or settlements, in other lands. The Europeans spread out, colonizing the New World while continuing to expand their trade with the Old World.

TIP

The first paragraph of each lesson in this book is designed as a review paragraph. This means that it reviews things you may have already learned. The paragraph on page 135, for example, reviews content from Unit 3. As you read paragraphs like this, try to remember as much as you can about the subjects they review. This will help you prepare for what you are about to read.

In just a few centuries, the world changed dramatically. The world grew both larger and smaller. It grew larger with the discovery, exploration, and colonization of the New World. But it also grew smaller with the increase of contacts and trade between Europe and many other parts of the world. The Age of Exploration had led to the **First Global Age**—a time when people from many parts of the globe, along with their goods and ideas, interacted.

PRACTICE 69: The Age of Exploration

Circle the letter of the correct answer to each of the following questions.

1. How did the world grow "larger" during the Age of Exploration?
   - **a.** by the discovery of the New World
   - **b.** by the increase of contacts and trade
   - **c.** by the conquest of Indian empires
   - **d.** all of the above

2. How did the world grow "smaller" toward the end of the Age of Exploration?
   a. by the discovery of the New World
   b. by the increase of contacts and trade
   c. by the conquest of Indian empires
   d. all of the above

Ships at Sea

By about 1600, the Age of Exploration gradually began to blend with the First Global Age. By 1700, European nations had trading partners and colonies all over the world. Europeans lived on every continent except for Antarctica.

At this time, there were no motorized vehicles—no automobiles, trains, or ships with engines. There were no forms of electronic communication, such as radios and telephones. Even steam engines did not exist. None of these things had been invented. How, then, did a global age develop without sophisticated methods of communication and transportation? How did Europeans stay in touch with their overseas colonies? How were trade goods transported?

The answer is by sailing ships. The Europeans came to be expert sailors. Their ships were the "high-tech" marvels of their day. Full-rigged ships carried European explorers to the far reaches of the globe. In their wakes came merchant vessels carrying trade goods. Overseas trade was becoming increasingly important to the Europeans. So, it was natural that they made the best trading ships they could.

In the mid-1500s, the Spanish developed a new type of ship. This was the famous Spanish **galleon.** You may have heard tales of sunken galleons and their golden treasures.

The galleon was larger than earlier ships. Its huge hold could carry many tons of cargo. It had a low forecastle, a huge stern castle, and up to four masts carrying six sails. A typical galleon might be about 175 feet long. Galleons also carried many cannons to defend themselves and their valuable cargoes from pirates and raiders from other countries.

In the 1600s, the Europeans built another new type of ship. In some ways this ship was similar to the galleon. But it was larger than the galleon and could carry more. It had more sails on taller masts to pull its great weight. This ship was called an **East Indiaman.** The unusual name came from what it was designed to do: carry trade goods between Europe and the East Indies, or the island nations of southeast Asia.

A Galleon

Galleons and East Indiamen were slow by today's standards. After all, they were bulky, heavy, sailing ships. But in those days, they were the most advanced transportation technology on the planet. And they got the job done. The great worldwide trade routes that developed during the 1500s, 1600s, and 1700s were sailed by these types of ships. They were the workhorses of European navies and trading companies.

■ PRACTICE 70: Ships at Sea

Circle the letter of the correct answer to each of the following questions.

1. What type of ship was developed during the First Global Age?

- **a.** the galleon
- **b.** the East Indiaman
- **c.** the full-rigged ship
- **d.** both a and b

2. In what way were the new ships of the First Global Age superior to older ships?

- **a.** They could carry more.
- **b.** They had more sails.
- **c.** They were larger.
- **d.** all of the above

Trade in Goods and Ideas

Galleons and East Indiamen traveled the waters of the world. From Europe they traveled to European colonies in the Americas, to city-states on the east coast of Africa, and to trading ports in Asia. The ships plowed the waters of the Atlantic Ocean, the Pacific Ocean, and the Indian Ocean.

From Asia, these ships brought porcelain, ivory, silks, a wide variety of spices, and many other goods. From the Americas came gold, silver, furs, and other things. As the European ships sailed the oceans of the world, they brought about the first global age in history.

The ships carried not only goods and money, they also carried people and ideas. Throughout history, the world has changed when people of different nations interact. New languages are learned, religious ideas are shared, and different ways of looking at the world are compared. Often, as you know, more powerful peoples force their ideas onto weaker peoples. On the other hand, sometimes the interaction is peaceful, and everyone benefits. The exchange of ideas between peoples of different cultures is called **cultural exchange.** Cultural exchange was a major feature of this period.

During the First Global Age—the 1500s, 1600s, and 1700s—the Europeans, as a rule, were the most powerful people on Earth. After all, it was they who sailed to other lands, and not vice versa. They had sophisticated ships and guns. But they also had a strong sense of **ethnocentrism.** This means that they believed that their culture was superior to all other cultures. They considered other peoples backward or primitive, or even savage and evil. This ethnocentrism, coupled with racism, led Europeans to do such things as massacre the peoples of the Americas and enslave the peoples of Africa. **Racism** is prejudice against people of other races. Both ethnocentrism and racism strongly affected the way Europeans dealt with the foreign peoples they met.

As part of their ethnocentric outlook, the Europeans also thought their religion, Christianity, was the only true religion. So, wherever the Europeans went, they tried to spread Christianity. Often the peoples the Europeans came in contact with accepted Christianity voluntarily. But the Europeans also often forced their religion on different peoples.

All of these things—the trade in goods, cultural exchange, and Europeans' forcing their culture onto others—happened during the First Global Age. They happened in some parts of the world more than others. But, together, they changed the face of Earth.

■ PRACTICE 71: Trade in Goods and Ideas

Circle the letter of the correct answer to each of the following questions.

1. What is cultural exchange?

- **a.** the sharing of religious ideas
- **b.** the comparing of world views
- **c.** the learning of languages
- **d.** all of the above

2. What is ethnocentrism?

- **a.** thinking one's own culture is the best
- **b.** cultural exchange
- **c.** trade in goods
- **d.** all of the above

Spain

By 1700, Spain was the most powerful nation in Europe. Part of the reason for its power was its large overseas holdings.

Look at the map on page 141 entitled "Europe's Overseas Possessions in 1713." This map shows Spain's colonies as of the early 1700s. As you can see, most of Spain's overseas territory was in the New World. Spain controlled almost all of the West Indies. It also controlled the southern part of North America, Central America, and much of South America.

The Spanish set up a complex system of government in the New World. **Viceroys,** who represented the king and queen of Spain, controlled various districts. Viceroys were advised by councils. But many had enormous power in the district they governed. The ultimate authority remained with the throne in Spain. However, it took weeks and even

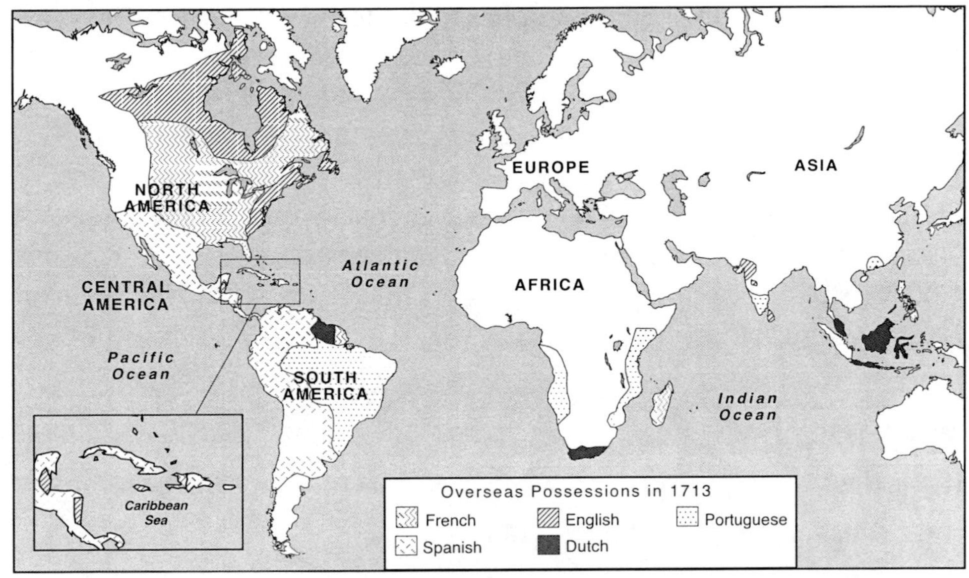

Europe's Overseas Possessions in 1713

months for news and orders to travel between Spain and the viceroys. As a result, viceroys had wide authority in making decisions.

The major reasons the Spanish were in the New World were "God and gold." They wanted to spread Christianity to the New World. As a result, many Spanish settlements were built around **missions**, or churches built to spread Christianity. Although the hope of finding gold also drew the Spanish to the New World, they had better luck with silver. In South America, in what is now Bolivia, they found a huge deposit of silver at Potosí. The wealth from the Potosí mines was so great that it became a mainstay of Spain's economy.

IN REAL LIFE

You have probably heard of the Alamo, in San Antonio, Texas. Although the Alamo is famed as the site of a battle, it was built as a Spanish mission. Many early Spanish missions still stand in Texas, the Southwest, and California. In fact, many American cities were founded on the sites of, and took their names from, early Spanish missions. Examples include San Antonio (Texas), San Bernardino (California), and San Francisco (California).

Sadly, one feature of Spanish presence in the New World was the Spaniards' terrible treatment of Native Americans. The early Spanish conquistadors treated them cruelly. This continued under the viceroys. Native Americans were killed, forced off their land, and enslaved. (The Potosí mines, for instance, were worked by enslaved Native Americans.) From the time Christopher Columbus, sailing for Spain, landed in the New World, the Spanish killed, harassed, and enslaved Native Americans. Unfortunately, the other European powers in the New World did not treat Native Americans any better.

■ PRACTICE 72: Spain

Circle the letter of the correct answer to each of the following questions.

1. Where were most of Spain's overseas possessions?

- **a.** Africa
- **b.** China
- **c.** the East Indies
- **d.** the New World

2. What was mined at Potosí?

- **a.** gold
- **b.** silver
- **c.** lead
- **d.** coal

3. What was a mission?

- **a.** a church
- **b.** a fort
- **c.** a capitol
- **d.** a viceroy's residence

France

The overseas holdings of France during the First Global Age were, like Spain's, concentrated in the New World. Look again at the map on page 141. This map also shows France's overseas colonies. France claimed much of Canada and what was to become the central United States. Its first permanent settlement in the New World was established at Quebec in 1608. From Quebec the French slowly expanded their holdings. They established several settlements around the Great Lakes and along the St. Lawrence River.

France developed a profitable trade with both the Native Americans and the French settlers. Most of the trade was in furs. These were highly prized by the Europeans. The fur trade greatly enriched France. The French also fished the rich waters off the eastern coast of Canada.

France's real breakthrough in the New World came when **Robert de La Salle** explored the length of the Mississippi River between 1679 and 1683. He named the land surrounding the great river Louisiana, after the French king, Louis XIV. France now laid claim to almost the entire inland area of the huge North American continent.

■ PRACTICE 73: France

Circle the letter of the correct answer to each of the following questions.

1. For whom did Robert de La Salle claim the land surrounding the Mississippi?

- **a.** England
- **b.** Spain
- **c.** France
- **d.** Italy

2. What did La Salle call the land around the Mississippi?

- **a.** Canada
- **b.** Quebec
- **c.** Louisiana
- **d.** Montreal

3. What was the major item traded by the French?

- **a.** fish
- **b.** gold
- **c.** furs
- **d.** tobacco

England

France's great rival in North America was England. Look back at the map on page 141 to find England's overseas colonies. It should not surprise you to learn that England set up colonies in what was to become the eastern United States. In fact, as you probably know, these colonies *became* the United States. The first permanent English settlement in the New World, Jamestown, was built in 1607. The second settlement, at Plymouth, was founded by the Pilgrims in 1620.

The English settled in North America in hopes of making England more self-sufficient. They wanted the colonies to provide goods that England, an island nation, had been forced to import from other countries. One of the most valuable products was sugar. Sugar had been almost unknown in Europe before the Renaissance. By the 1600s, it was a popular luxury item. There were great profits to be made in the sugar trade.

The idea of having colonies exist solely for the benefit of the home country is called **mercantilism.** Eventually, mercantilist policies helped drive the English colonies to rebel, and to form the United States of America.

At the same time they pursued mercantilism, however, the English allowed their colonies a larger degree of self-government than did the Spanish or the French. The colonies were allowed to make many local decisions themselves, without approval from England.

The English also established strong trading ties with India. In 1600, the **British East India Company** was chartered to conduct trade with India. This company, working under the authority of the government, set up trading posts in Bombay, Calcutta, and Madras. It also set up trading posts in the East Indies.

As you will learn, England established an empire that stretched around the world. It owed the success of that empire to the seafaring skills it was developing at this time. Strong ships and stronger men were making England a major sea power. Famous English captains, called **sea dogs**, regularly raided Portuguese and Spanish ships. With its sea power growing, England would soon be the most powerful nation on Earth.

■ THINK ABOUT IT

You have just read that English sea captains raided Portuguese and Spanish ships. Why do you think they attacked these ships? Write your answer on a separate sheet of paper.

■ PRACTICE 74: England

Circle the letter of the correct answer to each of the following questions.

1. What was England's first permanent settlement in the New World?

a. Calcutta
b. Jamestown
c. Plymouth
d. Bombay

2. Which country did the British East India Company trade with?

a. Portugal
b. Spain
c. India
d. all of the above

3. Who were the sea dogs?

a. Portuguese sea captains
b. Spanish sea captains
c. English sea captains
d. French sea captains

Portugal

It was Portugal, through Vasco da Gama, that first established sea trade with India. Portugal was to maintain and increase this trade throughout the 1500s and 1600s.

In India, Arab traders resented the Portuguese presence. They did not want to have to compete with European traders. But the Portuguese, with their superior ships and tactics, drove off the Muslim traders. They forced their way into Indian trade and profited greatly from it.

Soon, Portugal dominated European trade with Asia and the East Indies. For a while, Portugal imported more Asian goods—especially spices—than any other European country.

Unlike Spain, France, and England, Portugal did not establish many colonies at first. Instead, Portugal relied on trading bases and relatively good relations with its trading partners. Thus, Portugal avoided the expense of maintaining colonies.

Portugal did, eventually, establish settlements along the eastern coast of South America, in what was to become Brazil. These territories are shown on the map on page 141. Portuguese is still spoken in Brazil today. In Africa, the Portuguese controlled trade with great East African city-states and some areas of western Africa. As you will read later, much of this trade consisted of human cargo, slaves.

■ PRACTICE 75: Portugal

Decide if each statement below is true (**T**) or false (**F**). Write the correct letter on the line before each statement.

_____ **1.** Arab traders welcomed the Portuguese in India.

_____ **2.** Portugal imported more Asian goods than any other European country.

_____ **3.** Unlike other European countries, the Portuguese did not establish many colonies at first.

The Netherlands

Like the Portuguese, the **Dutch** (the people of the Netherlands) did not have extensive overseas holdings. They did, however, control many islands in the East Indies. These islands came to be called the Dutch East Indies.

In the 1600s, the Dutch became the leading sea power in Europe. All told, Dutch ships carried about half of the world's sea trade. **Amsterdam,** the capital of the Netherlands, became the most prosperous trading city in the world.

In 1602, the Dutch formed the **Dutch East India Company.** It traded in India and the East Indies. It founded a city there, in what is now Indonesia, that would grow into Jakarta. Today, Jakarta is the capital of Indonesia. The Dutch East India Company was an enormous success. It eventually drove British and Portuguese traders out of the area. It colonized Ceylon, an island in the Indian Ocean. It also colonized the area around the Cape of Good Hope, at the southern tip of Africa.

Another Dutch company, the **Dutch West India Company,** conducted trade with the New World and western Africa. It established colonies in North and South America. Look back at the map on page 141 to find these territories. One of these settlements, New Amsterdam, would one day become New York City.

The First Global Age was underway. Spain, France, England, Portugal, and the Netherlands had become the great **trading nations of Europe.**

■ PRACTICE 76: The Netherlands

Circle the letter of the correct answer to each of the following questions.

1. What city in the Netherlands became the most prosperous city in the world?
  a. Jakarta
  b. Ceylon
  c. Amsterdam
  d. New Amsterdam

2. Where did the Dutch East India Company conduct trade?
  a. the East Indies
  b. the West Indies
  c. the Netherlands
  d. both *a* and *b*

3. Where did the Dutch West India Company conduct trade?
  a. the East Indies
  b. the New World
  c. western Africa
  d. both *b* and *c*

LESSON 12: The Response of China and Japan to European Expansionism

GOAL: To explain expansionism; to discuss how China and Japan responded to European nations' attempts to trade with them

WORDS TO KNOW

expansionism **trading station**

porcelain

PLACES TO KNOW

Guangzhou **Macao** **Nagasaki**

European Expansionism

Expansionism is the term for a country's policy of expanding its territory and influence. All of the great European trading nations you have been reading about—Spain, France, England, Portugal, and the Netherlands—were following expansionist polices during the 1500s, 1600s, and 1700s.

The countries were expanding in many ways. They were expanding economically as they traded more and more goods in more and more places. They were expanding geographically as they established colonies and trading posts around the world. And they were expanding their influence as their peoples and their ideas came to these places.

TIP

You know that when something *expands,* it grows larger. This gives you a clue to what expansionism means.

It is important to remember that the Europeans never went into "uninhabited lands." There were already native peoples nearly everywhere they went. After all, the Europeans were seeking trade—trade with other people. In the New World, the great tracts of lands the Europeans claimed for themselves were already inhabited by Native Americans. Whenever a nation expands, it usually does so at the cost of other peoples. This was certainly true in the case of European expansionism in the 1500s, 1600s, and 1700s.

In this lesson, you will see how two nations—China and Japan—coped with the European desire to trade with them.

■ PRACTICE 77: European Expansionism

Circle the letter of the correct answer to each of the following questions.

1. What is *expansionism?*
   - **a.** when a country's policy is to expand its territory and influence
   - **b.** when a country trades with other countries
   - **c.** when a country thinks its culture is the best
   - **d.** all of the above

2. What European nations participated in expansionism?
   - **a.** Spain, France, and Portugal
   - **b.** England and the Netherlands
   - **c.** Japan and China
   - **d.** both *a* and *b*

Trade with China

Europeans had traded with China on a limited basis for centuries. Ever since Marco Polo returned from his voyage there, Europeans had been fascinated with China—and with Chinese goods. One of the trade goods that so fascinated Europeans was **porcelain**, or "china." It was not available anywhere else in the world. How it was made remained a mystery to the Europeans until about 1700.

But China was not an easy nation with which to trade. Within China, merchants were members of the lowest social class. Merchants did not produce anything, as craftspeople and peasant farmers did. Because they made their living selling the results of the labor of others, they were held in low regard. Moreover, the Chinese had long considered agriculture, not trade, to be the basis of their economy.

Chinese rulers had a similar outlook on foreign trade. They did not believe that foreign trade would increase the wealth of the empire. Instead, they were used to receiving tribute, or taxes, from outlying nations that they had conquered. Furthermore, foreign trade might mean foreign influence. Such influence might corrupt Chinese culture and turn the peasants against the Chinese government.

Despite these obstacles, Europeans were determined to open a maritime, or sea-based, European-Chinese trade.

■ PRACTICE 78: Trade with China

Decide if each statement below is true (**T**) or false (**F**). Write the correct letter on the line before each statement.

_____ **1.** China was an easy nation with which to trade.

_____ **2.** The Chinese held merchants in low regard.

_____ **3.** Chinese rulers were afraid of foreign influence.

Portuguese and Dutch Trade with China

The first European nation to open maritime trade with China was Portugal. Portuguese ships first reached Chinese shores in 1514. But, it wasn't until 1557—some 43 years later—that the Chinese agreed to trade with the Portuguese. After decades of negotiation, they allowed the Portuguese to establish a tiny trading station at **Macao.** (A **trading station** was a small group of buildings where traders lived, goods were stored, and trades took place.) Over time, many similar trading stations would spring up around eastern Asia.

As you have already learned, Chinese rulers feared that foreigners would change Chinese culture. And, as you've also read, Europeans continually sent missionaries to other lands in hopes of spreading

Christianity. The Chinese fear and the European hope collided when Portugal opened trade with China.

The Portuguese sent Christian missionaries to their trading station in Macao. The missionaries, who were educated men, impressed the Chinese emperor and his court. They added to Chinese knowledge about astronomy and the calendar. Because of this contribution, they were allowed to stay. Many even served in important posts in the Chinese government.

Over time, however, many powerful Chinese began to resent the missionaries. They thought foreigners had no role in the Chinese government. They were concerned that the missionaries would spread their religion. As a result, in the 1700s, all Portuguese were forced to withdraw from China.

Another reason for the Portuguese withdrawal was the growth of Dutch trade in the region. The Dutch were coming in greater numbers, and they provided stiff competition for the Portuguese.

■ PRACTICE 79: Portuguese and Dutch Trade with China

Match each description with a term from the list below. Write the letter of the correct term on the line before each description.

a. missionaries **b.** Macao **c.** trading station

_____ **1.** a small compound of buildings where traders lived, goods were stored, and trades took place.

_____ **2.** the Portuguese trading station in China

_____ **3.** learned men who impressed the Chinese emperor and his court

British Trade with China

The British established maritime trade with China in 1699. They built a small trading station at **Guangzhou** (formerly known as Canton). The company that traded with China was the British East India Company.

Like the Portuguese before them, the British faced severe restrictions in China. They were not allowed to leave the trading station, which was built outside of the city. They could only trade with a few merchants, who were handpicked by the Chinese government. And their ships were only allowed to dock at Guangzhou. Goods had to be carried hundreds of miles to the coast, adding to the cost.

Why would the British sail so far for such limited trade? The answer is tea. The Europeans—especially the British—had developed a tremendous thirst for this new drink. Chinese tea was the best, and it commanded a handsome price in the markets back in England. Chinese silk was also in demand.

Over the next two centuries, British trade with China continued to grow. Hundreds of ships, loaded with tea and other goods, brought a taste of China to England.

■ PRACTICE 80: British Trade with China

Circle the letter of the correct answer to each of the following questions.

1. Where was the British trading station in China?

- **a.** Macao
- **b.** Beijing
- **c.** Shanghai
- **d.** Guangzhou

2. What did the British want to buy from the Chinese?

- **a.** corn
- **b.** tobacco
- **c.** tea
- **d.** coffee

Trade with Japan

As you learned in Lesson 6, Japan remained isolated from other countries for centuries. This began to change in the mid-1500s with the arrival of European traders. The first to arrive were the Portuguese.

Many Japanese noblemen, called daimyos, welcomed the Portuguese traders. Here was a chance for the daimyos to increase their wealth. For decades, Portugal engaged in successful trade with Japan.

But, not surprisingly, the traders were followed by the Christian missionaries. These missionaries concentrated on converting the daimyos. Then newly Christian daimyos encouraged the people they led to adopt the religion. The tactic worked well. Half a million Japanese converted to Christianity.

The rulers of Japan viewed the spread of Christianity as a threat to Japanese culture and their rule. They also felt that the foreign traders were influencing Japanese culture in other ways.

Meanwhile, the Dutch—Portugal's constant rival for trade in eastern Asia—also began to trade with the Japanese. The Dutch set up a small trading station in the port city of **Nagasaki**. Spain and Britain also set up trading posts.

Now there were people from several foreign countries on Japanese soil. This, combined with the spread of Christianity brought by the foreigners, was too much for the Japanese rulers. They decided to stop all foreign trade, despite the wealth it brought.

And stop it they did, in a dramatic fashion. In about 1640, the leaders of Japan simply closed the country to foreigners. Under the new rules, no foreigner was allowed into Japan. No Japanese were allowed to leave the country.

The years of isolation were also years of peace in Japan. A rich Japanese culture was formed. The type of drama called Kabuki developed. It included exciting plots and lively action on the stage. Another art form that developed in these years was the woodblock print. These prints could be made cheaply enough to reach a wide audience. They quickly became popular, and have stayed popular ever since.

Even without foreign trade, the economy was healthy. More and more, Japan's economy moved from farming to manufacturing and trade. This was good news for the growing merchant class. But it was bad news for the daimyos and samurai. Their wealth was based on land. As the economy changed, their wealth grew less. Also, the clear class lines began to blur. Rich merchants bought the rank of samurai. Some samurai and farmers went to cities and became merchants themselves. The rigid structure of Japanese society was starting to fall apart.

IN REAL LIFE

Even today Japan remains relatively "closed" to outside trade. American businesses often complain about how the Japanese government makes it difficult for Americans to conduct business there. In part, this is a result of Japan's long-standing preference for isolation.

PRACTICE 81: Trade with Japan

Decide if each statement below is true (**T**) or false (**F**). Write the correct letter on the line before each statement.

_____ **1.** Portuguese traders arrived in Japan in the mid-1500s.

_____ **2.** Japan closed itself to European traders in about 1640.

_____ **3.** The Japanese rulers closed Japan because they were afraid of foreign influence.

_____ **4.** Without foreign influence, Japanese culture grew weak.

LESSON 13: Expansionism in India

GOAL: To explain the role the British East India Company played in India after the downfall of the Mogul Empire

WORDS TO KNOW

British India

NAME TO KNOW

Warren Hastings

PLACES TO KNOW

Bombay

Madras

Calcutta

EVENT TO KNOW

Battle of Plassey

The East India Trading Companies

As you have already learned, two of the major trading companies during the First Global Age were the Dutch East India Company and the British East India Company. These companies did not operate like companies today. For one thing, they were closely tied to the governments of their countries. Both were created under royal charter, which means they operated on behalf of the king and queen. Both companies were huge and powerful. They built their own fleets of armed trading ships. The soldiers who worked for the companies were also armed. Rich, well armed, and well connected, the trading companies were powerful forces.

These two companies, and the nations they traded for, also traded beyond India into eastern Asia. But the Indian trade was especially important. And the power of the trading companies would change the face of India for centuries.

The names of these two companies give you important information about them. The *Dutch* East India Company came from the Netherlands.

The *British* East India Company came from England. Both were *companies*—private firms that made their money from trade. Both companies traded in the *east.* And, as you might have guessed, both companies traded with India.

■ PRACTICE 82: The East India Trading Companies

Match each description with a term from the list below. Write the letter of the correct term on the line before each description.

a. the Dutch East India Company

b. royal charter

c. the British East India Company

____ **1.** company from the Netherlands that traded with India

____ **2.** company from England that traded with India

____ **3.** permission to operate on behalf of the king and queen

Portuguese Trade in India

The Portuguese were the first to establish a sea route to India. Vasco da Gama, sailing around the Cape of Good Hope at the southern tip of Africa, reached Calicut, India in 1498.

But da Gama was not welcomed in India. The Muslim merchants there did not want to have to compete with Europeans in trade. Da Gama and his men were harassed and threatened. They returned to Portugal in 1499. However, da Gama came back in 1502. He returned to India with 15 ships, ready to trade. Da Gama also brought soldiers, who attacked and killed any Muslim traders or Indians who would not trade with them. From then on, Portugal was a major trading nation in India.

Portugal went so far as to seize ports along the coast of India. Any local rulers who interfered with trade were attacked. The Portuguese also fought with English, Dutch, and French traders. Their goal was not just to control trade with India, but also to protect their sea routes to eastern Asia.

The Portuguese prospered from the trade with India for about a century. Over time, however, their trade decreased. Bad management, the anger of the Indians, and the growing power of European trading rivals contributed to this decline. By the early 1600s, another European power came to the forefront in India: England.

PRACTICE 83: Portuguese Trade in India

Circle the letter of the correct answer to each of the following questions.

1. When did the Portuguese dominate European trade with India?

- **a.** the early 1400s to the early 1500s
- **b.** the early 1500s to the early 1600s
- **c.** the early 1600s to the early 1700s
- **d.** the early 1700s to the early 1800s

2. What European nation came to control trade in India after Portugal?

- **a.** France
- **b.** Italy
- **c.** Spain
- **d.** England

British Trade in India

The British East India Company, formed in 1600, set its sights on trade with India. Within 100 years, it had established thriving trading stations at **Bombay**, **Calcutta**, and **Madras**.

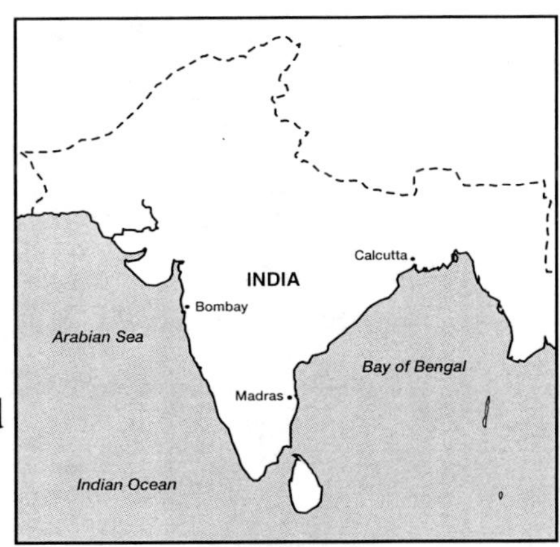

British India

Along with the trading stations, the British built forts. That they felt the need to build forts should tell you something about the situation. Remember that the Portuguese had fought rival Muslim traders and the Indians themselves.

Now the British were in a similar situation. Europeans also often fought each other to control the trade to India and eastern Asia. Most of these fights, however, had been small skirmishes. The British soon raised such wars over trade to new heights.

THINK ABOUT IT

As you are learning, the Europeans of the 1400s, 1500s, and 1600s were eager to buy such goods as spices, silks, gold, and furs from Asia, the New World, and Africa. These goods were very valuable to Europeans of that time. Often, European nations went to war to protect their ability to trade these goods. What types of goods do you think are as valuable today? What trading goods might countries go to war with each other to protect? Write your answers on a separate sheet of paper.

PRACTICE 84: British Trade in India

Circle the letter of the correct answer to each of the following questions.

1. Which of the following was a major British trading port in India?

- **a.** Bombay
- **b.** Madras
- **c.** Calcutta
- **d.** all of the above

2. Why did the British build forts in India?

- **a.** to protect themselves against attacks by rival trading nations
- **b.** to protect themselves against attacks by the Indians
- **c.** both *a* and *b*
- **d.** neither *a* nor *b*

The Mogul Empire

When the Portuguese and the British began trading in India, India was ruled by the Mogul Empire. As you learned in Lesson 5, the Mogul Empire was founded in north central India in 1526. Within 200 years, this empire stretched across almost all of India.

The leaders of the Mogul Empire were Muslims, followers of the religion of Islam. But most Indian people were followers of Hinduism. For a time, this caused great tension in the empire. But during the rule of the emperor Akbar, from 1556 to 1605, the tension decreased. Akbar promoted harmony in India. The result was a peaceful, strong empire.

Trouble came when Aurangzeb came to control the Mogul Empire. The Mogul Empire reached its greatest size in the early 1700s during his rule. But within the empire, the previous harmony began to break down.

Aurangzeb was a devout Muslim. Under Akbar, Hindus and other non-Muslims had lived in peace in the empire. But Aurangzeb persecuted non-Muslim peoples. He ordered many of their temples destroyed.

Of course, many people in the Mogul Empire resented Aurangzeb. Revolts broke out that weakened the empire. Also, the empire had grown so large that it was hard to rule. Some states within the empire wanted to be independent. When Aurangzeb died in 1707, he left behind a weak and divided empire.

Within 50 years, Mogul rulers could no longer hold the empire together. India was a weak and divided land—easy prey for foreign invaders. And the British were ready to take advantage of the situation.

■ PRACTICE 85: The Mogul Empire

Circle the letter of the correct answer to each of the following questions.

1. What empire ruled India when the European traders came?
   - **a.** the Mogul Empire
   - **b.** the British Empire
   - **c.** the Maratha Empire
   - **d.** the Persian Empire

2. What emperor's cruel rule helped destroy central government in India?
    a. Sikh
    b. Aurangzeb
    c. Akbar
    d. Maratha

The British East India Company in India

As long as the Mogul Empire held together, the influence of the British East India Company in India was limited to coastal trading stations. With the disintegration of the empire after Aurangzeb, however, the British pressed their advantage. By the mid-1700s, the British had moved deep into India.

IN REAL LIFE

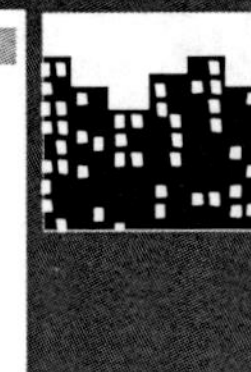

Aurangzeb's disastrous rule of the Mogul Empire led to its disintegration—and to the British takeover of India. For one man to have such a major influence on the history of a nation is not unusual. In the United States, the federal government is designed specifically to keep the president from becoming too powerful. The reason is to avoid the catastrophes that can happen when one person has too much power.

Since there was no strong central government in India, local Indian rulers were free to do as they pleased. Many entered into alliances with the British East India Company. The Indian rulers knew that they could grow rich trading with the British.

These agreements were not one-sided. The British East India Company demanded—and got—enormous powers when it entered into these alliances. The Indian rulers saw the possible trade opportunities and were happy to comply. In some cases, they appointed British traders to government positions. The British even collected taxes from the Indians.

As they gained the confidence of local Indian rulers, the British expanded their role in India. They played devious political games, turning

Indian rulers against one another. The British would trade with both sides, but pretend to be on just one side. Once one ruler defeated the other, the British would claim to have been on his side all along. Sometimes the British East India Company provided troops to support local Indian rulers.

Any local ruler who refused to accept British rule was attacked. Time and again, forces of the British East India Company defeated the Indian armies. The British were better trained and had better weapons. Quickly, the British East India Company took over India.

■ PRACTICE 86: The British East India Company in India

Circle the letter of the correct answer to each of the following questions.

1. How did the British East India Company gain control of India?
   a. by taking advantage of a weak and divided country
   b. by making alliances with local rulers
   c. by conducting warfare
   d. all of the above

2. Why did the Indians allow the British East India Company to take over?
   a. Local Indian rulers wanted to make money from trade.
   b. The Indian armies were not as well equipped or well trained as the British.
   c. India had no central government to oppose the British.
   d. all of the above

British India

Aurangzeb died in 1707, leaving behind a weak empire. Just 50 years later, much of what had been his empire was controlled by the British East India Company.

The final blow came in 1757. In that year, forces of the British East India Company fought Indian troops at the **Battle of Plassey**. With this victory, the British East India Company became the most powerful force in India—more powerful than any local ruler.

Less than 20 years later, the British were confident of their control over much of India. In 1774, they went so far as to appoint a governor general of India. Although **Warren Hastings** was a member of the British East India Company, his real role was to rule India. He and his successors ruled **British India** harshly to promote the interests of the British East India Company. They continued to lead wars to secure and expand their rule.

Eventually, all of India came under British rule. In 1858, it became an official part of the British Empire, controlled by the British government instead of by the British East India Company. But for 200 years, this proud and ancient land had been controlled by a foreign trading company.

IN REAL LIFE

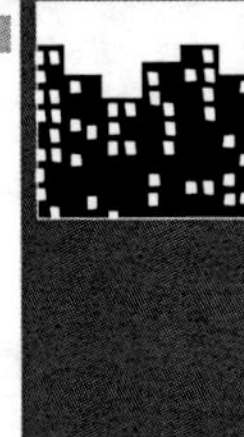

Have you ever read any stories or poems by Rudyard Kipling? He was an English writer who was born in India and spent much of his life there. Some of his best-known books set in India are *Kim, Plain Tales from the Hills,* and *The Jungle Books.* They give an interesting picture of life in British India.

PRACTICE 87: British India

Circle the letter of the correct answer to each of the following questions.

1. Who won the Battle of Plassey?
- **a.** India
- **b.** the British East India Company
- **c.** Warren Hastings
- **d.** Aurangzeb

2. Who was Warren Hastings?
- **a.** the emperor of India
- **b.** a member of the British East India Company
- **c.** a governor general of India
- **d.** both *b* and *c*

LESSON 14: Expansionism in Africa

GOAL: To discuss the European slave trade in Africa as part of the triangular trade; to define *Europeanization*

WORDS TO KNOW

Europeanization

plantations

slave trade

triangular trade

PLACES TO KNOW

Cape Town

Ceuta

Africa Before European Contact

By the time European traders came to Africa, hundreds of different cultures had developed there. These many peoples spoke different languages, had different traditions, and practiced different religions. Each culture was unique. Despite their differences, early African peoples also had many things in common. For example, most Africans were farmers who lived in villages. All maintained an oral tradition. And most practiced traditional religions that included a belief in ancestral spirits and magic. In North Africa, though, Islam had become the dominant religion.

From about 900 to about 1500, three great kingdoms arose in western Africa: Ghana, Mali, and Songhai. They are called the West African Kingdoms because they were in western Africa, just south of the Sahara Desert. The great kingdoms of West Africa were all based on trade. The Kingdom of Ghana was the first West African Kingdom. It lasted more than 1,000 years. By the 1200s, the Mali Empire had replaced Ghana as the most powerful trading kingdom in West Africa. It was the supreme power in West Africa until the 1500s. Eventually, the Songhai Empire became the largest of the great trading kingdoms of West Africa. At its peak in the late 1400s and early 1500s, it covered an area the size of western Europe.

Other great trading centers were growing along the east African coast. There many city-states developed. (A city-state is a large city that is independent.) All of the East African city-states earned their wealth through trade. Two of the more powerful city-states were Kilwa and Mombasa. The city-states of East Africa prospered from the early 700s through the 1300s.

In short, the peoples of Africa had enjoyed a long and proud history before the European traders came. They had no way of knowing that the Europeans would forever alter the life of every African man, woman, and child.

PRACTICE 88: Africa Before European Contact

Circle the letter of the correct answer to each of the following questions.

1. Which statement about Africa is TRUE?

- **a.** Africa was a backward land before the Europeans came.
- **b.** No great kingdoms ever arose in Africa.
- **c.** Trade was unknown in Africa until the Europeans came.
- **d.** Africa had a long and rich history before European contact.

2. Which of the following was a great kingdom in West Africa?

- **a.** the Ghana Empire
- **b.** the Mali Empire
- **c.** the Songhai Empire
- **d.** all of the above

The Portuguese and Others in Africa

As you know, the Portuguese were the first Europeans to establish sea trade with Asia. Their route to Asia—which curved around the southern tip of Africa—was established by Vasco da Gama in 1498. But the Portuguese didn't sail nonstop to India. Instead, they did it one step at a time, sailing down the western coast of Africa and up the eastern coast.

The Portuguese captured **Ceuta** in North Africa in 1415. It was the first European toehold on the African continent. By 1460, they had voyaged south, beyond Muslim North Africa, to black Africa. Within 30 years, they had rounded the Cape of Good Hope and were sailing up the eastern coast of Africa.

All along the way, the Portuguese set up trading stations. As they inched their way down one coast of Africa and up the other, the number of trading stations grew.

Sometimes the Portuguese established stations where no settlements existed. More often, however, they forcefully captured coastal towns and set up their own trading stations there. In East Africa, they captured the trading city-states.

The Portuguese were not the only Europeans interested in Africa. By the 1600s, other Europeans were joining them. The African coast was valuable as a stopover place on the way to India, as well as for African trade goods. The Dutch established a station at **Cape Town,** near the tip of Africa, in 1652. It soon grew into a colony. The British and the French also had a presence in Africa.

But the Portuguese led the way. In Africa, they found ivory, gold, silver, animal hides, and various craft goods. But as you know, their greatest wealth came from trading something completely different: human beings.

■ PRACTICE 89: The Portuguese and Others in Africa

Circle the letter of the correct answer to each of the following questions.

1. What was the first city in Africa to be captured by Europeans?
- **a.** da Gama
- **b.** Ceuta
- **c.** Cape Town
- **d.** Calcutta

2. What trade goods did Europeans want from Africa?
- **a.** gold and silver
- **b.** ivory and animal hides
- **c.** craft goods
- **d.** all of the above

3. Which Europeans were the first to explore Africa?
    a. the French
    b. the English
    c. the Spanish
    d. the Portuguese

The Slave Trade

As you already know, Europeans captured Africans and forced them to work as slaves. The **slave trade** lasted for four centuries, from the 1400s to the 1800s. It turned out to be the most profitable trade for the Portuguese, and later for the Spanish, in Africa. It also turned out to be one of the saddest chapters in human history.

The Portuguese began enslaving Africans soon after they captured Ceuta in 1415. But the slave trade did not really take off until the 1500s. By then, Europeans were colonizing the Americas in greater and greater numbers. They wanted African slaves to work the agricultural **plantations,** or large farms, of the New World.

No description of the European slave trade in Africa can accurately convey its horror. For centuries, Europeans captured innocent men, women, and children. They destroyed the lives of individuals, families, and even whole villages and cultures. In all, about 12 million Africans were taken as slaves.

Moreover, many Africans willingly took part in the slave trade. Slavery had existed in parts of Africa for centuries. (African slavery, however, was usually the result of warfare and was not as cruel as European slavery.) Because the Europeans paid well for slaves, many Africans went into the business of capturing slaves to sell to the Europeans.

Once slaves had been seized, they were marched to the slave-trading ports on the coast. There the slaves were packed into ships. They were treated as cargo, not as human beings. In many ships, slaves did not even have space to sit up. The trip across the Atlantic took two or three months. One in six slaves died on the way. Of the survivors, most were sent to the islands of the West Indies or to Brazil. About 1 in 20 ended up in North America. Every one of them lived a tragic life.

THINK ABOUT IT

Not all Europeans supported slavery. Many decent people spoke out against it. But they were unable to stop slavery for centuries. How do you think the people who participated in the slave trade supported their position against these critics? Was it pure racism? Think about what their arguments might have been. Write your answers on a separate sheet of paper.

PRACTICE 90: The Slave Trade

Decide if each statement below is true (**T**) or false (**F**). Write the correct letter on the line before each statement.

_____ **1.** The slave trade lasted for 400 years.

_____ **2.** The slave trade was the most profitable African trade for the Europeans.

_____ **3.** About 12 million black Africans were shipped to the New World as slaves.

The Triangular Trade

The demand for slaves by the Europeans was a direct result of the colonization of the New World by Portugal, France, England, and the Netherlands. The Europeans built huge plantations in the New World, many of them growing sugarcane. These plantations required a great deal of labor to run. At first, the Europeans used Native Americans as slave labor. But most died from European diseases and cruel treatment. That is when the Europeans in the New World looked to Africa for slaves.

Over time, the **triangular trade** developed. It was called this because ships traveled in a large triangle between America, Europe, and Africa. (It can also refer to the trade between North America, West Africa, and the West Indies.) From Europe, traders brought cheap manufactured goods to Africa. In Africa, they exchanged these goods for slaves. The slaves were then shipped to the Americas and sold. The money the traders got was used to buy the products of the slave-worked plantations: sugar (usually exported as rum), cotton, and tobacco. Finally, the traders sailed back to Europe, where they sold these goods. The vicious cycle then began again.

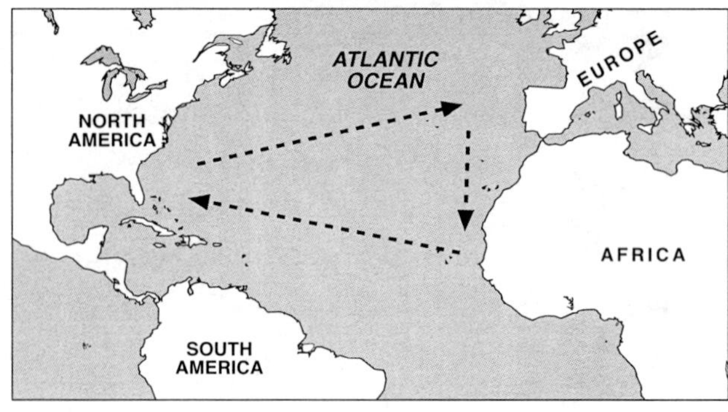

The Triangular Trade

TIP

The triangular trade is described on page 167 and above, both in writing and on a map. When ideas are presented in more than one way, take advantage of it. Read the description and study the map. This will make it easier for you to learn and remember the main ideas being presented.

PRACTICE 91: The Triangular Trade

Circle the letter of the correct answer to each of the following questions.

1. In the triangular trade, what was brought to Africa?
- **a.** cheap manufactured goods
- **b.** sugar or rum
- **c.** cotton
- **d.** slaves

2. In the triangular trade, what was brought to America?
- **a.** tobacco
- **b.** sugar or rum
- **c.** cotton
- **d.** slaves

3. In the triangular trade, what was brought to Europe?
   a. tobacco
   b. sugar or rum
   c. cotton
   d. all of the above

Lasting Effects

In this unit, you have read about how the First Global Age came about. European explorers found sea routes to many other parts of the world. Following them came missionaries and traders. From tiny trading stations, the influence of Europeans grew. In some places, such as Japan, they were pushed back. In other places, such as India and Africa, they completely took over.

By the end of the nineteenth century, a few European powers had set up colonies around the world. Great Britain had colonies on every continent. Much of Africa, South Asia, and Southwest Asia was under British rule.

Today, European languages, especially English, are spoken all over the world. European ideas and technologies are found nearly everywhere. The United States grew out of the European expansionism of the First Global Age. **Europeanization** is a term some historians use for the worldwide European influence that began during this period. This great change in world history started with small numbers of men setting out to explore and to trade.

IN REAL LIFE

Where do your ancestors come from? Many Americans are of European ancestry. This is a direct result of Europeanization. Many other Americans are of African ancestry. This is a direct result of the slave trade, which was a result of Europeanization. Without Europeanization, most of the people in this country today would be of Native American ancestry.

■ PRACTICE 92: Lasting Effects

Circle the letter of the correct answer to each of the following questions.

1. Which of the following places was completely taken over by Europeans during the First Global Age?
   a. Africa
   b. the New World
   c. India
   d. all of the above

2. What do some historians call the worldwide European influence that began during the First Global Age?
   a. ethnocentrism
   b. colonization
   c. Europeanization
   d. expansionism

UNIT 4 REVIEW

Circle the letter of the correct answer to each of the following questions.

1. Which European nation claimed ownership of Louisiana?
   a. the Netherlands
   b. Spain
   c. Italy
   d. France

2. Which nation founded the colonies of Jamestown and Plymouth?
   a. Italy
   b. Spain
   c. England
   d. France

3. What Chinese trade good did the British want more than any other?
   a. porcelain
   b. linen
   c. tea
   d. coffee

4. What religion did Europeans introduce in Japan?
   a. Christianity
   b. Shintoism
   c. Islam
   d. Buddhism

5. How did the Japanese rulers eventually react to Japan's contact with foreign countries?
   a. They stopped trading with anyone but the Portuguese.
   b. They closed the borders of Japan entirely.
   c. They carefully controlled which traders could enter Japan.
   d. They forced foreign traders to remain within small trading stations.

6. How did the British East India Company gain control of India?
   a. by taking advantage of a weak and divided country
   b. by making alliances with local rulers
   c. by conducting warfare
   d. all of the above

7. Why did the people of India allow the British East India Company to take over?
   a. Local Indian rulers wanted to make money from trade.
   b. The Indian armies were not as well equipped or well trained as the British.
   c. India had no central government to oppose the British.
   d. all of the above

8. Why was the Battle of Plassey significant?
   a. It marked the first time the British fired on the Indians.
   b. It marked the first time the Indians fought back against the British.
   c. It established the British East India Company as the most powerful force in India.
   d. It marked the end of the Mogul Empire.

9. Which statement about Africa is TRUE?
   a. Africa was a backward land before the Europeans came.
   b. No great kingdoms ever arose in Africa.
   c. Africa had a long and rich history before European contact.
   d. Trade was unknown in Africa until the Europeans came.

10. In the triangular trade, what was NOT brought to Europe?
   a. tobacco
   b. sugar (or rum)
   c. cotton
   d. slaves

UNIT 4 APPLICATION ACTIVITY

European Place-names in North America

You have read that North America was claimed and colonized by several European nations. The three most successful colonizers of North America were England, France, and Spain.

The legacy of these countries lives on in many place-names in the United States. For example, New London is a city in Connecticut that was founded and named by the English. New Orleans, a city in Louisiana, was founded and named by the French. In both of these cases, the American city was named after a city in the colonizer's country. London is the capital of England, and Orleans is a city in France.

Find a map of the United States. Choose a state to study. If your state is along the East Coast, you will also need a map of England. If your state is in the Midwest, you will need a map of France. If your state is in the Southeast, the Southwest, or the West, you will need a map of Spain.

Once you have copies of both maps, study the place-names in the U.S. state. Now, look on the map of the European country. Do any of the names look similar? Go back and forth between the two maps. Make a list below of each American place-name that is related to a city in the European country. See how many you can find.

American city	**European city it is named after**

UNIT 5

New Ideas Lead to Revolution

LESSON 15: The Age of Reason in Europe

GOAL: To identify the major thinkers and ideas of the Age of Reason, or Enlightenment

WORDS TO KNOW

Age of Rationalism	**mechanical universe**
Age of Reason	**philosopher**
balance of powers	**rational will**
deism	**reason**
deists	**revolution**
"enlightened" monarchs	**separation of powers**
Enlightenment	**universal laws**

NAMES TO KNOW

Catherine the Great	**Frederick the Great**	**Jean-Jacques Rousseau**
Queen Christina	**Joseph II**	**Voltaire**
René Descartes	**John Locke**	
Denis Diderot	**Montesquieu**	

Reason and Revolution

Two words will stand out as you read this lesson: **reason** and **revolution.** In many ways, these two terms describe much of what happened in Europe and the Americas in the 1700s and 1800s.

Think about the word *reason.* By "reason," we don't mean "the reason things happen" or "the reason somebody did something." Here, we will refer to reason as the human ability to think rationally, as when someone "reasons out a problem." During the 1700s and 1800s, the human power to reason was celebrated as never before. Reason was applied in science, in literature, and in politics and government. In fact, the period of European history from the 1600s to the late 1700s is called the **Age of Reason.**

The other word that stands out is *revolution.* As you know, a revolution is the overthrow of an established government. The American Revolution, for example, gave birth to the United States of America. That revolution occurred in the 1770s. Several other modern countries, such as France and Mexico, were also born out of the revolutions of this period.

So, remember the two words: *reason* and *revolution.* And read carefully to see how, in many cases, it was peoples' very ability to reason that led to revolution!

■ PRACTICE 93: Reason and Revolution

Decide if each statement below is true (**T**) or false (**F**). Write the correct letter on the line before each statement.

_____ **1.** In this lesson, the word *reason* is used to mean the *reason* the revolution happened.

_____ **2.** A revolution is the overthrow of an established government.

The Age of Reason

The Age of Reason was a period of European history that lasted from the 1600s to the late 1700s. European thinkers of this period believed that reason—careful, logical thought—was the best way to learn about people and the world.

The Age of Reason is sometimes called the **Enlightenment.** This is because leading thinkers of the time were thought to be enlightened, or "lit up" by the power of thought and education. This period is also called the **Age of Rationalism.** This is because leading thinkers of the time relied on the power of rational, or careful and logical, thought. Of the three names, you will probably hear Enlightenment and Age of Reason more often. Both will be used in this lesson.

Many important philosophers lived during the Age of Reason. A **philosopher** is someone who thinks and writes about important ideas of human existence. The philosophers of this time thought that reason could improve human life. Other great thinkers of this period included scientists, mathematicians, writers, educators, and even revolutionaries. They thought and wrote about many different things. But they all had in common a firm belief in the power of human reason.

THINK ABOUT IT

You have just read that the Age of Reason also has two other names: the Enlightenment and the Age of Rationalism. Many other historical periods and events also have more than one name. This is because history is complex and often cannot be described by one term. For example, what name would you give the current period of time? Can you sum up the entire feeling of our age in only one term? Write your answers on a separate sheet of paper.

PRACTICE 94: The Age of Reason

Decide if each statement below is true (**T**) or false (**F**). Write the correct letter on the line before each statement.

_____ **1.** The Age of Reason was a period of Chinese history.

_____ **2.** Another name for the Age of Reason is the Enlightenment.

Ideas of the Age of Reason

The thinkers of the Age of Reason worked in different fields. But they had many ideas in common.

One of these ideas was a belief in the orderliness of the universe. This means that the universe is not a random collection of things but has a pattern. Although the universe is large and complex, there is an order to nature.

A related idea was that there are **universal laws,** or rules, at work in the universe. Everything in the universe—living and nonliving alike—acts according to these laws. For example, Isaac Newton had discovered the law of gravity in the mid-1600s. Gravity acts the same way on everything in the universe. Enlightenment thinkers thought that by identifying these universal laws they could make clear the way the universe worked.

To understand these laws, people had to use reason. Enlightenment thinkers thought that every person has a **rational will.** By this, they meant that everyone can think rationally. They knew, of course, that not everyone thinks rationally all the time. But Enlightenment thinkers thought that by using their rational will, people could unlock and understand universal laws. The key to using rational will was education.

This marks another main idea of the Enlightenment: opposition to superstition and ignorance. Enlightenment thinkers thought that superstition and ignorance had caused many of the world's problems. They thought the "Dark Ages," or the Middle Ages, had been caused by widespread ignorance. They also thought that ignorance and superstition kept people from solving many problems. Education and the use of rational will, they argued, could overcome problems in all human activities.

It isn't surprising that many great thinkers of the Age of Reason had confidence in the power of mathematics and science. They had seen the wonderful achievements made in these fields by such men as Galileo, Kepler, and Copernicus. They saw how mathematics was critical to the success of these and other men. Mathematics and science seemed to yield unarguable truths. Two plus two, for example, always equals four. These thinkers believed that nature works the same way. Find the laws of nature, they thought, and you will find the truth.

Many of these ideas are probably familiar to you. This is because they help form the basis of much of our modern worldview. In fact, the modern world, in many ways, began with these ideas of the Age of Reason.

IN REAL LIFE

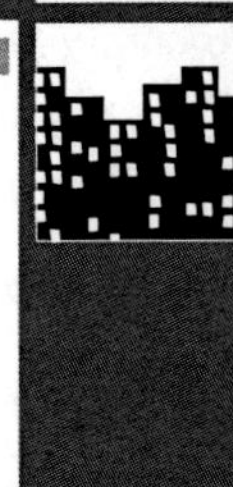

The view that education is the key to moving ahead, solving the world's problems, and having a better quality of life is even more widely held today. The more adept you become at the process of learning, the more flexible you can be in finding a job you enjoy, trying more than one career, and exploring new possibilities in your life.

PRACTICE 95: Ideas of the Age of Reason

Complete each sentence with a term from the list below. Write the letter of the correct term on the line.

a. science **b.** rational will **c.** modern **d.** order **e.** universal laws

1. The thinkers of the Age of Reason thought that the universe had a(n) _____ to it.
2. They thought that everything in the universe acted according to _____.
3. They thought that the pattern of the universe and the rules that ran it could be discovered if people used their _____.
4. Successes in mathematics and _____ seemed to prove the power of reason.
5. Many of the ideas of the Age of Reason are part of our _____ worldview.

Deism

Deism is a theory about God and the universe. Many thinkers of the Age of Reason were **deists,** or believers in deism. Understanding deism will help you understand the basic ideas of the Age of Reason.

Deists sometimes referred to God as a "great clock maker." Just as a clock maker makes a clock, they believed, God created the universe. Once a clock maker makes a clock, he or she leaves it alone. The gears and other parts determine how the clock runs. In a similar way, God created the universe and then left it alone. Universal laws, such as the law of gravity, determine how the universe runs.

Deists believed that identifying these universal laws would reveal how the universe works. People could identify these laws by using mathematics, science, and rational will.

Moreover, deists believed that the very purpose of human existence was to uncover these laws. They believed that God could have made the universe and the human mind any way God wanted to. And God created people with the power of reason. So, this power was intended to be used.

As you can see, most of the main ideas of the Age of Reason are expressed in deism. The universe is ordered, it runs according to universal laws set in motion at creation, and these laws are understandable to people if they use their rational will and the tools of mathematics and science.

■ PRACTICE 96: Deism

Decide if each statement below is true (**T**) or false (**F**). Write the correct letter on the line before each statement.

_____ **1.** Most of the main ideas of the Age of Reason are expressed in deism.

_____ **2.** Deists believed that people should rely on faith, not on rational thought and understanding.

_____ **3.** Deists believed in a natural order of the universe.

René Descartes

René Descartes was a French philosopher, scientist, and mathematician. He lived from 1596 to 1650. Descartes is often called "the first modern philosopher." He was a major figure of the Age of Reason.

Descartes did much to champion the idea of deism and the power of human thought. In contrast to earlier thinking, which stressed faith, Descartes stressed doubt, or skepticism. To find out about the universe, he said, people should begin by doubting. How can we know that what we see is real? he asked. How do we know that our senses aren't tricking us? Descartes determined that the only thing we can be sure of is that we think. Because we think, we must exist. In one of the most famous statements of history, Descartes declared, "I think, therefore I am."

From this idea, Descartes constructed a whole way of learning about the world. His method was based on observation and logical thinking. He applied his method to a variety of areas, such as physical science, anatomy, optics, and meteorology.

Like all other deists, Descartes believed that the universe operated according to universal laws. He believed in God and was a Catholic, but he believed that God did not continuously affect how the universe worked. Descartes believed in an idea called the **mechanical universe.** This was like the "universe as a clock" idea of deism.

Descartes became very influential. His idea of the mechanical universe, his belief that people should doubt things until they were proved, and his support of mathematics and science all have had a major impact on philosophers, scientists, and mathematicians even to the present day.

■ PRACTICE 97: René Descartes

Circle the letter of the correct answer to each of the following questions.

1. Where was Descartes from?

a. England
b. France
c. Spain
d. Italy

2. Which statement about Descartes is TRUE?

a. Descartes believed in a mechanical universe.
b. Descartes was a psychologist.
c. Descartes did not believe in God.
d. Descartes stressed belief over skepticism.

Jean-Jacques Rousseau

Descartes was perhaps the leading scientific thinker of the Age of Reason. A leading writer of this period was **Jean-Jacques Rousseau.** Rousseau lived from 1712 to 1778.

Rousseau came to fame when he won an essay contest. The issue for the contest was whether arts and sciences supported morality and society. Rousseau argued that they did not. He won the contest. He became immediately famous and wrote many books.

THINK ABOUT IT

The topic of the essay contest Rousseau entered was whether or not arts and sciences support good morals and values. This issue is still being debated today. For example, some people believe that the lyrics of certain types of music promote violence in teens. And the medical practice of abortion is still highly controversial. What do you think? Does the art and science of today help or hurt society? Why? Write your answers on a separate sheet of paper.

Rousseau was a social critic. In his writings, he attacked social issues such as inequality and the lack of morals in society. He wrote on topics ranging from political science to religion to government. All of his writings are marked by a passionate desire for social institutions that are fair and just.

Rousseau was one of the most influential writers who ever lived. His ideas about education—that a child's emotional needs and interests should be supported—have influenced educators ever since. And his celebration of the human spirit helped give rise to the literary movement called Romanticism.

But Rousseau's most important contributions were his writings about the individual, society, and government. Rousseau argued that people in their "natural state" are just and moral. Flawed social institutions, such as churches and governments, corrupt this basic goodness. Rousseau thought that society should be changed to support the individual spirit and not damage it. In a famous line, he said, "Man is born free, and everywhere he is in chains."

He argued that government should express the will of the people. This idea influenced the leaders of the American and French Revolutions.

■ PRACTICE 98: Jean-Jacques Rousseau

Circle the letter of the correct answer to each of the following questions.

1. What did Rousseau believe to be the "natural state" of people?
  a. religious and scientific
  b. corrupted
  c. passionate
  d. just and moral

2. What did he believe changed people from this state?
  a. flawed social institutions
  b. government
  c. churches
  d. all of the above

3. How did Rousseau's writings influence leaders of the American and French Revolutions?
  a. by arguing that government should express the will of the people
  b. by arguing that there should be no rulers or governments
  c. by arguing that people are born evil and need to be taught how to behave
  d. by arguing that government leaders should be supported, no matter what the cost

Montesquieu and Voltaire

Montesquieu was a French philosopher who wrote during the Age of Reason. He lived from 1689 to 1755. Like other Enlightenment thinkers, Montesquieu believed that certain laws control the operation of the universe. He believed, too, that universal laws govern human behavior. Montesquieu thought that people could identify these laws and build a good society based on them.

Montesquieu applied these ideas to government. He put forth the idea that the powers of government should be separated among three branches: legislative, executive, and judicial. These powers, Montesquieu argued, should be balanced so that no one part of government becomes too powerful. Only through such **separation of powers** and **balance of powers** could the freedom of the individual be protected. As you may know, these two ideas are a fundamental part of American government.

IN REAL LIFE

If you ever get a speeding ticket, you'll experience the separation and balance of powers in our government firsthand. The legislative branch (Congress and your state legislature) determined the speed limit. The executive branch (the president of the United States and state governors) had to approve it. The executive branch also enforces the speed limit (through the police). If you think the ticket is unfair, you can appeal to the judicial branch by going to court.

Of all the French thinkers of the Age of Reason, **Voltaire** is perhaps the most famous. Voltaire lived from 1694 to 1778. As a writer of essays, plays, novels, and philosophical books, Voltaire embodied the spirit of the Age of Reason.

Both during his own time and today, Voltaire has been recognized as witty, clever, and extremely bright. All told, his writings contributed more than 30,000 pages of insight to history.

Voltaire wrote on a variety of subjects. But three ideas color most of his work. The first one is a passionate support of freedom of speech. His dedication to this idea is best summed up by his famous statement: "I disagree with what you say, but I will defend to the death your right to say it." Voltaire also supported the freedom of the press. Finally, like many other thinkers of the period, Voltaire was also horrified at the religious persecution that was common in Europe at the time. He spoke out frequently for freedom of religion.

In addition, Voltaire, through the power of his personality and writing, made many Enlightenment ideas popular. His work was read and admired by leaders of the French and American Revolutions. His satirical novel *Candide* is still widely read and enjoyed today.

■ PRACTICE 99: Montesquieu and Voltaire

Circle the letters of the correct answers to each of the following questions. (*Hint:* Each question has more than one correct answer.)

1. What features did Montesquieu say governments should have to keep them from becoming too powerful and to protect individual freedom?

- **a.** separation of powers
- **b.** spirit of laws
- **c.** universal laws
- **d.** balance of powers

2. Which of the following ideas did Voltaire support?

- **a.** freedom of the press
- **b.** freedom from insight
- **c.** freedom of religion
- **d.** freedom of speech

John Locke

Most of the thinkers you have been reading about—Rousseau, Montesquieu, and Voltaire—were important leaders of the Age of Reason in France. Yet all of them were influenced by a man who was perhaps the most influential thinker of the Age of Reason—an Englishman named **John Locke.**

John Locke lived before these other writers, from 1632 to 1704. As you have read earlier, other Enlightenment writers celebrated ideas such as a separation of powers, a just government, and individual liberty. But it was Locke who first put forth the idea of a democracy under a constitution as the best form of government.

Locke argued for religious freedom. While others argued for freedom for different Christian sects, Locke argued that all religions should be tolerated.

Even more important were Locke's ideas in his *Two Treatises on Government.* Locke argued that people have natural rights, including the right to life, liberty, and the ownership of property. Government should protect the rights of the people, since governments obtain the right to govern from the consent of the people. People have the right to overthrow governments that are unjust. The majority should rule, but a majority cannot deprive a minority of its rights. A government cannot take people's property without their consent.

These ideas should sound familiar: They are the principles on which the Constitution of the United States of America is based. Locke's belief in the right of people to revolt was also a major influence on Thomas Jefferson and other leaders of the American Revolution. A true genius, Locke was the first to express many ideas that still sweep the world today.

■ PRACTICE 100: John Locke

Check each statement below that is TRUE.

☐ **1.** Locke was from France.

☐ **2.** Locke thought a democracy under a constitution was the best form of government.

☐ **3.** The United States government is based largely on Locke's principles of government.

☐ **4.** Locke had little influence outside of his own country.

☐ **5.** Locke did not believe in religious freedom.

The "Enlightened" Monarchs

Many ideas of the Age of Reason can be summed up in three words: nature, reason, and freedom. Nature is important because it involves the world people live in, which is governed by natural laws. By discovering these laws and living in a "natural state," these thinkers told us, people would be happiest. Reason is important because it is the key that unlocks these laws. And freedom is necessary for people to use their reason and to act on the results of their reasoning.

Today, these ideas seem almost commonplace. But at the time, they were new and revolutionary. Also, today it seems unlikely that only a few thinkers could radically reshape the world. But that is just what the thinkers of the Age of Reason did. As you have read, they greatly influenced leaders of the French and American Revolutions.

These thinkers also influenced leaders of their own time. For example, Voltaire stayed for a long time as adviser to **Frederick the Great**, the king of Prussia. Descartes was the private tutor of **Queen Christina** of Sweden. **Catherine the Great** of Russia supported **Denis Diderot**, a thinker who put together an encyclopedia. Such work was important to the thinkers of the Age of Reason because gathering and publishing what people had learned advanced human knowledge.

Catherine the Great

Many of these rulers were interested in Enlightenment ideas. But most failed to reform their governments. One European leader, **Joseph II** of the Holy Roman Empire, did apply some Enlightenment ideas. Joseph II promoted religious toleration and free speech. He reformed the legal system to make it more fair. And he tried to give the poorest people more rights.

Catherine of Russia began her reign with ideas for reform. She allowed some religious freedom and tried to improve education. She brought Western culture to Russia by hiring European architects, musicians, and artists. However, Catherine also extended serfdom, which kept poor peasants at the mercy of their landlords. She took land from the Church and gave it to officials. And she gave Russia's nobles even more rights.

These rulers are sometimes called the **"enlightened" monarchs.** Although they remained in absolute control of their countries, they were "enlightened" enough to consider Enlightenment ideas and even implement some of them. However, it took a revolution for these ideas to take hold on a large scale. You will read about this revolution in the next lesson.

■ PRACTICE 101: The "Enlightened" Monarchs

Decide if each statement below is true (**T**) or false (**F**). Write the correct letter on the line before each statement.

_____ **1.** The ideas of the Age of Reason included nature, reason, and freedom.

_____ **2.** Catherine the Great was one of the "enlightened" monarchs.

_____ **3.** All of the "enlightened" monarchs immediately reformed their governments in response to Enlightenment ideas.

_____ **4.** Joseph II of the Holy Roman Empire did apply some Enlightenment ideas to his empire.

_____ **5.** Catherine of Russia freed peasants who were at the mercy of their landlords.

_____ **6.** These rulers are considered "enlightened" because they were willing to consider new ideas.

LESSON 16: Revolutions in British America and France

GOAL: To discuss the causes and consequences of the American and French Revolutions; to explain how both revolutions were inspired by ideas of the Age of Reason

WORDS TO KNOW

American Revolution

Bastille

Battles of Lexington and Concord

Boston Tea Party

colonists

Committee of Public Safety

Constitution

Declaration of Independence

Declaration of the Rights of Man and of the Citizen

Directory

divine right

estates

Estates-General

First Continental Congress

First Estate

French and Indian War

French Revolution

National Assembly

National Convention

Reign of Terror

Second Estate

Third Estate

Treaty of Paris

NAMES TO KNOW

Napoleon Bonaparte

Thomas Jefferson

Louis XVI

Maximilien Robespierre

George Washington

Two Revolutions

In this lesson, you will read about the **American Revolution** and the **French Revolution.** The American Revolution gave birth, as you know, to the United States of America. The French Revolution radically changed French government and also helped lead to other revolutions throughout Europe. Both of these revolutions continue to serve as inspirations to peoples around the world.

It is important to remember that the American and French revolutions were wars, but they were also revolutions about ideas. You have read that many important ideas developed during the Age of Reason: freedom of the individual, the right of people to overthrow unjust governments, and freedoms of religion, speech, and the press. All of these ideas had a huge impact on the thinking of the leaders of both revolutions.

As you read about the causes, course, and impact of these revolutions, keep two things in mind. First, these revolutions were in many ways a direct outgrowth of the ideas of the Age of Reason. Second, these two revolutions altered the world in ways that few other events in history have. The way the world is today, not just in the United States and in France but all over the globe, is largely a legacy of these two revolutions.

■ PRACTICE 102: Two Revolutions

Decide if each statement below is true (**T**) or false (**F**). Write the correct letter on the line before each statement.

_____ **1.** The way the world is today is largely a result of the French and American revolutions.

_____ **2.** The French and American revolutions were directly related to the ideas of the Age of Reason.

The Causes of the American Revolution

As you know, the Americas were colonized by European powers. For a long time, Spain, France, and Britain fought for control of the Americas. In the **French and Indian War** (1754–1763), Britain defeated France and became the most important power in North America.

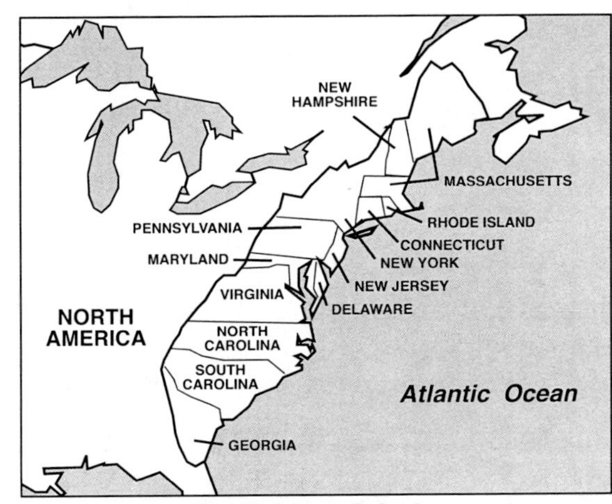

The Thirteen Colonies

Britain controlled 13 colonies along the east coast of North America. These colonies eventually revolted against Britain and became the original 13 states.

But for a long time, the British **colonists**—people who lived in the colonies—had no desire to break free from Britain. They were happy and proud to be members of the British Empire. They considered themselves more British than American. A lively trade took place between the "mother country," Britain, and its "children," the colonies.

For years, the British government allowed the colonies a great degree of independence. During the French and Indian War, Britain was busy fighting France. It largely left the American colonies alone. After the war, however, Britain wanted to tighten its control over the colonies.

In the ten years after the war ended, tensions between the colonists and the British government grew and grew. These tensions had many causes.

First, the colonists were feeling more independent from Britain. Separated by an ocean, they had developed their own views and ways of life. They were used to a degree of self-government, and resented any attempts by the British to control their lives.

Second, Britain tried to control the colonists' expansion. Many settlers wanted to head west. But Britain feared war with the Indians and so prevented the settlers from moving west.

Third, Britain took many steps to try to increase its income from the American colonies. In 1764, it passed the Sugar Act, which taxed American molasses. Another tax, the Stamp Act (1765), required colonists to buy tax stamps that were placed on a variety of documents. The Stamp Act was repealed in 1766, but further acts only increased colonists' resentments. In 1765, Britain passed the Quartering Act. This act required colonists to help pay the costs of British soldiers in America and to provide them with food and lodging.

The Townshend Acts in 1767 required Americans to pay taxes on imported goods. The colonists protested, crying "no taxation without representation." Most of the taxes were repealed. The tax on tea, however, remained. The colonists took to smuggling tea to avoid paying the British tax. Britain responded with the Tea Act. The Tea Act let the British East India Company sell tea in the colonies at a very low price. Britain hoped to force Americans to buy British tea and pay British taxes.

The colonists protested at the famous **Boston Tea Party,** in which they threw British tea into Boston Harbor. In response, Britain passed another set of acts, which the Americans called the Intolerable Acts. These acts restricted the freedom of the people of Massachusetts and gave the British authorities there more power.

These many acts infuriated the colonists. They began to see Britain as an enemy instead of a caring mother country. Leaders of the colonies held the **First Continental Congress** to demand fairer treatment.

THINK ABOUT IT

Consider all of the British actions toward the American colonists in the years leading up to the Revolution. Why would these actions cause resentment in the colonists? What did all of these actions have in common? Write your answers on a separate sheet of paper.

PRACTICE 103: The Causes of the American Revolution

Circle the letter of the correct answer to each of the following questions.

1. Which of the following British actions caused resentment in the American colonies?
   - **a.** the Sugar Act
   - **b.** the Stamp Act
   - **c.** the Townshend Acts
   - **d.** all of the above

2. Which event caused Britain to largely leave the American colonies alone?
   a. the American Revolution
   b. the Crusades
   c. the French and Indian War
   d. exploration of the New World

The Course of the American Revolution

In 1775, Britain declared the colony of Massachusetts to be in rebellion against Britain. This declaration gave British soldiers the right to shoot colonists. The British ordered their troops to capture Boston, to control the rebels, and to arrest their leaders. At the **Battles of Lexington and Concord,** the colonists resisted. The American Revolution was under way.

The American Revolution lasted from 1775 to 1783. In 1776, the colonists, thinking they could never work things out with Britain, published the **Declaration of Independence.** They claimed that they were no longer under British control. Instead, they were an independent nation.

The Declaration of Independence was written by **Thomas Jefferson.** He incorporated many ideas of the Age of Reason into this famous document. For example, he referred to the Enlightenment idea that people could overthrow any government that did not express the people's will. He also referred to human rights as universal laws.

The colonial army was led by **George Washington.** As the war went on, the army grew strong under his leadership. But the key to the colonists' success was the support of the French. The French were longtime enemies of the British. They were happy to cause the British trouble by supporting the Revolution. France gave the Americans money and weapons. And, eventually, the French even provided troops and ships.

This aid, along with the devotion of the colonists to the cause of independence, contributed to an American victory. In 1781, the British surrendered their forces at Yorktown. The war would soon be over.

■ PRACTICE 104: The Course of the American Revolution

Decide if each statement below is true (**T**) or false (**F**). Write the correct letter on the line before each statement.

_____ **1.** The Battles of Yorktown and Concord were the first battles of the American Revolution.

_____ **2.** Thomas Jefferson wrote the Declaration of Independence.

_____ **3.** The leader of the American troops in the Revolution was George Washington.

_____ **4.** The help of France was key to the colonists' success.

The Impact of the American Revolution

In 1783, the Americans and the British signed the **Treaty of Paris,** which ended the war. The treaty gave the colonies independence. A new country was formed: the United States of America.

The American Revolution was to have a worldwide impact. Its first, and foremost, effect was that it led to the creation of the United States of America.

The American Revolution also led to the creation of the United States **Constitution,** or plan of government. The United States Constitution was unlike anything the world had seen before. It put into practice the Enlightenment ideas of freedom and limited government. Ever since it was adopted in 1789, it has served as a model for constitutions around the world.

Finally, the American Revolution made clear that democracy can triumph over an oppressive government. Ever since the American Revolution, peoples around the world have taken inspiration from the victory of the colonists.

One revolution that the American Revolution helped inspire was the French Revolution. You will read about this revolution in the next section.

■ PRACTICE 105: The Impact of the American Revolution

Circle the letter of the correct answer to each of the following questions.

1. What formally ended the American Revolution?
   a. the signing of the Declaration of Independence
   b. the creation of the U.S. Constitution
   c. the signing of the Treaty of Paris
   d. the battles of Lexington and Concord

2. Which statement about the American Constitution is TRUE?
   a. It put into practice the Enlightenment ideas of freedom and limited government.
   b. It serves as a model for constitutions around the world.
   c. It is a plan of government for the United States of America.
   d. all of the above

The Causes of the French Revolution

For centuries, Europe had been ruled by monarchs. These kings and queens held almost unlimited power. Many also claimed a **divine right** to rule. That is, they claimed that their power to rule came from God.

During the Enlightenment, new ideas spread about government. Philosophers such as Locke and Rousseau thought that government should represent the people, not oppress them. These ideas became widespread. Eventually, these new ideas would help bring about the French Revolution.

A second cause of the French Revolution was economic trouble. The French government spent huge sums of money during the French and Indian War and during the American Revolution. By the late 1780s, the government had almost run out of money. This financial crisis contributed to instability.

Perhaps the most important cause of the French Revolution was inequality among the people of France. The French people were divided into three classes, called **estates**. The **First Estate** was made up of religious officials. The **Second Estate** was made up of nobles. The **Third Estate**—by far the largest—was made up of middle-class merchants, urban workers, government officials, and peasants.

The Third Estate resented members of the other two estates. Most members of the Third Estate were poor peasants who lived hard lives, while members of the other two estates lived well. Even the middle-class members of the Third Estate were resentful because they had to pay high taxes and because they lacked social status.

These three factors—Enlightenment ideas about government, the financial crisis, and a resentful Third Estate—reached a breaking point in 1789. This was when the French Revolution began.

■ PRACTICE 106: The Causes of the French Revolution

Circle the letter of the correct answer to each of the following questions.

1. Which of the following was a cause of the French Revolution?
- **a.** economic trouble in France
- **b.** inequality among the people of France
- **c.** the spread of Enlightenment ideas about government
- **d.** all of the above

2. Who made up the Third Estate in France?
- **a.** nobles
- **b.** religious officials
- **c.** middle-class merchants, government officials, urban workers, and peasants
- **d.** philosophers of the Enlightenment

The Course of the French Revolution

In 1789, King **Louis XVI** of France called a meeting of the **Estates-General.** The Estates-General was a body that included representatives of all three estates. He called the meeting because he wanted to raise taxes and borrow money to solve the government's financial crisis.

At the meeting, members of the Third Estate took the opportunity to express their resentments. They demanded that a constitution be written and that they be given rights similar to those of the other estates. When their demands were refused, they formed their own body: the **National Assembly**.

The king planned to destroy the National Assembly. But peasants rose up around the country to demand their rights. They stormed the **Bastille,** a prison and fort in Paris. They hoped to obtain weapons to defend themselves against the king's army. The attack on the Bastille became a symbol of the people's power. Such uprisings occurred all over France. Fearful of rebellion, the king let the National Assembly meet.

The Bastille

IN REAL LIFE

Have you ever heard of Bastille Day? Bastille Day is a holiday celebrated in France every July 14. It honors the people's takeover of the Bastille. The French celebrate it as we celebrate Independence Day—fireworks and all. It is their most important national holiday.

The National Assembly adopted a document called the **Declaration of the Rights of Man and of the Citizen.** It guaranteed basic rights to all members of all estates. It also abolished many of the privileges of the first two estates. The Declaration was an expression of many of the ideas of the Enlightenment.

But King Louis XVI still opposed the revolution. He encouraged French nobles who had left the country to help overthrow the new government. He also encouraged other European countries to attack France. They did so because they were afraid of revolution spreading to their own countries.

In response, the French people captured Louis XVI and his family. At this point, the revolution became out of control. France was threatened by foreign armies. The new government had little control over the people. The leaders of the revolution disagreed with one another.

Hoping to restore order, the leaders of the revolution called the **National Convention** in 1792. It declared France to be a republic, whose slogan would be "Liberty, Equality, Fraternity."

Unfortunately, the National Convention came under control of one of its committees, the **Committee of Public Safety**. This committee was led by radicals. It suspended civil rights and declared war on anyone who opposed it. The Committee sentenced nearly 20,000 people to death by guillotine (a machine that cut off people's heads). It also jailed hundreds of thousands of other people. This period became known as the **Reign of Terror**. Its most notorious leader was **Maximilien Robespierre**.

In time, other leaders turned against the Reign of Terror. Robespierre, who had ordered so many executions, was executed himself. The National Convention was replaced by a new governmental body called the **Directory**. The Directory took power in October 1795.

The Directory ruled France from 1795 to 1799. But France still faced economic problems, instability, and the threat of foreign armies. The stage was set for yet another change in French government. In 1799, a young hero of the French Revolution named **Napoleon Bonaparte** took control of the government. His seizing of power ended the French Revolution.

■ PRACTICE 107: The Course of the French Revolution

Decide the order of the following seven events. Write **1** on the line before the first event, **2** before the second event, and so on.

_____ **1.** When the demands of the Third Estate were refused, members of the Third Estate formed the National Assembly.

_____ **2.** The peasants stormed the Bastille hoping to get weapons.

_____ **3.** Other countries helped King Louis XVI try to overthrow the new government.

_____ **4.** The Directory replaced the National Convention.

_____ **5.** Thousands of people were killed during the Reign of Terror.

_____ **6.** The French people captured King Louis XVI.

_____ **7.** Napoleon took control of the government.

The Impact of the French Revolution

The course of the French Revolution was very complex. After all, the government of France went from an absolute monarchy to the Estates-General, to the National Assembly, to the Committee of Public Safety, to the Directory, to Napoleon's seizing of power—in just ten years!

You might think that all of this turmoil would keep the French Revolution from achieving much. But the French Revolution did have an effect on the people. For one thing, the majority of the French people participated in government for the first time. The National Convention promoted free education and a fair tax system. It also authorized public assistance for poor people. Of course, many of these reforms failed because of the unstable government.

Nonetheless, the French Revolution changed France forever. The people of France felt that they had a greater say in their future. And the seizure of the government by Napoleon would have a great impact at home and throughout Europe, as you will see.

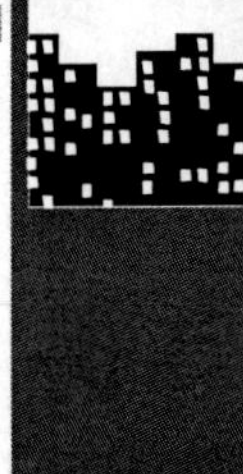

One far-reaching result of the French Revolution was the metric system. Before the French Revolution, France had no consistent units of measure. In 1790, the French government asked the Academy of Science to develop a simple system for measuring things. The Academy came up with the metric system. Today, this system is used in many countries around the world.

PRACTICE 108: The Impact of the French Revolution

Decide if each statement below is true (**T**) or false (**F**). Write the correct letter on the line before each statement.

_____ **1.** The government of France went from an absolute monarchy to Napoleon's seizure of power in just ten years.

_____ **2.** A major effect of the French Revolution was that poor people were taken off public assistance.

LESSON 17: The Napoleonic Era in Europe

GOAL: To explain Napoleon's rise to power and the major events of his rule

WORDS TO KNOW

Code Napoleon	**coup d'état**	**Napoleonic Era**
Consulate	**Emperor of France**	**Napoleonic Wars**
Continental System	**the Hundred Days**	

EVENT TO KNOW

Waterloo

The Rise of Napoleon Bonaparte

The seizing of the French government by Napoleon Bonaparte in 1799 marked the end of the French Revolution. By this time, Napoleon had already proved himself one of the most capable leaders and military men who ever lived.

Napoleon Bonaparte was born in 1769 on the island of Corsica in the Mediterranean Sea. At age 9, he entered military school. When he was 15, he entered an elite military academy. Fresh out of the academy, he entered the French army as a lieutenant of artillery. He was 16 years old.

The French Revolution began in 1789. Eventually, Napoleon came to support Robespierre and the other radicals of the French Revolution. In 1793, he commanded the artillery that helped to stop an uprising against Robespierre and his regime. For his service, Napoleon was promoted to brigadier general. He was only 24 years old.

Napoleon Bonaparte

Later, Napoleon led French troops against mobs who were trying to attack the National Convention. Napoleon ordered his cannon to fire directly into the crowd. He is said to have remarked that a "whiff of grapeshot" would disperse the crowd. It worked, but hundreds were killed or wounded. Again, Napoleon was rewarded with a promotion, this time to major general. The man who promoted Napoleon became a member of the new government, the Directory.

At this point, Napoleon was still remarkably young—only 26 years old. Yet he was already a major general in the French army. He also had very close political ties to the leaders of the new government. His military skill, combined with his political connections, soon made his star rise even higher.

THINK ABOUT IT

Napoleon rose to a position of tremendous power at a remarkably young age. Do you think it would be possible for anyone in the United States today to achieve such political greatness when so young? Why or why not? Write your answer on a separate sheet of paper.

PRACTICE 109: The Rise of Napoleon Bonaparte

Circle the letter of the correct answer to each of the following questions.

1. How old was Napoleon when he first became a general?

- **a.** 16
- **b.** 24
- **c.** 26
- **d.** 45

2. Which statement about Napoleon is TRUE?

- **a.** Napoleon was born on the island of Corsica.
- **b.** Napoleon distinguished himself at an early age.
- **c.** Napoleon had military, but not political, ties with government leaders.
- **d.** both *a* and *b*

The Consulate

France was at war during much of the ten years of the French Revolution (1789–1799). The leaders of other European nations saw the opportunity to conquer a weakened and divided France. They also hoped to prevent the ideas of the French Revolution from spreading to their own countries and then weakening their monarchies.

These wars occurred from 1792 to 1795. Napoleon became a general only one year after these wars began. By 1796, the country that was the biggest threat to France was Austria. Napoleon led French troops against tremendous odds to defeat Austria in less than a year. He won four battles, each against armies much larger than his own. It was during this war that Napoleon established himself as a military genius. By holding most of his forces in reserve, and then attacking at the right time and in the right place, he was able to win battles that, by all rights, he should have lost.

When Napoleon returned to Paris after defeating Austria, he was hailed as a hero. He was so incredibly popular that he considered taking over the French government. But he still wasn't ready. To enhance his reputation further, he sailed to Egypt in 1798. His plan was to attack British forces there and interfere with Britain's trade with the Middle East. Napoleon thereby hoped to weaken Britain, which was at war with France.

Napoleon's campaign in Egypt was a failure. However, the French people celebrated some of his victories there and remembered his defeat of the Austrians. When he returned to France, he was again given a hero's welcome.

At this point, Napoleon seized his opportunity. With others in 1799, he staged a **coup d'état,** or takeover of the government. The new government was called the **Consulate.** It had a constitution, and it was supposed to be ruled by three leaders, called consuls. Napoleon was one of the consuls. In reality, though, Napoleon now had absolute power over France. Just six years earlier, he had been an unknown military officer. He was just 30 years old.

A new era of French history—and European history—began with Napoleon's takeover of the government. It is called the **Napoleonic Era.** It lasted from 1799 to 1815.

TIP

You have just read that the Napoleonic Era in Europe lasted from 1799 to 1815. Earlier, you read that the Age of Reason lasted from the 1600s to the late 1700s. Do you remember reading about other periods in the history of Europe? The Renaissance lasted from about 1300 to about 1600. The Middle Ages lasted from about 500 to about 1500. Try to memorize the names and dates of such large periods of history. They will give you a good overview of European history. Also, try to connect each period to events going on at that time. This will help the string of dates make sense.

PRACTICE 110: The Consulate

Check each statement below that is TRUE.

☐ **1.** A coup d'état is a takeover of the government.

☐ **2.** Napoleon's new government was called the Third Estate.

☐ **3.** Napoleon was in his 40s by the time he rose to power.

☐ **4.** Napoleon shared power equally with the other two consuls.

Napoleonic Reforms

Napoleon came to power after France had suffered ten years of turmoil and revolution. The French people welcomed Napoleon as a strong leader, which the country badly needed.

Napoleon began his rule by bringing peace to Europe. He accomplished this by defeating the Austrians in a final battle. Their allies, the Russians and British, agreed to peace soon thereafter. The wars that had raged during the Revolution finally subsided. For the first time in ten years, Europe was at peace.

As a ruler, Napoleon made many important reforms. He restructured the French government to make it more efficient. He centralized the government and divided the country into areas similar to states. His reforms altered the legal, judicial, and financial parts of the government. Napoleon created a national bank, the Bank of France, to help stabilize the economy. He also created a new university, the University of France. All of these changes strengthened France.

Napoleon knew that people liked to be honored for what they did. He created the Legion of Honor to reward people's contributions to society.

Napoleon also created a new system, or code, of civil laws. It was called the **Code Napoleon.** Many historians think that the Code Napoleon is Napoleon's most lasting contribution. This is because it has been adapted for use in many countries around the world. And it still serves as the basis for civil law in France.

The Code Napoleon abolished feudalism in France. All citizens could now enter into legal contracts and choose their own occupations. The Code protected religious freedom and provided equal treatment under the law. The Code also took away many rights that women had gained during the revolution. Still, in many ways, the Code was a compromise between the ideals of the revolution and the need for a practical system of law.

PRACTICE 111: Napoleonic Reforms

Circle the letter of the correct answer to each of the following questions.

1. How did Napoleon reform the French government?

- **a.** He weakened it.
- **b.** He centralized it.
- **c.** He turned it into a democracy.
- **d.** He created a university.

2. What was the Code Napoleon?

- **a.** a system of law
- **b.** a famous book
- **c.** a code of behavior
- **d.** a revolutionary handbook

The Napoleonic Empire

In 1804, Napoleon had himself declared **Emperor of France.** As emperor, he was not content just to govern France. As a lifelong military man, he had dreams of conquering Europe and creating an empire. By 1812, his empire covered most of Europe.

But first, Napoleon wanted to extend French influence in the Americas. In 1800, he had forced Spain to give most of central North America to France. This territory was called Louisiana. But the French army was unable to take control of the territory. In 1803, Napoleon sold the territory to the United States in the Louisiana Purchase, to raise money for his campaigns in Europe.

Napoleon then turned all of his energy to conquering Europe. Of course, the other European nations fought against him. Britain, Austria, Russia, and Sweden joined forces to prevent French expansion.

From 1803 to 1815, Europe was rocked by battles of the **Napoleonic Wars.** At first, Napoleon won victory after victory. With each victory, he added land to his empire.

Napoleon set up a policy called the **Continental System**. Under the Continental System, countries on the European continent were forbidden to trade with Britain. The Continental System did not work. The British set up a blockade of their own. The United States refused to trade with either France or England. The French government lost the income from duties paid on imported goods. And Europe had to do without all the goods that came from British colonies, such as coffee, sugar, cocoa, and cotton. People began to resent the French for making these things unavailable.

Spain was the first to act against Napoleon. In 1808, Napoleon made his brother king of Spain. This made people in Spain angry. Within a few months, a rebellion broke out. The British sent soldiers to help Spain. A long, costly war began.

While the war in Spain continued, France's relations with Russia grew worse. Russia's ruler, Tsar Alexander I, withdrew from the Continental System. Napoleon had defeated a Russian army before. He was sure he could do it again. In 1812, Napoleon led an army of 600,000 men into Russia.

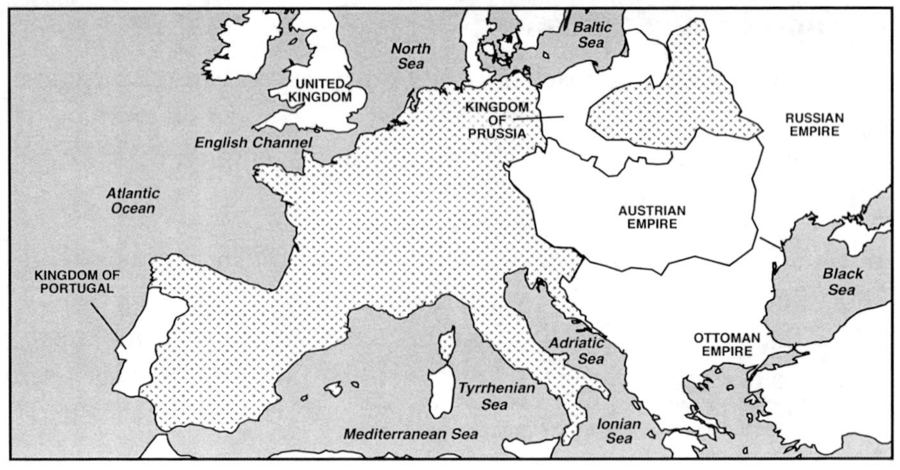

The Napoleonic Empire in 1810

At first, the Russians retreated, and the French moved forward. When the two armies met, thousands of soldiers on both sides were killed. Finally, Napoleon reached Moscow. He waited there for Alexander to surrender. The surrender never came. By the time the army began to march back to France, the Russian winter had set in. Thousands of French soldiers died of cold and hunger on the long march home. Of the 600,000 soldiers who had set out for Russia, about 100,000 returned.

Napoleon's fortunes were turning for the worse. The disasters in Spain and Russia hurt his armies and his prestige. They also encouraged his enemies. After he lost battles in Germany, enemy armies pursued and captured Napoleon in Paris. They sent him to live in exile on Elba, a small island in the Mediterranean. It was 1814.

But one year later, in 1815, Napoleon and a small group of loyal followers returned to Paris. It was a triumphant return. Soldiers of the French army were overjoyed and wanted to follow him again as their emperor. Napoleon was once more the leader of France. This period, though, lasted only about three months. It is called **the Hundred Days.**

The Hundred Days ended with Napoleon's famous defeat at **Waterloo,** at the hands of the British and Prussians. This time, Napoleon was exiled to a barren island in the Atlantic Ocean called St. Helena. He died there in 1821, at the age of 52.

It is difficult to sum up the impact of Napoleon. His many victories on the battlefield mark him as one of the greatest military geniuses of all time. Yet he lost some major battles and made some disastrous decisions, such as invading Russia. He himself always claimed to be defending the French Revolution. But he was really a dictator. He was an able leader of the French government, yet he allowed many abuses to continue. Perhaps these contradictions are what make him one of the most fascinating people in history.

IN REAL LIFE

Today, you might still hear the phrase that people "met their Waterloo." This means they met their final defeat. People might also say "that will be your Waterloo" to warn you against a disastrous step. Whenever you hear the word "Waterloo," pay attention! It is widely used as a symbol of crushing, final defeat.

PRACTICE 112: The Napoleonic Empire

Circle the letter of the correct answer to each of the following questions.

1. What was the Continental System?
- **a.** a plan of invasion
- **b.** a trade policy
- **c.** a system of French government
- **d.** the group of countries who united against Napoleon

2. Where did Napoleon suffer his final defeat?
- **a.** Moscow
- **b.** Elba
- **c.** Waterloo
- **d.** Paris

3. When did the Napoleonic Empire end?
- **a.** 1805
- **b.** 1810
- **c.** 1815
- **d.** 1830

LESSON 18: Revolution in Latin America

GOAL: To describe how many countries in Latin America became independent from European control in the early 1800s

WORDS TO KNOW

"the Liberator"

NAMES TO KNOW

Simón Bolívar

Miguel Hidalgo y Costilla

José María Morelos y Pavón

Pedro

José de San Martín

Toussaint-Louverture

PLACES TO KNOW

Argentina

Bolivia

Brazil

Colombia

Costa Rica

Ecuador

El Salvador

Gran Colombia

Guatemala

Haiti

Honduras

Latin America

Mexico

Nicaragua

Saint Domingue

United Provinces of Central America

Venezuela

European Colonies in the New World

As you have read, two revolutions rocked America and Europe in the late 1700s. The American Revolution and the French Revolution were fired by the ideas of the Age of Reason. In America, the revolution led to a new, independent country: the United States. In France, the revolution had very different results, leading to the empire of Napoleon.

In **Latin America**, as Central and South America are called, news of these revolutions had a major effect. Colonists were inspired by the success of the American Revolution. They were also inspired by the ideals of the French Revolution, if not its actual results. The effect was a growing movement for independence from European rule in Latin America.

THINK ABOUT IT

Have you ever wondered where Latin America got its name? Latin America was settled chiefly by Europeans. Today, the people of Latin America speak mostly Spanish, Portuguese, or French. Each of these languages developed from the same ancient language. What do you think this ancient language was? Write your answer on a separate sheet of paper.

The two major colonial powers in Latin America were Portugal and Spain. The British, French, and Dutch had smaller holdings in Latin America. But all of these countries were weakened by their wars with Napoleon. The peoples of Latin America took this opportunity to fight for their freedom.

PRACTICE 113: European Colonies in the New World

Decide if each statement below is true (**T**) or false (**F**). Write the correct letter on the line before each statement.

_____ **1.** In Latin America, colonists did not know about the American and French Revolutions.

_____ **2.** The major colonial powers in Latin America were Portugal and Spain.

Toussaint-Louverture and Haitian Independence

Haiti is a country on the island of Hispaniola in the West Indies. It was originally colonized by the Spanish. Then it was taken over by the French in 1697. The French called their colony **Saint Domingue.** Most of the people there, though, were not French. They were Africans. They were slaves and the descendants of slaves captured in Africa and forced to work on plantations. By 1788, there were 500,000 black slaves in Saint Domingue, along with about 50,000 French people.

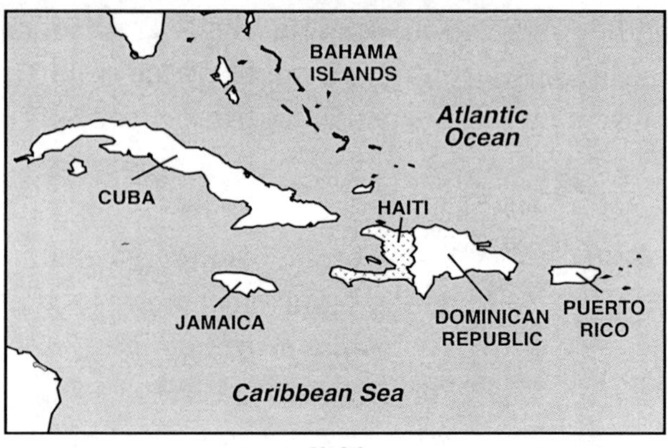

Haiti

News of the French Revolution reached Saint Domingue by ship soon after it began. The news filtered down to the slaves, who had suffered generations of cruel treatment. The ideas of liberty and equality inspired the slaves to revolt. Uprisings broke out throughout the colony. The man who became their leader was **Toussaint-Louverture.**

Toussaint-Louverture had been a slave all his life. Now, at 50, he became the leader of a revolution and a general. He led his black army to victory over the French troops. He came to control the colony in 1799. Under his rule, there was peace and order, and Haiti prospered.

In 1802, Napoleon decided to take back control of Haiti. French troops captured Toussaint-Louverture and imprisoned him in France. But the people of Haiti had enjoyed their taste of independence. Their new leader, Jean-Jacques Dessalines, defeated the French and declared Haiti independent in 1804.

IN REAL LIFE

Revolutions may seem like pages from history. But Haiti has experienced unstable politics as recently as the 1990s. A military coup took control of the country from 1991 to 1994, encouraging thousands of Haitians to flee. Between 1991 and 1992, some 35,000 Haitian refugees tried to enter the United States but were turned away by the U.S. Coast Guard. Most of these refugees were returned to Haiti.

■ PRACTICE 114: Toussaint-Louverture and Haitian Independence

Circle the letter of the correct answer to each of the following questions.

1. What was Toussaint-Louverture before he became a general?
   - **a.** a politician
   - **b.** a student
   - **c.** a slave
   - **d.** a revolutionary

2. When did Haiti win its independence from France?
   - **a.** 1697
   - **b.** 1799
   - **c.** 1802
   - **d.** 1804

Independence for Mexico and Central America

Six years after Haiti became independent, **Mexico** began its bid for independence from Spain. On September 16, 1810, a priest named **Miguel Hidalgo y Costilla** called for Mexican independence. The next day, the peoples of Mexico began to fight the Spanish. Today, Mexicans still celebrate September 16 as their Independence Day.

Hidalgo's followers attacked the Spanish. But they were no match for the trained soldiers. They were defeated, and Hidalgo was captured and killed.

Another priest, **José María Morelos y Pavón,** took up the fight. He and his followers made a formal declaration of independence from Spain and even drew up a constitution. But he, too, was captured by the Spanish and put to death.

By 1816, Spain had succeeded in putting down all of the rebels. But in 1820, there was a widespread revolt in Spain. Rebels in Mexico saw yet another chance to obtain independence. A leader of the Spanish forces in Mexico was sympathetic to the Mexican rebels. He met with the rebels and agreed to their independence. So, in 1821, Mexico became an independent country.

The Spanish colonists in other Central American colonies also wanted to break away from Spain. The Spanish saw little advantage in fighting to keep them as colonies, because they provided Spain with little wealth. As a result, Spain did not interfere, and they joined Mexico in 1821.

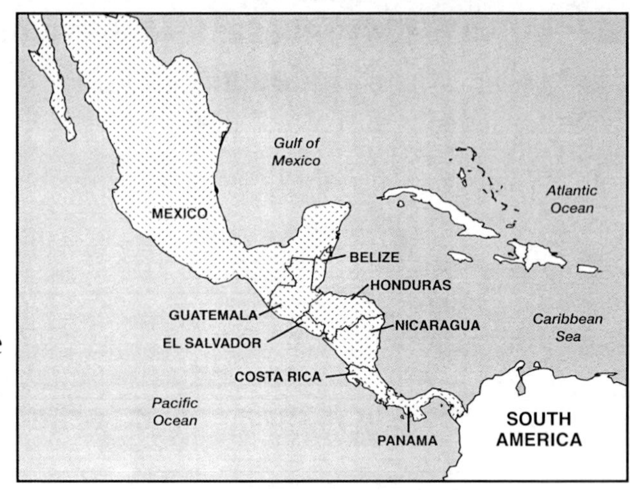

Mexico and Central America Today

In 1823, these countries broke away from Mexico and formed the **United Provinces of Central America.** Within 15 years, however, this organization fell apart, and each of the countries became independent. The countries that grew out of the United Provinces of Central America were **Costa Rica, El Salvador, Guatemala, Honduras,** and **Nicaragua.**

PRACTICE 115: Independence for Mexico and Central America

Circle the letter of the correct answer to each of the following questions.

1. Which European country controlled Mexico and Central America?
- **a.** Spain
- **b.** France
- **c.** England
- **d.** Portugal

2. When did Mexico begin its bid for independence?
- **a.** 1810
- **b.** 1816
- **c.** 1821
- **d.** 1906

3. When did Mexico win its independence?
   a. 1810
   b. 1816
   c. 1821
   d. 1906

4. Which country was originally a member of the United Provinces of Central America?
   a. Guatemala
   b. Nicaragua
   c. Honduras
   d. all of the above

Independence in South America

The greatest leader of the revolutions of South America was **Simón Bolívar.** In a remarkably short time, Bolívar and other revolutionaries freed most of South America from Spanish rule. Bolívar led armies that helped achieve independence for **Bolivia, Colombia, Ecuador,** Peru, and **Venezuela.**

Bolívar began by declaring Venezuela's independence in 1810. He became the dictator of that country in 1816. Marching from Venezuela, he liberated Colombia from Spanish rule in 1819. He organized a new country, **Gran Colombia,** with himself as president. In the early 1820s, Bolívar captured Ecuador and Peru. In 1824, he crushed the Spanish army at the Battle of Ayacucho. This effectively ended Spanish rule in South America.

South America in the Mid-1800s

Part of Peru was soon declared a new country—Bolivia. Bolívar had hoped to join all of Latin America into a grand union, but Gran Colombia soon fell apart. In 1830, it split into Colombia, Ecuador, and Venezuela.

Although Bolívar failed in his dream of a united Latin America, he succeeded in his dream of independence. This great general is still remembered as **"the Liberator"** of South America.

Another great leader for independence in South America was **José de San Martín.** He helped win independence for **Argentina** in 1816. In 1818, he also drove the Spanish out of Chile. Like Bolívar, San Martín is still remembered as a great leader in the wars for independence from Spain.

PRACTICE 116: Independence in South America

Circle the letter of the correct answer to each of the following questions.

1. Who was "the Liberator"?
- **a.** Miguel Hidalgo y Costilla
- **b.** José de San Martín
- **c.** José Mariá Morelos y Pavón
- **d.** Simón Bolívar

2. How many countries did "the Liberator" help win their independence from Spain?
- **a.** seven
- **b.** five
- **c.** three
- **d.** one

3. What was Gran Colombia?
- **a.** a Latin American country formed by Bolívar
- **b.** a battle site
- **c.** an alliance of revolutionary armies
- **d.** the region that became South America

TIP

Here's a tip to help you remember Simón Bolívar's name. Think of the South American country *Bolivia.* This country was named after Simón *Bolívar.*

Independence for Brazil

Between 1810, when Mexico's bid for independence began, and 1824, with Bolívar's victory at Ayacucho, Spain lost control of all of its territories in Central and South America. For more than 300 years, Spain had ruled colonies in the New World. But it lost all of its possessions there in just 14 years.

A large part of South America, however, had never been controlled by Spain. **Brazil** was a Portuguese colony. It also became independent during this remarkable period.

Portugal was invaded by the French under Napoleon in 1807. Portugal's ruler, Prince John, escaped Napoleon by fleeing to the Portuguese colony of Brazil. There, he ruled the colony, waiting for Napoleon's defeat. Finally, in 1821, Prince John returned to Portugal. His son, **Pedro,** was left in charge of Brazil.

In 1822, Pedro declared Brazil to be independent, and himself to be emperor. Brazil would suffer under Pedro's rule. But it had won its independence from Portugal. South America, once entirely controlled by Europeans, was now a continent of almost completely independent countries.

PRACTICE 117: Independence for Brazil

Decide if each statement below is true (**T**) or false (**F**). Write the correct letter on the line before each statement.

_____ **1.** Brazil fought a long war for independence.

_____ **2.** Brazilian independence was declared by the son of the leader of Portugal.

_____ **3.** Brazil became independent of Portugal in 1822.

Ideas That Changed the World

At the beginning of this unit, you read about the main ideas of the Age of Reason. These ideas helped cause all of the events you have been reading about.

Philosophers such as John Locke argued that government should follow certain principles, such as separation of powers and democracy. These principles were based on ideas about the laws of the universe. Leaders of the American Revolution took these ideas to heart. Their success inspired leaders of the French Revolution, who also believed in the ideas of the Age of Reason. The French Revolution opened the way for Napoleon to become an emperor, and to change the face of Europe.

In Central and South America, colonists followed the lead of these revolutions to achieve independence for themselves. Many countries that exist today were born of the wars for independence fought against the Spanish in the early 1800s.

TIP

When you look at a map of the world, you see more than just lines and words. You see history in action. Any modern map of the world shows the results of the ideas and events you have just read about. In fact, today's world was largely shaped by the reason and revolutions that shook Europe and the Americas in the late 1700s and early 1800s.

PRACTICE 118: Ideas That Changed the World

Circle the letter of the correct answer to each of the following questions.

1. Who provided the ideas of government that led to so many revolutions?

a. the military leaders of the revolutions
b. the philosophers of the Age of Reason
c. the king of Portugal
d. Toussaint-Louverture

2. Which European country ruled most of Latin America before the wars of independence?
   - **a.** Spain
   - **b.** Portugal
   - **c.** France
   - **d.** Italy

UNIT 5 REVIEW

Circle the letter of the correct answer to each of the following questions.

1. Which of the following is a main idea of the Age of Reason?
   - **a.** The universe has an order to it.
   - **b.** The universe follows certain laws.
   - **c.** Mathematics is a useful tool.
   - **d.** all of the above

2. Whose ideas formed much of the foundation of the American government?
   - **a.** Diderot
   - **b.** Joseph II
   - **c.** Voltaire
   - **d.** Locke

3. What was the purpose of the Stamp Act, the Townshend Acts, and the Sugar Act?
   - **a.** to punish the colonists
   - **b.** to declare America's independence
   - **c.** to raise money for Britain
   - **d.** to treat the colonists more fairly

4. What event marks the end of the French Revolution?
   - **a.** the storming of the Bastille
   - **b.** the Reign of Terror
   - **c.** Napoleon coming to power
   - **d.** the king calling the Estates-General

5. What do the American and French revolutions have in common?
   a. They were both inspired by Enlightenment ideas.
   b. Both had far-reaching results.
   c. One helped inspire the other.
   d. all of the above

6. What was the Code Napoleon?
   a. a system of law
   b. a famous book
   c. a code of behavior
   d. Napoleon's capital

7. The Continental System was designed to hurt the trade of which country?
   a. the United States
   b. Spain
   c. Russia
   d. Britain

8. What two European countries controlled almost all of South America?
   a. Spain and Portugal
   b. Spain and Britain
   c. France and Britain
   d. France and Portugal

9. What were most of the people of Saint Domingue?
   a. peasants
   b. French merchants
   c. slaves
   d. sailors

10. Which country below was a member of the United Provinces of Central America?
   a. Guatemala
   b. El Salvador
   c. Honduras
   d. all of the above

UNIT 5 APPLICATION ACTIVITY
The Birth of a Country

As you learned in Unit 5, many Latin American countries gained independence from European control in the early 1800s. Simón Bolívar, "the Liberator," led independence movements in some of these countries.

Imagine you are a reporter. Your editor has asked you to write a story about Bolívar's independence movement in one of the Latin American countries. Choose one of the countries Bolívar helped liberate. Then do some research about Bolívar's activities in that country. You can use the library or the Internet to find information. Take notes on the lines below.

Finally, write a news story about Bolívar and the country's independence movement. Write your story on a separate sheet of paper. Don't forget to include a headline.

Name of country: ______________________________

Notes: ______________________________

____

____

____

____

____

____

____

____

____

____

____

____

UNIT 6

The Industrial Revolution

LESSON 19: Revolutions in Agriculture

GOAL: To define the Industrial Revolution and discuss the major changes brought about by two agricultural revolutions

WORDS TO KNOW

agriculture

Britain

crop rotation

drill

enclosure movement

First Agricultural Revolution

industrial

Industrial Revolution

industry

reaper

Second Agricultural Revolution

NAMES TO KNOW

John Deere **Cyrus McCormick** **Jethro Tull**

The Industrial Revolution

In this unit, you will read about the Industrial Revolution. The **Industrial Revolution** was one of the most dramatic periods of change in history. At the start of this period, most people in Europe lived in rural areas. Most goods were made by hand, at home. And the way to wealth lay in owning land. Within 100 years, all this had changed. The city, not the country, was the source of wealth. And most goods were made by machines, in factories. The Industrial Revolution affected nearly every country on Earth, and it continues to shape your life today. Understanding the changes brought by the Industrial Revolution is key to understanding the modern world.

TIP

Think about each word in the term *Industrial Revolution.* A *revolution* is a great change. ***Industrial*** means "having to do with industry." (***Industry*** is the production, or making, of goods.) Now, put the two words together. The Industrial Revolution was a great change in the way goods were made.

The Industrial Revolution was the birth of modern industry. It paved the way for all of the things you associate with industry and working today: factories, powered machinery, time clocks, even people going to work for paychecks—all of this is the result of the Industrial Revolution.

The Industrial Revolution also led to other changes—changes in where and how people live, changes in people's values and priorities, and even changes in government. The term *Industrial Revolution* refers both to the birth of modern industry and to the social changes the revolution brought.

As you will see, the Industrial Revolution did not occur in one specific time or place. It began in **Britain** in the 1700s, but it spread throughout the rest of Europe, to America, and around the world. Usually, the dates given for the Industrial Revolution are the 1700s and early 1800s.

■ PRACTICE 119: The Industrial Revolution

Circle the letter of the correct answer to each of the following questions.

1. What was the Industrial Revolution?
- **a.** a movement to put computers everywhere
- **b.** a major change in the way goods are made
- **c.** a new way of powering machinery
- **d.** a Latin American independence movement

2. When was the Industrial Revolution?
- **a.** the 1900s
- **b.** the 1500s
- **c.** the 1700s and early 1800s
- **d.** the 1600s and early 1700s

Changes in Agriculture

To understand what the Industrial Revolution means, you need to start by understanding not industry, but agriculture.

Agriculture is the growing of food, or farming. People didn't always grow food. For thousands of years, the peoples of the world lived by hunting and gathering wild plants. Then, about 10,000 years ago, people learned how to farm. Instead of roaming about looking for food, they settled down to tend their crops. This great change from a wandering lifestyle to a settled lifestyle based on farming is sometimes called the **First Agricultural Revolution**. Like the Industrial Revolution, it was one of the great changes in human history.

Slowly, over thousands of years, the Agricultural Revolution took hold around the world. More and more people became farmers. Eventually, most people in the world lived by agriculture. Fewer and fewer people lived by hunting and gathering.

At first, farmers all over the world grew food just for themselves and their families. Slowly, agriculture became a business. Farmers grew food to sell. Merchants sold food in cities. City people who never set foot on a farm bought their food in stores and marketplaces.

For centuries, there was little advancement in agricultural technology. Then, in the early 1700s, many important changes occurred in agriculture in a very short time. These changes are called the **Second Agricultural Revolution**. Like the Industrial Revolution that was to accompany and follow it, the Second Agricultural Revolution started in Britain.

Three important changes in farming technology occurred during the Second Agricultural Revolution.

1. Improved methods of growing crops. Farmers learned that by using **crop rotation**, or changing the crops grown in each field each growing season, they could produce more food.

2. Improved methods of breeding livestock. People had long known about breeding. But, during the 1700s, British farmers learned how to breed intensively to produce cheaper animals that yielded more and better products.

3. The invention of new farming equipment. For thousands of years, farmers had spread seeds by hand. In 1700, an Englishman named **Jethro Tull** invented a machine called a **drill** that would plant seeds. Another important invention was the **reaper**, or harvesting machine. It was invented by an American, **Cyrus McCormick**, in 1831. A few years later, another American, **John Deere**, invented the steel plow. It was much more efficient than earlier iron and wood plows.

■ IN REAL LIFE

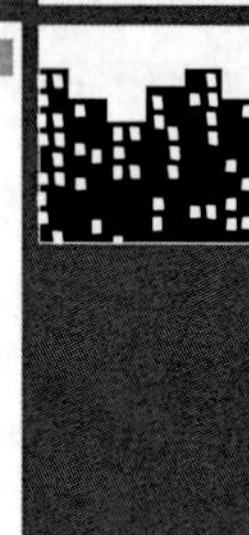

Today, the John Deere Company is one of the largest manufacturers of farm equipment in the world. The company uses a picture of a deer as its symbol, which makes it easy to recognize John Deere products. Cyrus McCormick's company merged with other companies to form International Harvester, another giant of the farm equipment industry today.

Along with these technological developments in Britain came a fourth change, called the **enclosure movement.** This was a reorganization of farmland. Before this, all fields had been open. During the enclosure movement, landowners enclosed, or fenced in, this land. As a result, some private farms became very large.

These important developments of the Second Agricultural Revolution made farms in Britain much more efficient than ever before. Farmers could produce far more with fewer people.

What does this agricultural revolution have to do with a revolution in industry? The answer is that it dramatically decreased the need for farm workers. By the time the Industrial Revolution was really under way in the late 1700s, British farming was so efficient that fewer people were needed on farms. These people moved to the cities. There, they became the world's first industrial workers.

■ PRACTICE 120: Changes in Agriculture

Decide if each statement below is true (**T**) or false (**F**). Write the correct letter on the line before each statement.

_____ **1.** In the First Agricultural Revolution, people stopped hunting for food and settled down to tend their own crops.

_____ **2.** In the Second Agricultural Revolution, farming technology changed the way people produced food.

LESSON 20: The Industrial Revolution in Britain

GOAL: To identify and describe the main events of the Industrial Revolution in Britain

WORDS TO KNOW

coal
Communications Revolution
cottage industry
cotton
cotton gin
decentralized
domestic system
flying shuttle
hand loom
iron
mechanization
mills
Morse Code
roller-spinning machine
smelting
spinning
spinning jenny
spinning mule
spinning wheel
steam engine
steam-powered loom
telegraph
textile industry
Transportation Revolution
water frame
weaving

NAMES TO KNOW

Richard Arkwright
Alexander Graham Bell
Edmund Cartwright
Samuel Crompton
Nicholas Cugnot
Abraham Darby
Abraham Darby II
James Hargreaves
Samuel F. B. Morse
James Watt
Eli Whitney

The Cottage Textile Industry

As you have read, the Industrial Revolution began in Britain. Within Britain, the Industrial Revolution started in the **textile industry**.

Before the Industrial Revolution, cloth in Britain was made using what is called the **domestic system**. Another term for the domestic system is **cottage industry**. These two terms are used because the work was done in people's homes (*domestic* means "at home"; a cottage is a small home). Under this system, merchants bought raw materials and gave them to workers. Often, the merchants also provided the workers with the tools they needed.

There were (and still are) two basic steps in creating cloth. They are spinning and weaving. In the British cottage textile industry, workers usually specialized in one of the two steps.

Spinning Wheel

In **spinning,** raw fiber is turned into thread and yarn. Workers used spinning wheels to accomplish this task. A **spinning wheel** is a foot-powered machine that spins raw material, such as cotton or wool, into thread. Once the thread was spun, the merchants gave it to other workers to weave.

IN REAL LIFE

Today, we use the word *homespun* to say that something looks simple, crude, or homemade. It can also refer to "folk" wisdom or humor. The word *homespun* comes from the days when yarn was *spun* at *home.* Homespun thread was uneven compared with thread spun in a factory, where machines produced thread that was always the same.

In **weaving,** threads are woven into cloth. Workers in the British cottage textile industry used hand looms to accomplish this task. A **hand loom** is a framework on which threads are woven together. Once the cloth was woven, it was ready to be cut and sewed into clothing and other products.

The British cottage textile industry remained unchanged for centuries. But there were many problems with the industry. First, it was slow. Individual workers using crude, human-powered machines, could produce only so much cloth. Second, it was inefficient. The work was done at many different homes. Merchants had to transport raw fiber to one group of homes, thread to another group, and cloth to a third. In other words, the work was **decentralized.** This means that it was not located at one central place. It was difficult for merchants to regulate the workers. Merchants also had to compete for a limited number of workers.

These inefficiencies led merchants to ask the same question, over and over again: What could they do to make more cloth, more efficiently? The answer would come in the form of some amazing new inventions. These inventions would make the Industrial Revolution a reality.

■ PRACTICE 121: The Cottage Textile Industry

Circle the letter of the correct answer to each of the following questions.

1. In what industry in Britain did the Industrial Revolution begin?
- **a.** agriculture
- **b.** textile
- **c.** tool
- **d.** cottage

2. Which step happens first when creating cloth?
- **a.** spinning
- **b.** weaving
- **c.** making clothing
- **d.** wheeling

3. Where did people work in the domestic system?
- **a.** in factories
- **b.** in their homes
- **c.** in offices
- **d.** in industrial parks

Changes in Spinning

As you remember, the first step in making cloth is spinning. For centuries, spinning was done on spinning wheels. An individual working at a spinning wheel could make only one single thread at a time. Then, in the 1700s, a remarkable series of inventions revolutionized spinning. All of these inventions were created in Britain.

In 1738, Lewis Paul invented a new machine to make spinning more efficient. The **roller-spinning machine** was the first successful attempt at mechanization of the spinning process. **Mechanization** is the use of automated machinery to increase production. Mechanization proved to be one of the most important features of the Industrial Revolution. So, Paul's machine was an important breakthrough. But it was still an awkward and inefficient machine.

In 1764, **James Hargreaves** invented the **spinning jenny.** His machine could spin 16 threads at once, instead of just one. Five years later, **Richard Arkwright** invented a machine called the **water frame.** It provided an efficient way to spin a certain kind of thread.

Together, the spinning jenny and the water frame revolutionized the spinning industry. They made the production of thread faster and more efficient, and solved the problems of the roller-spinning machine.

But soon even these two machines were surpassed. **Samuel Crompton** invented the **spinning mule** in 1779. The mule combined the best features of the spinning jenny and the water frame. Soon, very large spinning mules were built. They could spin hundreds of threads at once.

TIP

The spinning jenny has a woman's name because women did most of the spinning at home. In fact, this is where the word *spinster* (an older, unmarried woman) comes from. The spinning mule was named after the mule—a hard-working animal.

British merchants built **mills,** or textile factories, to house the new spinning machines. The first mills appeared in the 1740s and housed roller-spinning machines. By 1800, there were hundreds of mills in Britain, filled with thousands of spinning mules. This quickly led to the end of the cottage industry in spinning.

The change from a cottage industry in spinning to spinning in mills was a major change in the textile industry. The Industrial Revolution was now under way.

■ PRACTICE 122: Changes in Spinning

Circle the letter of the correct answer to each of the following questions.

1. Which of the following machines came first?
  - **a.** the spinning jenny
  - **b.** the roller-spinning machine
  - **c.** the water frame
  - **d.** the spinning mule

2. How did the invention of new spinning machines change the textile industry?
  - **a.** It transformed spinning from a cottage industry to a factory-based industry.
  - **b.** It slowed the production of threads and cloth.
  - **c.** It forced many spinners out of work.
  - **d.** It brought the spinning industry back inside the home.

Changes in Weaving

The second step in making cloth is weaving. For centuries, weaving was done on hand looms. Hand looms are slow and inefficient.

Just as a series of inventions led to increased production in spinning, the same happened in weaving.

In 1733, John Kay invented a **flying shuttle.** This was a machine that would weave mechanically. Suddenly, there was a machine that could do work once done by hand. Kay had succeeded in mechanizing the weaving process.

In the 1780s, **Edmund Cartwright** took the mechanical loom and powered it with a steam engine. This was the **steam-powered loom.** This loom made weaving faster and more efficient. Soon there were thousands of steam-powered looms operating across Britain.

Hand Loom

Just as they had done with spinning, British merchants housed these new machines in large mills. This quickly led to the end of the cottage industry in weaving.

Let's summarize what you have just read. In the 1730s, the textile industry in Britain was a cottage industry. Spinning and weaving were done on simple, human-powered machines at home. Less than a century later, the work was done in mills on complex, steam-powered machines. The making of textiles in Britain had turned into a modern industry. It was the first industry in the world to undergo mechanization. It was at the forefront of the Industrial Revolution.

PRACTICE 123: Changes in Weaving

Circle the letter of the correct answer to each of the following questions.

1. What powered Cartwright's loom?

- **a.** a foot treadle
- **b.** steam
- **c.** a flying shuttle
- **d.** coal

2. What happened to the cottage weaving industry after mills filled with powered looms were built?

- **a.** It flourished.
- **b.** It moved to other towns.
- **c.** It disappeared.
- **d.** It moved to other countries.

Eli Whitney and the Cotton Gin

The development of the spinning mule and the steam-powered loom dramatically increased the efficiency of the British textile industry. Textile mills grew in size, number, and output.

This, of course, created a demand for more **cotton,** from which most cloth was (and still is) made. During the Industrial Revolution, Britain imported a great deal of cotton from the United States. The United States grew cotton in the South, on plantations worked by slaves.

Eli Whitney

Before cotton can be spun into thread, it has to have its seeds removed. In the United States, this very slow and tedious work was done by slaves working by hand. It took a whole day to get the seeds out of just one pound of cotton.

Plantation owners and merchants knew that if this process could be speeded up, they could sell more cotton and make more money. The solution came in 1793 with the invention of the cotton gin in America by **Eli Whitney**. A **cotton gin** is a machine that separates cotton fiber from the seeds. (Actually, simple gins had been used for centuries, but they were nowhere near as efficient as Whitney's.) Whitney's cotton gin could separate seeds from cotton 50 times faster than someone doing the work by hand.

The cotton gin radically changed American agriculture. Cotton became the "king" of the South, where it was grown. More important, it made the Industrial Revolution in Britain possible. Because of the cotton gin, there was plenty of cotton to run through the mills in Britain. In fact, the cotton gin is one of the most important inventions of the Industrial Revolution.

A Cotton Gin

THINK ABOUT IT

You have just read that Eli Whitney's cotton gin enabled people to remove seeds from cotton fiber 50 times faster than before. Can you think of another machine that has increased productivity so much? Write your answer on a separate sheet of paper.

PRACTICE 124: Eli Whitney and the Cotton Gin

Circle the letter of the correct answer to each of the following questions.

1. What does a cotton gin do?

- **a.** picks cotton
- **b.** separates cotton fiber from the seeds
- **c.** spins cotton
- **d.** turns cotton into alcohol

2. Why was the cotton gin important to the Industrial Revolution?

- **a.** It was the first machine.
- **b.** It provided cotton for the textile industry.
- **c.** It was steam-powered.
- **d.** It assisted cottage industries.

The Steam Engine

A **steam engine** is powered by the steam from boiling water. By hooking belts to the steam engine, any other machine can be powered.

The steam engine became the workhorse of the Industrial Revolution. It was cheap and efficient. It didn't get tired, like human workers or animals. The steam engine was the first great step in motorizing the world.

The first steam engine was invented in Britain by Thomas Savery in 1698. It powered a pump. But it was inefficient. His engine was greatly improved by Thomas Newcomen in 1712. By the 1720s, Newcomen's engine was used in coal

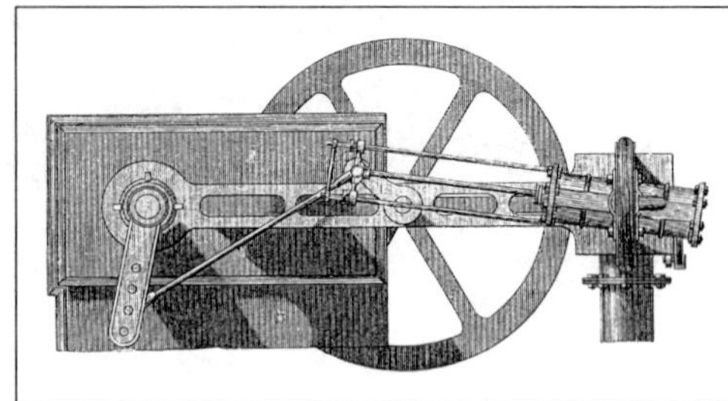

An Early Steam Engine

mines throughout Britain to power the pumps that drew water out of the mines.

Even Newcomen's engine, however, wasn't good for much other than powering pumps. Then, in the 1760s, 1770s, and 1780s, the Scottish inventor **James Watt** radically improved Newcomen's engine. Watt's engine was at least *four times* more efficient. Watt's steam engine wasted much less heat, steam, and moving energy. Watt's improvements were so important that he is often called the inventor of the steam engine.

Watt's steam engine was one of the most important inventions of the Industrial Revolution. This is because it marked the great change from muscle power to machine power. Watt's engine was used to power the looms that transformed the British textile industry. Without this power source, factories themselves could not exist. What's more, its importance as a power source for factories was matched by its importance as a power source for other things, as you will see.

■ PRACTICE 125: The Steam Engine

Circle the letter of the correct answer to each of the following questions.

1. Who did the most to make the steam engine practical for many uses?

- **a.** James Watt
- **b.** Thomas Newcomen
- **c.** Thomas Savery
- **d.** Eli Whitney

2. Why is the steam engine considered one of the most important inventions of the Industrial Revolution?

- **a.** It brought wealth and people to the farms of Britain.
- **b.** It marked the great change from human power to machine power.
- **c.** It allowed the textile industry to flourish.
- **d.** It marked the beginning of cottage industries throughout Britain.

The Transportation Revolution

Many inventors quickly realized the potential of Watt's steam engine. Edmund Cartwright used it to power looms in the 1780s. Across the English Channel, in France, another inventor used it to power something completely different: a tractor. This tractor was the first motorized vehicle in the world.

The tractor was built by **Nicholas Cugnot.** He built it at the request of the French government, which wanted a good way to move cannons. The tractor had awkward steering and weak brakes. Its steam engine could power the tractor for about 15 minutes at a time before it had to stop to build up more steam. It was primitive by today's standards. But for the first time in history, people traveled under the power of an engine.

The steam engine marked the beginning of the era of motorized vehicles. Cugnot built his tractor in 1770. In 1783, the first motorized boat, powered by a steam engine, was launched. In 1804, the first steam locomotive was built. By the early 1800s, both steam locomotives and steamships were common in Britain and America.

So, in just the few decades after Watt's work, the modern age of transportation—with motorized land vehicles, boats, and trains—had begun. All of these vehicles were powered by versions of Watt's steam engine: the engine that revolutionized industry—and transportation. In fact, these changes were so great that they are sometimes called the **Transportation Revolution**.

■ PRACTICE 126: The Transportation Revolution

Match each event with a date from the list below. Write the letter of the correct date on the line before each event.

a. 1804 **b.** 1770 **c.** 1783

_____ **1.** first motorized vehicle

_____ **2.** first motorized boat

_____ **3.** first steam locomotive

Coal and Iron

As you have read, the Industrial Revolution started in Britain. One of the reasons that the Industrial Revolution occurred in Britain is that the country has large deposits of coal and iron.

Coal was important for the Industrial Revolution because it was burned to power steam engines. Coal was also important because it was used to make iron. **Iron** was used to help build machines such as power looms and steam engines, and other things such as railroad tracks and fasteners. Iron was also used to make tools that were used to make machines.

Iron is an element found in rocks. To be usable as a metal, iron must be separated from other materials in the rock. This process is called **smelting**. In the early 1700s, **Abraham Darby** and his son, **Abraham Darby II**, developed a new process that made smelting much more economical and efficient. Before this, charcoal had been used to heat the rock. The supply of charcoal was limited. The new process used a type of coal. Coal was cheap and available in large quantities.

In the 1780s, another British inventor, Henry Cort, developed a furnace that also made iron-making more efficient. Together, the contributions of the Darbys and Cort made iron-making more than three times more efficient than before. As a result, there was plenty of metal to build the tools and machines of the Industrial Revolution.

TIP

As you read, look for recurring themes. These are major ideas that are repeated over and over again. One recurring theme in this unit is efficiency. You have just read how the Darbys made iron-making more efficient. You have also read about what other inventors, such as James Watt and Eli Whitney, did to improve efficiency. Throughout the Industrial Revolution, people worked to make industry as efficient as possible. Pay attention to recurring themes like this. They will help you to understand the main developments of any period in history.

■ PRACTICE 127: Coal and Iron

Decide if each statement below is true (**T**) or false (**F**). Write the correct letter on the line before each statement.

_____ **1.** Coal was important during the Industrial Revolution because it powered steam engines and was used to make iron.

_____ **2.** Iron was important during the Industrial Revolution because it was used to heat the factories in winter.

The Communications Revolution

So far, you have read about the Second Agricultural Revolution, the Transportation Revolution, and, of course, the Industrial Revolution. A fourth important revolution was the **Communications Revolution.**

The Communications Revolution was a series of inventions of the early and middle 1800s that improved communication. Before this revolution, communication had not changed much since ancient times. People carried the news with them as they traveled. So, it took information a long time to spread.

The first breakthrough came in 1811, when a German inventor used Watt's steam engine to power a printing press. The steam-powered printing press enabled newspaper publishers to print many copies at the same time and for little cost.

Samuel F. B. Morse

But newspapers could only travel as fast as people could transport them. What was wanted was an increase in the *speed* of communication. The development of the **telegraph** took communication to the speed of electricity. The first reliable telegraph was invented by American **Samuel F. B. Morse** in the 1830s. A telegraph sends coded electrical signals over wires. The code that Morse developed, a series of dots and dashes, is called the **Morse Code.**

Other inventions of the 1800s that improved communication include photography, the phonograph, improved printing machines, motion pictures, and the radio. One of the most important was the telephone, invented by **Alexander Graham Bell** in the United States in 1876. For the first time, people did not need to be in the same room in order to talk to one another.

Alexander Graham Bell

PRACTICE 128: The Communications Revolution

Check each statement below that is TRUE.

☐ **1.** The Communications Revolution occurred in the 1800s.

☐ **2.** The first breakthrough of the Communications Revolution was the invention of the telephone.

☐ **3.** The steam-powered printing press was important because it allowed newspapers to be printed quickly and cheaply.

☐ **4.** Samuel F. B. Morse invented the first reliable telegraph.

IN REAL LIFE

Fifteen years after the telephone was invented, there were five million telephones in the United States. Fifteen years after cell phones were introduced, more than 33 million of them were in use in the United States.

A World Transformed

In this lesson, you read about many important revolutions—the Second Agricultural Revolution, the Industrial Revolution, the Transportation Revolution, and the Communications Revolution. You also learned about some important inventions, such as the cotton gin and the steam engine.

Taken together, these revolutions and inventions changed the world. The difference between life in Britain in the early 1700s and life there in the early 1800s is nothing short of amazing. Muscle power was giving way to machine power. Cottage industry was giving way to factories. Handwork was giving way to machine work. Sailing ships were beginning to give way to steamships. Horses were beginning to give way to steam locomotives. Travel and communication went faster than ever before. The world had changed in many ways.

In the next lesson, you will read about how all of these changes affected everyday people. As you will see, their lives were changed dramatically—but not necessarily for the better.

PRACTICE 129: A World Transformed

Decide if each statement below is true (**T**) or false (**F**). Write the correct letter on the line before each statement.

_____ **1.** The Industrial Revolution had little effect on the lives of most people in Britain.

_____ **2.** During the Industrial Revolution, human power gave way to machine power.

_____ **3.** Transportation became faster during the Industrial Revolution.

_____ **4.** At the end of the Industrial Revolution, more goods were made in factories than in homes.

_____ **5.** The cotton gin and the steam engine were two important inventions of the Industrial Revolution.

LESSON 21: Life in Britain During the Industrial Revolution

GOAL: To discuss social changes brought about by the Industrial Revolution

WORDS TO KNOW

child labor **Luddites** **social changes**

factory system **migration** **tenement houses**

industrial cities

Life Before the Industrial Revolution

Before the Industrial Revolution, most people lived in rural areas. There were cities and towns, but they were relatively small. Most people worked on farms. There was some industry, but it was small and scattered. Many people made the things they needed themselves. Manufacturing was accomplished through cottage industries. Common public land was used for grazing livestock, which made it possible for people to survive on small farms.

Most people were poor. Life was hard. People often worked in farm fields from sunup to sundown. Craft workers kept similar hours. Today, you are familiar with the ideas of "being at home" and "going to work." For most people before the Industrial Revolution, home and work were one and the same, although how hard the work was depended on the season of the year.

The main sources of power were human and animal muscle. People powered simple machines, such as spinning wheels, themselves. Animals pulled wagons and plows. There were also water wheels, mostly used to power grain mills. But these sources of power were few and far between.

These conditions had existed for many centuries. With the coming of the Industrial Revolution, however, they all changed.

THINK ABOUT IT

The way of life described on page 243 existed for thousands of years before the Industrial Revolution. Within less than a century, however, much of it changed completely. How is this in keeping with the term Industrial *Revolution?* Write your answer on a separate sheet of paper.

PRACTICE 130: Life Before the Industrial Revolution

Circle the letter of the correct answer to each of the following questions.

1. Where did most people live and work before the Industrial Revolution?

- **a.** in rural areas
- **b.** in cities
- **c.** in small towns
- **d.** in Scotland

2. What was the main source of power before the Industrial Revolution?

- **a.** steam engines
- **b.** water wheels
- **c.** human and animal muscle
- **d.** slaves

Major Social Changes

Before the Industrial Revolution, manufacturing was done in people's homes and a few craft shops. During and after the Industrial Revolution, manufacturing was done in mills and factories.

The first mills, or textile factories, sprang up in Britain in the 1740s. By the end of the century, there were hundreds of mills and other types of factories across Britain.

The growth in factories brought many changes in the way people lived. Such changes in society are called **social changes.**

TIP

A good way to understand social changes is to imagine yourself going through them. As you read about the social changes of the Industrial Revolution, picture yourself going through each one. For example, imagine moving from a farm or a small community to a new city, working in a factory, and seeing your child working beside you. Remember, all of these were events that happened to real people, just like you.

Most of the social changes of this period resulted from the development of the **factory system.** In the factory system, people work in factories for wages. The factory system replaced the domestic system.

All of the new factories needed people to work in them. The people who took the new factory jobs used to work at home. This change from working at home to working in factories was a major social change. Suddenly, families no longer lived and worked together. At least one member of the family, and often more, went to work in a factory. (Sometimes, whole families worked together in a factory.)

Another social change was the increasing distance between bosses and workers. Under the cottage industry system, bosses and workers had close relationships. The merchants who hired the workers felt an obligation to help care for them. After all, they knew them personally and were in their homes often. Under the new factory system, bosses usually didn't know the workers. There were simply too many workers. Moreover, upper-class bosses thought themselves superior to lower-class workers. They felt little responsibility for them.

Poor working conditions were a fact of life in the factories. Wages were extremely low. Working conditions were harsh and often dangerous. Workers could not go at their own pace—they had to keep up with machines. The work was monotonous, hard, and crushing to the human spirit. Workers staggered home exhausted at the end of the day.

Many of the workers in the factories were women and children. Back then, there were no laws that prevented children from working. Children as young as ten, or even younger, worked up to 14 hours a day in the loud, dirty factories. **Child labor** in factories was an ugly fact of life during the Industrial Revolution.

IN REAL LIFE

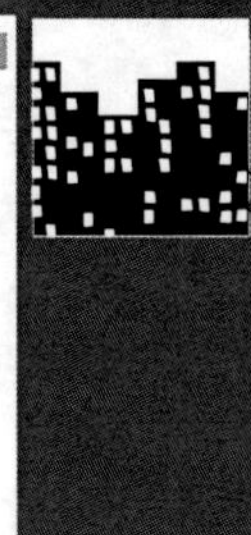

Child labor may seem like a problem from long ago, but it continues to be an issue in many countries today. Take a look at the labels in your clothes and shoes. Were most of them made in other countries? The United States has laws against child labor. But many other countries do not. Some people are concerned that many of the products sold in American stores are made in countries that do not have such laws, or do not enforce them.

PRACTICE 131: Major Social Changes

Decide if each statement below is true (**T**) or false (**F**). Write the correct letter on the line before each statement.

_____ **1.** A major social change brought about by the factory system was the change from working at home to working in factories.

_____ **2.** The factory bosses had close relationships with their workers and helped take care of them.

_____ **3.** Government agencies made sure that workers had safe, clean working conditions.

Industrial Cities and Tenement Houses

As you learned in Lesson 19, the Second Agricultural Revolution decreased the need for farm workers. Many people who used to work on farms came to the cities, looking for jobs in the new factories. Cities that are built around industries are called **industrial cities.** Many industrial cities were born and grew in Britain during the Industrial Revolution.

The growth of cities is called urbanization. Urbanization in Britain was fast and widespread. Factories grew extremely quickly. Recruiters went to the countryside to lure in the needed workers. There was a huge **migration,** or movement, of people from rural areas to urban areas.

Wherever factories were built, other buildings sprang up around them. There were apartments to house workers. There were shops so they could buy what they needed. But the pace of building could not keep up with the stream of new workers. There were too many people and not enough places to live. Serious overcrowding resulted.

Companies built large tenement houses for their workers. **Tenement houses** were unsafe, poorly maintained apartment buildings. Life in a tenement house was very difficult. There was little or no plumbing. Walls were thin. Several families often lived together in one room.

Dirty, crowded tenement houses were just one part of dirty, crowded industrial cities. The wealthy owners and managers of the factories lived extremely well. But most of the workers lived very hard lives.

■ PRACTICE 132: Industrial Cities and Tenement Houses

Match each definition with a term from the list below. Write the letter of the correct term on the line before each definition.

a. industrial cities **b.** urbanization **c.** migration **d.** tenements

_____ **1.** cities built around industries

_____ **2.** unsafe, poorly maintained apartment buildings

_____ **3.** the movement of people

_____ **4.** the growth of cities

The Luddites and Reform

At the beginning of the Industrial Revolution, the bosses had all the advantages. They were well-off and educated. Workers were often uneducated, and were always poor. They did not have the right to vote.

Laws were passed to keep workers from joining together to ask for more pay or fewer hours. People who tried to organize workers were sent to jail.

Many activists started to protest against the way workers were treated. One thing that angered people was the use of child labor. To a lesser extent, the poor treatment of female workers also enraged many people. At first, activists had limited success in helping workers.

Eventually, factory workers took matters into their own hands. Despite the fact that it was against the law, many formed unions. These workers went out on strike. Usually, the strikes got out of control. They quickly became riots. Workers attacked factories and destroyed machines. The rioting became so widespread that the British government passed a law that gave the death penalty to anyone who destroyed factory machinery.

THINK ABOUT IT

The British government passed a law that would punish with death anyone who wrecked factory equipment. Does that seem harsh to you? Is death a reasonable punishment for someone who wrecks factory equipment? What does the fact that the law was passed say about who had political power in Britain—the workers or the factory owners? Write your answers on a separate sheet of paper.

Between 1811 and 1816, a disorganized group of factory workers called **Luddites** rioted in many industrial cities. The Luddites usually wore masks and rioted at night. Their name came from their leader, known as King Ludd, who may have been an imaginary figure. The Luddites destroyed factory machines, blaming the machines for taking jobs away from people. Luddite riots were harshly broken up by the government.

Gradually, the widespread rioting and strikes began to have an effect. Working conditions slowly improved in the early 1800s. The government passed laws that gave more people the right to vote and legalized labor unions.

■ PRACTICE 133: The Luddites and Reform

Decide if each statement below is true (**T**) or false (**F**). Write the correct letter on the line before each statement.

____ **1.** Workers of the Industrial Revolution tried to improve their working conditions by joining unions, striking, and rioting.

____ **2.** The Luddites were a family who opposed unions.

____ **3.** Working conditions during the 1800s gradually improved.

Benefits of the Industrial Revolution

Many of the social changes associated with the Industrial Revolution were negative. Crowded cities, unsafe tenement houses, harsh working conditions, uncaring bosses—all came from the factory system.

But there were many benefits of the Industrial Revolution as well. One benefit was the greater availability of goods. The new factories produced a variety of things more quickly and more efficiently than ever before. For the first time, many people were able to afford certain goods that had been too costly before.

Another benefit of the Industrial Revolution was an increase in wealth. At first, only factory owners made money from the Industrial Revolution. But over time others, such as managers, inventors, and engineers, benefited as well. Many people grew rich during the Industrial Revolution.

This new wealth gave Britain a powerful middle class. As people grew in wealth, they also grew in political power. For a long time, the British government had responded only to the rich. Now, the growing middle class had a greater influence on government.

The educational system of Britain also benefited. Factories needed trained engineers, technicians, clerks, and other workers. Many new schools, libraries, and universities were created to respond to this demand.

So the Industrial Revolution, like many things in history, had both negative and positive consequences. Whether the effects were good or bad, most people in Britain knew they were witnessing a period of historic change. Soon those changes would travel beyond Britain's shores to much of the rest of the world.

■ PRACTICE 134: Benefits of the Industrial Revolution

Circle the letter of the correct answer to each of the following questions.

1. Which of the following was a result of Britain's factory system?

- **a.** a greater availability of goods
- **b.** harsh working conditions
- **c.** overcrowding in cities
- **d.** all of the above

2. How did the educational system benefit from the Industrial Revolution?

- **a.** New schools and libraries were created to meet industry's demands for skilled, educated workers.
- **b.** Britain required all children to attend school.
- **c.** Trained factory workers became teachers.
- **d.** Teachers shared in the industrial wealth.

3. How did British society change because of the Industrial Revolution?

- **a.** The middle class gained more power.
- **b.** The rich gained more power.
- **c.** The working class had more comfortable lives.
- **d.** The middle class grew smaller.

4. Which groups of people benefited from the Industrial Revolution?

- **a.** factory owners
- **b.** inventors
- **c.** engineers
- **d.** all of the above

LESSON 22: The Spread of the Industrial Revolution

GOAL: To describe how the Industrial Revolution spread from Britain to other countries; to identify the Industrial Revolution as a major change in human history

WORDS TO KNOW

Agricultural Age

Hunting and Gathering Age

Industrial Age

industrialized

Lowell Girls

urban working class

NAMES TO KNOW

Moses Brown

Francis Lowell

Samuel Slater

PLACES TO KNOW

Belgium

France

Germany

Lowell, Massachusetts

Manchester

Merrimack River

British Attempts at Secrecy

The Industrial Revolution started in Britain. It spread to other countries, but not for more than a century. The second country to industrialize, Belgium, did not really begin to do so until the 1830s.

You might find this puzzling. Today, technology and new ideas spread quickly. Why did the ideas of industrialization spread to other countries so slowly?

One reason is that communication and transportation were much slower than they are today.

Another reason was that Britain tried hard to *keep* the Industrial Revolution from spreading. Knowledge of industry gave Britain an enormous advantage. It brought the British great wealth. The city of **Manchester** alone produced most of the cotton cloth in the world.

Britain was the world's leading textile producer, and it wanted to remain in this role.

In fact, the British government made it illegal for anyone with any knowledge of industry to leave Britain. One law prevented craft workers from moving away. Another law made it illegal to export British machinery.

For a while, these measures worked. But soon, despite such laws, Britain's know-how began to spread. As early as 1750, an Englishman settled in France and introduced the roller-spinning machine there. But one of the greatest examples of the escape of know-how was a man who brought knowledge of the Industrial Revolution to America. His name was **Samuel Slater**.

IN REAL LIFE

If you have a great new idea, you might do one of two things. You might try to keep it to yourself, so that you can be the only one to make money from it—as Britain tried to do. Or, you might let other people pay to use your idea. This is called *licensing* or *franchising*. Many very successful companies do this. For example, every McDonald's restaurant is franchised by the McDonald's Corporation. The restaurant owners must agree to follow all of McDonald's rules.

PRACTICE 135: British Attempts at Secrecy

Circle the letter of the correct answer to each of the following questions.

1. What did Britain want to do with its knowledge of industry?
   - **a.** sell it to other countries
   - **b.** keep it a secret
   - **c.** distribute it around the world
   - **d.** incorporate it in the educational system

2. How did Britain attempt to keep its knowledge secret?
   a. by inviting experts to Britain from all over the world
   b. by passing laws preventing anyone with industrial knowledge from leaving the country
   c. by making it illegal to write any information about industry on paper
   d. by paying people to keep their knowledge to themselves

Samuel Slater

Samuel Slater was born in Britain in 1768. As a young man, he worked in a textile mill. He started as an apprentice. Eventually, he became the superintendent of the mill. There he learned all about the new spinning machine called the water frame, invented by Richard Arkwright. At one time, he even worked for Arkwright.

When Slater was 21, he felt that the textile industry in England had reached its peak. He decided to go to America. As you have read, British citizens with knowledge about machines and industry were not allowed to leave the country at this time. So, Slater had to travel in disguise. Likewise, he could not carry any written information about the water frame. Such documents would have given him away. In one of history's most amazing feats, Slater *memorized* how the water frame and other textile machines worked, down to the tiniest details.

Samuel Slater

In America, Slater met **Moses Brown,** a merchant. Slater oversaw the construction of a cotton spinning machine for Brown. Brown built a factory on the Blackstone River in Pawtucket, Rhode Island. The factory used waterwheels turned by the river to power the machines. The factory was soon a financial success.

The Pawtucket factory was the first factory in the United States. When it went into operation, the Industrial Revolution had begun in the United States.

■ TIP

Geography is a major force in history. Understanding the geography of an area can help you understand its historical development. When you think about the geography of New England, for example, you can see why it was a good place to build factories that were run by water power. Much of New England is hilly, so rivers run fast. This speed was harnessed to turn the water wheels that powered the factories. A slow-moving river, such as the Mississippi, would not have done the job as well.

■ PRACTICE 136: Samuel Slater

Circle the letter of the correct answer to each of the following questions.

1. Where did Samuel Slater get his knowledge of spinning machines?
   - **a.** Britain
   - **b.** France
   - **c.** Germany
   - **d.** Mexico

2. Where was the first factory in the United States located?
   - **a.** Rhode Island
   - **b.** New York
   - **c.** Massachusetts
   - **d.** North Carolina

The Industrial Revolution in the United States

Industrialization first spread rapidly throughout New England. New England's **Merrimack River** was nicknamed "the hardest-working river in the world" because it turned the waterwheels of many factories all down its length.

One of the factory towns built along the Merrimack River was **Lowell, Massachusetts.** The city was named in honor of **Francis Lowell,** a Boston merchant and one of the leaders of the Industrial Revolution in

America. The city of Lowell was planned from the beginning to be an industrial city. It was made up of textile mills and buildings to house the mill's workers. Construction of the city started in 1822.

The city of Lowell became a symbol of the Industrial Revolution in the United States. It had all the marks of the American Industrial Revolution: factories, an urban working class, an industrial city. At its peak, Lowell was home to 40 mill buildings, 10,000 looms, and 10,000 workers.

Most of the workers in the Lowell mills were young, single women recruited from local farms. They became known as the **Lowell Girls.** Their lives, strictly monitored by older women, were regulated by the clock. Bells sounded for them to get up, go to work, eat, and go to bed. They worked 14 hours a day. Despite their harsh schedule, they developed a remarkable society. They printed their own newspaper, put on plays, and formed literary circles.

IN REAL LIFE

Today, much of Lowell, Massachusetts, is a National Historical Park. The mills, boarding houses, and other buildings of the period have been preserved. You can see where the Lowell Girls lived and worked. Visiting such sites is a good way to make history come to life.

The Lowell Girls were among the first group of a new social class in America: the **urban working class.** This class is made up of people who live in cities and work at nonprofessional jobs. They form the bulk of union membership in the United States. To many Americans, the urban working class is the backbone of America. And this class began with the Industrial Revolution.

In the 1830s, industry spread beyond New England down the eastern coast. As the country grew toward the west, industry moved with it. In 1800, industry accounted for less than one tenth of everything made in the United States. By 1860, it accounted for one third. In 1800, about 1 in 20 Americans lived in cities. By 1860, almost 1 in 4 did. The urbanization of America, as in Britain, was a chief result of the Industrial Revolution.

The Industrial Revolution in the United States brought with it the same benefits and drawbacks that it had brought to Britain. Child labor was one of the drawbacks. The machines in Slater's and Brown's mill, for example, were run by children as young as seven years old.

TIP

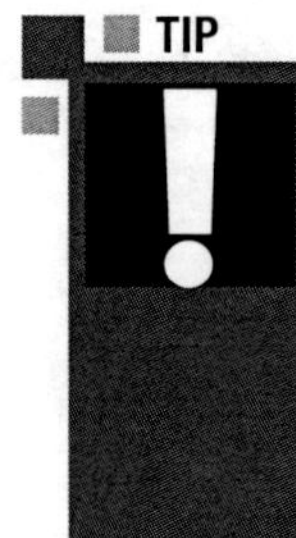

You might wonder why child labor was tolerated. The answer is that children had always worked on farms. To the people of the time, working in a factory was just a different kind of work for the children. Also, children did not have to be paid as much as adults. Factory owners wanted labor to be as cheap as possible. There were no laws requiring children to go to school.

Today, the United States is an industrial giant. Its economic success and its influence around the world are direct descendants of the American Industrial Revolution that took place in the early 1800s.

PRACTICE 137: The Industrial Revolution in the United States

Circle the letter of the correct answer to each of the following questions.

1. Where did the Industrial Revolution in the United States first take hold?
   - **a.** the South
   - **b.** New England
   - **c.** all down the east coast
   - **d.** New York City

2. What new class of people emerged from the Industrial Revolution in the United States?
   - **a.** the middle class
   - **b.** the urban working class
   - **c.** the very poor
   - **d.** the Luddites

Industrialization in Belgium and France

Soon after the Industrial Revolution happened in Britain, nearly all European countries had some industry. But only when industry becomes widespread and important do we say that a country has **industrialized.**

The next country to industrialize after Britain was **Belgium.** Like Britain, Belgium had a long tradition of textile-making. For this reason, it was natural that Belgium soon industrialized.

Another reason for Belgium's industrialization was government support. The Belgian government spent great sums of money to obtain and use textile industry know-how. It financed the development of machinery and built many factories.

The Belgian government's investment paid off. Major industrial cities developed in Belgium. The newly industrialized textile industry provided jobs and incomes to the growing nation.

Belgium's neighbor, **France,** also industrialized, although much more slowly. In the late 1700s, France was rocked by the French Revolution. Afterward, Napoleon came to power, and France was involved in the Napoleonic Wars. All of this turmoil slowed industrialization. Vital transportation links, such as roads and canals, fell into disrepair. Money was spent on warfare instead of on industry.

France remained largely agricultural far into the 1800s, and even beyond. It wasn't until the twentieth century, and even after the two world wars, that widespread industrialization took hold in France.

■ PRACTICE 138: Industrialization in Belgium and France

Decide if each statement below is true (**T**) or false (**F**). Write the correct letter on the line before each statement.

_____ **1.** After Britain, the first country to be industrialized was France.

_____ **2.** The French Revolution and the Napoleonic Wars slowed industrialization in France.

_____ **3.** The Belgian government spent a great deal of money to help Belgium industrialize.

Industrialization in Germany and the Rest of Europe

Today, **Germany** is an industrial powerhouse. But, as in France, industrialization there was a slow process.

Today, Germany is a single country. But in the early 1800s, this area was broken into a number of separate states. Each state had its own government. Each state also charged duties on imports. This made it difficult to bring raw materials and finished goods from one region to another. Commerce in the region was hurt by Napoleon's Continental System. Many raw materials were just not available.

One advantage that Germany had was large deposits of coal and iron. As you recall, these two materials are critical to industry. Coal was needed to power steam engines and to make iron. Iron was used to make the machines of the Industrial Revolution.

Throughout the 1800s, Germany's coal and iron production increased. By the end of the century, it had surpassed even Britain in the production of these two industrial ingredients.

All through the 1800s, other countries in Europe also began to industrialize. The pattern of industrialization remained basically the same. Work by hand was replaced by machines. In other words, production was mechanized. These machines were powered by water or, more frequently, by steam. Urbanization occurred as people moved from farm to factory.

Industrialization occurred at different rates in different countries. By about 1870, though, all of the countries that were to industrialize showed the hallmarks of the Industrial Revolution.

■ PRACTICE 139: Industrialization in Germany and the Rest of Europe

Circle the letter of the correct answer to each of the following questions.

1. What were the two resources that helped Germany to industrialize?

- **a.** coal and iron
- **b.** cotton and slaves
- **c.** an urban working class and cottage industries
- **d.** school-aged children and single women from farms

2. By what year did all of the countries that were to industrialize show the hallmarks of the Industrial Revolution?
   a. about 1810
   b. about 1830
   c. about 1850
   d. about 1870

Thinking About the Industrial Revolution

The Industrial Revolution changed the world. Like the First Agricultural Revolution, it marked a great change in history. In fact, some historians divide world history into three great eras. The first era was when small groups of people lived by hunting and gathering. This is sometimes called the **Hunting and Gathering Age.** The second great era, brought about by the First Agricultural Revolution, was when people developed agriculture, cities, and civilization. This is sometimes called the **Agricultural Age.** The third great era, brought about by the Industrial Revolution, was when people developed industry. This is sometimes called the **Industrial Age.** Some historians say that we are still living in the Industrial Age today. Others argue that we have entered a fourth era—the Post-Industrial Age, or Information Age.

As you have learned, the Industrial Revolution started in the textile industry in Britain. Work done by hand was then done by powered machines. Mills and factories were built. People who used to work on farms worked in factories instead. Cities grew as these workers migrated to the industrial cities. This caused great social changes. And this pattern was repeated in many countries, and in many industries, around the world.

The Industrial Revolution is still going on today in some parts of the world. In some African and Asian countries, for example, industrialization is in its early stages. These countries are facing the benefits and drawbacks of industrialization that other countries have already experienced.

The chart that follows will help you think about and remember the great changes brought by the Industrial Revolution. It provides a summary of much of what you have read. It will also remind you of the truly revolutionary changes in human life brought about by the Industrial Revolution.

The Industrial Revolution: Before and After

Before	After
most work done by hand	most work done by machines
domestic system	factory system
most power supplied by humans and animals	most power supplied by machines
most people work on farms	most people work in factories
most people live in rural areas	most people live in urban areas
few goods available	more goods available

■ PRACTICE 140: Thinking About the Industrial Revolution

Decide if each statement below is true (**T**) or false (**F**). Write the correct letter on the line before each statement.

_____ **1.** The Hunting and Gathering Age was followed by the Agricultural Age.

_____ **2.** The Industrial Age lasted from the 1800s to the early 1900s.

_____ **3.** In much of Africa, industrialization is still in its early stages.

_____ **4.** The Industrial Revolution is still going on today in some parts of the world.

UNIT 6 REVIEW

Circle the letter of the correct answer to each of the following questions.

1. Where did the Industrial Revolution begin?

a. the United States
b. France
c. Britain
d. Belgium

2. Which of the following is an improved method of growing crops developed during the Second Agricultural Revolution?
   a. crop rotation
   b. planting by hand
   c. farming
   d. growing food to sell

3. Which of the following is a result of the Second Agricultural Revolution?
   a. improved livestock breeding
   b. factories
   c. discovery of crop rotation
   d. all of the above

4. During the Industrial Revolution, what happened to textile production?
   a. It moved from mills to homes.
   b. It moved from homes to mills.
   c. It moved from city to country.
   d. It moved from factories to homes.

5. What are the two most important inventions of the Industrial Revolution?
   a. the telephone and the telegraph
   b. the steam engine and the cotton gin
   c. the water frame and the spinning jenny
   d. the loom and the mill

6. What system replaced the domestic system in the British textile industry?
   a. the cottage industry system
   b. the factory system
   c. the Industrial Revolution system
   d. the union system

7. What social change is associated with the Industrial Revolution?
   a. the change from working at home to working in factories
   b. the movement of people from rural areas to cities
   c. less communication between bosses and workers
   d. all of the above

8. Which of the following was a benefit of the Industrial Revolution?
   a. greater availability of goods
   b. the growth of educational institutions
   c. sudden wealth for the workers
   d. both *a* and *b*

9. Where was the first factory in the United States?
   a. Lowell, Massachusetts
   b. Pawtucket, Rhode Island
   c. New York, New York
   d. Boston, Massachusetts

10. Who were most of the employees in Lowell, Massachusetts?
   a. young men from farms
   b. young women from farms
   c. British immigrants
   d. slaves

UNIT 6 APPLICATION ACTIVITY
Machines in Our Lives

The machines invented during the Industrial Revolution changed, or "revolutionized," the world. Cars, trains, telephones, elevators—machines like these have become part of almost everyone's daily life. Machines include anything that is automated, such as an alarm clock, a washing machine, a car, or a computer. In this activity, you will think about the importance of machines in your own life.

First choose a three-hour block of time in a typical day. Then make a list of every machine you use during that block of time. For example, you might make a list of every machine you use between 9 A.M. and noon.

Try to pay close attention to your actions, and list every machine you use. Write your list on the lines below.

Day and time studied: ______________________________

List of machines used:

UNIT 7

Nationalism and Social Reform

LESSON 23: Social Reform and Socialism

GOAL: To define and discuss laissez-faire economics, socialism, and Marxism, and explain how they came to be

WORDS TO KNOW

bourgeoisie
capital
capitalism
capitalists
communism
The Communist Manifesto
dictatorship of the proletariat
economist
Factory Act
free enterprise system
ideal communities
laissez-faire
law of competition
law of supply and demand
Marxism
Marxists
means of production
natural laws of economics
proletariat
reform movement
revolution of the proletariat
Romantic Movement
Romanticism
socialism
socialists
strikes
Ten Hours Act
unions
utopian socialists

NAMES TO KNOW

Ludwig van Beethoven
Johannes Brahms
Frédéric Chopin
John Keats
Thomas Malthus
Karl Marx
Sir Thomas More
Robert Owen
David Ricardo
Percy Bysshe Shelley
Adam Smith
William Wordsworth

The Industrial Revolution

As you have read, in the late 1700s and early 1800s, Europe was transformed by the Industrial Revolution. More and more people lived in cities. They depended on wages from employers. There was a greater social and economic distance between bosses and workers.

Many workers of the Industrial Revolution endured terrible working conditions. For 14 hours a day, they worked at mind-numbing jobs amid the loud noise of machines. Often, the jobs were dangerous. Even more often, the wages were low. Most workers were poor.

The Industrial Revolution also had some benefits. Countries that industrialized enjoyed more wealth overall. More and cheaper goods were available. Businesspeople and inventors grew rich. So did the factory owners.

As the Industrial Revolution progressed, there was a growing conflict between two groups of people. One group was made up of factory owners, managers, and others who benefited from the Industrial Revolution. They wanted workers to do their jobs without complaining, to work according to schedule, and to work for as low a wage as possible. The other group was the workers. They wanted decent wages, safe workplaces, and reasonable hours.

Many workers joined unions, went on strike, and even rioted in attempts to be treated fairly. They hoped to get the government to pass laws to protect them. But at first, most governments did nothing. These governments were deeply influenced by certain ideas of the Enlightenment. These ideas convinced them that government should stay out of the economy. You will read more about these ideas in the next section.

IN REAL LIFE

Do the conflicts between the factory owners and the workers sound familiar to you? Many issues that emerged at the very beginning of the Industrial Revolution are still with us today. These include conflicts over wage rates, hours of work, and the safety of the workplace.

■ PRACTICE 141: The Industrial Revolution

Decide if each statement below is true (**T**) or false (**F**). Write the correct letter on the line before each statement.

_____ **1.** The two groups that came into conflict during the Industrial Revolution were factory owners and workers.

_____ **2.** Both groups wanted to keep wages as low as possible.

_____ **3.** At first, most governments did nothing to help workers.

_____ **4.** Workers joined together to get better treatment.

Three Economists and the Laissez-Faire View of the Economy

The Enlightenment was a period in which many people believed that rational thinking would uncover the natural laws of the universe. Society, they argued, should be run according to natural laws.

Enlightenment thinkers greatly influenced many European leaders of the time. One influential group was the economists of the Enlightenment. An **economist** is someone who studies and writes about the economy (the use of resources). Economists of the Enlightenment thought that natural laws were at work in nations' economies. The best economies, they said, were those that followed these natural laws.

One such economist was **Adam Smith,** of Scotland. Smith argued that there were certain **natural laws of economics.** They were the **law of supply and demand** and the **law of competition.** To Smith, these laws were a natural part of the way economies operated. Any attempt to interfere with them would cause economic disaster.

The basic idea behind Smith's laws is this: If everyone—workers and owners alike—were free to do as they pleased, then the laws of economics would operate properly. Businesses would come and go, people would be hired and fired, prices would increase and decrease, but the economy would grow. Smith believed that people wanted to succeed. And if all citizens of a country were trying to achieve personal success, the whole country would succeed. Such an economy, where everyone is free to make choices and profits, is called a **free enterprise system.**

Many of Smith's ideas still form the basis of the free enterprise system today. He is known as "the father of modern economics."

Two other economists largely agreed with Smith. One was **Thomas Malthus,** an Englishman. Malthus wrote that the human population always increases much faster than food supplies. As a result, he said, disasters such as famines (mass starvation) and wars are unavoidable. They are a natural part of human life that serves to control the population. This was a brutal natural law, but it made sense to many people.

Another English economist, **David Ricardo,** argued that the idea of free enterprise should extend to trade between nations. He also said that workers' wages would always be low as long as there was a large supply of workers.

Taken together, the ideas of these three economists would not please any wage-earning worker. These economists said that low wages and unemployment were a natural part of the economy.

More importantly, they said that any attempt to interfere with the way the economy operates would end in disaster. This approach to the economy is called **laissez-faire,** which is French for "let it be." In other words, these economists argued that the government should leave the economy alone. Any government regulation, even safety regulations, would interfere with natural law.

As you might imagine, rich factory owners liked these ideas. To them, it seemed that their wealth was somehow "natural." These ideas also kept the government from interfering in their businesses. They were free to force workers to work long hours on unsafe machinery, to hire children, and to pay low wages.

Government officials were also influenced by these ideas. In earlier years, English society had tried to help poor people. Many rural towns gave money to unemployed workers so that their families would not starve. The new economic ideas said that these payments hurt everyone, rich and poor alike. They went against the natural laws of economics. So governments did virtually nothing to help abused workers in the early years of the Industrial Revolution.

■ PRACTICE 142: Three Economists and the Laissez-Faire View of the Economy

Match each definition with a term from the list below. Write the letter of the correct term on the line before each definition.

a. the free enterprise system
b. Adam Smith
c. Thomas Malthus
d. laissez-faire
e. David Ricardo

_____ **1.** an economy where everyone is free to make profits

_____ **2.** the idea that the government should not interfere in the economy

_____ **3.** an economist who said that free enterprise should extend to trade between nations

_____ **4.** the father of modern economics

_____ **5.** an economist who thought disasters were unavoidable

Romanticism

The logic of the Enlightenment economists was cruel. They argued that human suffering, especially among the working class, was inevitable. It was a result of the natural laws of economics.

This sort of thinking—the elevation of cold logic above humanitarian concern—was Enlightenment thinking at its worst. Yet, all of the Enlightenment thinkers stressed reason and logic and science as the best way to view life.

In the early 1800s, though, the Enlightenment was giving way to a new intellectual movement. This new movement was called **Romanticism,** or the **Romantic Movement.** Romantic writers and artists emphasized the innate goodness of human beings. They emphasized feeling over thinking. They emphasized beauty over efficiency. As you can see, Romanticism was largely a reaction to the Enlightenment. In many ways, it was the direct opposite of the Enlightenment.

During the Enlightenment, books and paintings tended to be complex. They were made to be enjoyed by educated people. Toward the end of the 1700s, a new interest in folk music, stories, and art began. People studied folk songs and ballads. In Germany, two professors collected folktales from different regions. Some people felt that these simple works had just as much to offer as the more complex works of the Enlightenment.

Johannes Brahms

Some of the most famous people in history belonged to the Romantic Movement. Great Romantic writers include the British poets **William Wordsworth, John Keats,** and **Percy Bysshe Shelley**.

In Austria, Germany, and France, Romantic composers captured the Romantic mood in music. Great Romantic composers include **Ludwig van Beethoven, Johannes Brahms,** and **Frédéric Chopin**.

The works of the Romantic poets and composers can give you a better understanding of the term "Romanticism" if you experience them yourself. Your library has books of their poetry and stories of their lives. It may also have CDs of their music that you can borrow. Your local classical music radio station is another source of such music.

As you just read, Romanticism was largely a reaction to the reason of the Enlightenment. But it was also a reaction to the ugliness of the Industrial Revolution. The factories and industrial cities of the Industrial Revolution were engineering marvels, but they were also crowded, noisy, and polluted. These cities stressed function over form. They were practical and not beautiful.

In contrast, Romantic poetry and music stressed form and beauty, as did Romantic art. Many painters of the period created vibrant landscapes that expressed the bright colors, natural beauty, and harmony of nature. These images stood in sharp contrast to the cold thinking of the Enlightenment and the ugly industrial cities.

■ PRACTICE 143: Romanticism

Circle the letters of the correct answers to each of the following questions. (*Hint:* Each question has more than one correct answer.)

1. What was Romanticism a reaction to?
   a. the Enlightenment
   b. laissez-faire
   c. William Wordsworth
   d. the Industrial Revolution

2. Which of the following was a Romantic writer?
   a. John Keats
   b. Percy Bysshe Shelley
   c. William Wordsworth
   d. e. e. cummings

3. Which of the following was a Romantic composer?
   a. Ludwig van Beethoven
   b. Frédéric Chopin
   c. Barry Manilow
   d. Aaron Copland

The Reform Movement

In the world of art, people reacted against the Industrial Revolution by creating the Romantic Movement. In the industrial world, people reacted with another kind of movement: a reform movement.

A **reform movement** is an attempt to reform, or change, existing conditions. Reformers in the early 1800s wanted to change the terrible working conditions of workers in factories.

Early reformers in Britain and other industrialized countries wrote and spoke about the need for change. They publicized the terrible working conditions in the factories. They pointed out how inhumane they were. The reformers argued for two chief goals: that the government should limit working hours and should set a minimum wage.

At first, the governments did not respond. They believed that they should stay out of the economy (laissez-faire). They thought that government regulation would slow or stop economic growth and the creation of wealth.

It was the poor working conditions of children and women that finally led the British government to act. Very young children—sometimes four and five years old—were working in factories as much as 14 hours a day. Women, too, were working long hours in dangerous conditions.

In 1819, the British government passed the **Factory Act.** It prohibited employing children younger than 9 years old. Children between 9 and 18 could work no more than 12 hours a day.

Then, in 1847, the government passed the **Ten Hours Act.** This act limited the work day to ten hours.

But these and similar laws were not always enforced. Besides, working conditions remained harsh, and wages remained very low. Unable to achieve their goals through the law, the workers tried another tactic: going on strikes.

■ PRACTICE 144: The Reform Movement

Decide if each statement below is true (**T**) or false (**F**). Write the correct letter on the line before each statement.

_____ **1.** Reformers wanted to get government to limit working hours and provide a minimum wage.

_____ **2.** The Ten Hours Act said that children under ten could work no more than ten hours a day.

Strikes and Unions

Unions, or workers' organizations, were illegal in most industrial countries for most of the Industrial Revolution. They weren't made legal in Britain until 1825. In other European countries, another 50 years would pass before unions were legally allowed.

Even before unions were formed, workers went on **strikes**. This means that they would refuse to work until their wages were increased and their working conditions improved. Often, these strikes turned into riots. The governments put down many riots with force.

The strikes also grew into more general protests about the nature of society. The strikers wanted more than better wages and working conditions. They wanted society to change so that wealth was spread more equally. They wanted all workers to be as rich as the factory owners, or at least to have a greater share of the wealth. The success of the strikers varied from country to country and from industry to industry. Sometimes, factory owners simply hired other workers to replace the strikers. Other times, the workers got some or all of what they wanted.

Although their successes varied, the workers of the industrialized world were becoming more powerful. Soon they would take on more than just the factory owners. They would take on society itself.

■ PRACTICE 145: Strikes and Unions

Match each definition with a term from the list below. Write the letter of the correct term on the line before each definition.

a. strikes **b.** unions

_____ **1.** workers' organizations

_____ **2.** workers' refusing to work until their demands are met

Socialism

Laissez-faire economics and the Industrial Revolution had many effects. But to a poor worker of the time, perhaps the most obvious was that only a few people were very rich, while most were extremely poor.

More and more people argued that this was not the way "natural law" was supposed to work. They thought that the wealth of society should be shared among all the people.

To share the wealth, they argued, ownership of the means of production would have to be shared. The **means of production** are the tools, equipment, and investment money used to produce goods. A factory, the land it stands on, the machines it contains, the raw materials it uses, and the money needed to run it are all examples of the means of production.

In a free enterprise laissez-faire system, the means of production are owned by private citizens. For example, a private businessperson, or group of businesspeople, owns a factory. The owners often make large profits while workers toil away for very low wages.

But what if the factory were owned by the government, instead of private citizens? And what if the government truly represented the people? Couldn't the government then fairly distribute the profits among everyone? Wouldn't the workers then get a fair wage? Wouldn't all of the people in society become equal? The people who answered "yes" to these questions believed in socialism.

Socialism is a political and an economic idea that says that governments should run the means of production. The government would then run the factories and businesses for the benefit of everyone. Everyone would share in the ownership of the means of production. In socialism, it is society that owns the means of production. People who believe in socialism are called **socialists.**

The first socialists thought that socialism could work, at least at first, only on a small scale. They thought that people should live in small, cooperative communities. Everyone in the communities would share in the ownership of the means of production. These communities are sometimes called **ideal communities.**

Early supporters of ideal communities were called **utopian socialists.** Their name came from a book called *Utopia* written by **Sir Thomas More** in 1516. In *Utopia,* More describes an ideal community.

Robert Owen

One important utopian socialist was **Robert Owen,** a factory owner who lived in Britain. Owen was an exception among factory owners: He cared about his workers and tried hard to improve their lives. He built good housing for them and paid good wages. He even set up schools for their children. Owen thought that if people were treated well, their natural goodness would come out.

Owen, as you see, put his ideas into practice in his factory. But he went a step further. He actually established ideal communities, both in Britain and in the United States. The community of New Harmony was in Indiana.

Although these communities failed, they are important. They were nearly heroic efforts to improve the lives of working people, at great personal cost. Another man who cared about working people would have a much greater impact than Robert Owen. In fact, his ideas would touch billions of people around the world. You may have heard of this "workers' hero." His name was Karl Marx.

■ PRACTICE 146: Socialism

Circle the letter of the correct answer to each of the following questions.

1. What are the means of production?

- **a.** tools and equipment used to produce goods
- **b.** money invested to produce goods
- **c.** raw materials used to manufacture goods
- **d.** all of the above

2. What is the name of the idea that all people, through the government, should own the means of production?

- **a.** socialism
- **b.** means of production
- **c.** ideal communities
- **d.** laissez-faire

Karl Marx

Karl Marx, who lived from 1818 to 1883, was one of the most influential people of all time. His ideas about the economy, society, and government were adopted by countries around the world. Today, rebels in many countries continue to fight to try to put his ideas into practice. And, the former Soviet Union was founded largely on some of his ideas. In fact, much of the history of the twentieth century is a result of Marx's work.

Marx was a journalist and a social critic. In a pamphlet called **The *Communist Manifesto*,** he outlined his basic ideas. Together, Marx's ideas are called **Marxism.** Believers in Marxism are called **Marxists.**

Like others of his time, Marx was outraged at the abuses of poor workers by the rich owners of the means of production. The rich owners were known as **capitalists.** This was because they owned the **capital,** or money, that was invested in the means of production. The term **capitalism** describes an economy in which the means of production are privately owned. A capitalist economy is one that is driven by a desire for profit. It is similar to the free enterprise and laissez-faire systems you read about earlier.

Marx believed that capitalism was doomed to failure because it resulted in a society that was divided into rich and poor. Throughout history, Marx argued, such inequality always led to conflict and struggle.

The rich owners of the means of production and those who supported them were called the **bourgeoisie.** The poor workers were called the **proletariat.** Marx thought that, in capitalist economies, conflict between the bourgeoisie and the proletariat was inevitable. He pointed to the growth of strikes and unions as examples of this conflict. Marx thought that society would soon be divided completely into a few rich bourgeoisie and masses of poor proletariat.

Once that had happened, Marx thought that a revolution would occur. Enraged by inequality, the proletariat would seize the means of production by force. They would take over the government. This would be the **revolution of the proletariat.**

At first, the proletariat would have to use force to stay in power, because the bourgeoisie would not accept the new order. Marx called this stage the **dictatorship of the proletariat**. Eventually, though, everyone would be educated to the benefits of the new order. A completely equal society, free of social and economic classes, would result. This final stage would be called **communism.** Under communism, each individual would both contribute to and benefit from society.

Marx's theory had wide appeal. It argued that a wonderful, equal, peaceful society could be a reality. Marx's vision stood in sharp contrast to the ugliness and inequality that capitalism had brought forth.

It is no wonder, then, that groups of socialists and others around the world tried to put Marxist ideas into practice.

THINK ABOUT IT

Marx believed in the possibility of an ideal society in which everyone was equal. Do you think that such a society is possible? Why or why not? Write your answer on a separate sheet of paper.

PRACTICE 147: Karl Marx

Circle the letter of the correct answer to each of the following questions.

1. What term refers to the ideas of Karl Marx?

- **a.** communism
- **b.** capitalism
- **c.** Marxism
- **d.** laissez-faire

2. Why did Marx believe that capitalism was doomed to failure?

- **a.** because of conflicts between the rich and the poor
- **b.** because the factories could not handle the demand for new goods
- **c.** because the government was controlled by corrupt officials
- **d.** because the factory workers were unable to work efficiently

3. What did Marx say would be the final stage of the revolution of the proletariat?

- **a.** communism
- **b.** capitalism
- **c.** the dictatorship of the proletariat
- **d.** Marxism

LESSON 24: Nationalism and Liberalism in Europe

GOAL: To explain how the Metternich system worked and how nationalism and liberalism spread across Europe in the 1800s

WORDS TO KNOW

absolute monarchy

Age of Liberalism

Age of Metternich

compensation

Congress of Vienna

European balance of power

legitimacy

liberal

liberalism

Metternich system

nationalism

Quadruple Alliance

Red Shirts

weakened France

NAMES TO KNOW

Count Camillo Benso di Cavour

Giuseppe Garibaldi

Giuseppe Mazzini

Prince Klemens von Metternich

Otto von Bismarck

Victor Emmanuel II

PLACES TO KNOW

Italy

Prussia

Sardinia-Piedmont

The Defeat of Napoleon and the Congress of Vienna

Between 1789 and 1799, France was rocked by the French Revolution. In 1799, Napoleon came to power. Napoleon launched a series of wars, conquering nearly all of Western Europe. Only by combining forces were the other countries of Europe finally able to defeat him.

Napoleon claimed to carry the ideals of the French Revolution into the areas he conquered. These included freedom, equality, and a constitutional government. The rulers of other European nations feared that Napoleon would bring revolutionary ideas to their countries. This desire to keep the French Revolution from spreading, and to keep Napoleon from conquering them, led several European nations to fight, and ultimately to defeat, Napoleon.

The wars against Napoleon had thrown Europe into disarray. Political leaders from throughout Europe decided to meet to do two things: restore order to Europe and halt the spread of revolutionary ideas.

European leaders met at the **Congress of Vienna** in 1814 and 1815. The congress, or meeting, was held in Vienna, the capital of Austria. Hundreds of political leaders from throughout Europe attended.

The members of the Congress of Vienna decided to put into practice four principles, or guiding ideas, to achieve their goals.

TIP

You have just read that there were four principles of the Congress of Vienna. When you read such things, you should make a list on a separate sheet of paper. Your list will help you understand, review, and remember the ideas you are reading about. After you have read more about these ideas, go back to your list. You can then decide whether each principle was achieved, and what its effects were.

The first principle was called **legitimacy.** By this, the participants meant that the legitimate, or rightful, rulers of Europe were nobles and ruling families. These families had lost power when Napoleon built his empire. The congress restored these rulers to power.

The second principle was a **European balance of power.** By this, they meant that the economic, political, and especially military power of European nations should be balanced. They did not want one country to become too powerful and try to take over the continent, as France had done.

The third principle was a **weakened France.** The congress wanted to weaken France so that its expansion under Napoleon would not be repeated under another ruler.

The fourth principle was **compensation.** The congress wanted countries that had suffered losses in land, men, and money while fighting Napoleon to be compensated.

The leaders at the Congress of Vienna argued about how these principles should be put into place. They especially argued over how territory should be divided. Eventually, though, they reached an agreement. France lost the territory it had gained under Napoleon, and the map of Europe took on a new form.

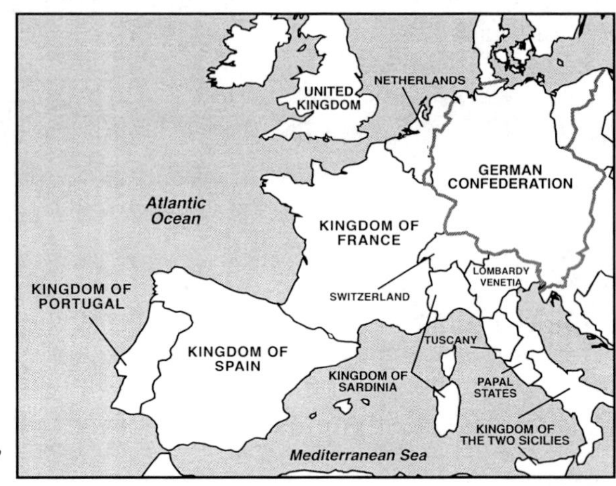

Western Europe after the Congress of Vienna, 1815

PRACTICE 148: The Defeat of Napoleon and the Congress of Vienna

Decide if each phrase below was a goal (**g**) or principle (**p**) of the Congress of Vienna. Write the correct letter on the line before each phrase.

_____ **1.** legitimacy

_____ **2.** European balance of power

_____ **3.** to restore order to Europe

_____ **4.** a weakened France

_____ **5.** to halt the spread of revolutionary ideas

_____ **6.** compensation

Metternich Versus Liberalism

The leader of the Congress of Vienna was **Prince Klemens von Metternich** of Austria. Metternich had enormous influence over the congress. His influence continued to shape European politics for another 30 years. In fact, the period of European history from 1815 to 1845 is sometimes called the **Age of Metternich.**

Metternich strongly opposed the ideas of the French Revolution. He opposed freedoms of the press, religion, and speech. He also opposed elections and constitutions. His firm belief was in the power of an **absolute monarchy**, in which the monarch had complete power. In other words, he was opposed to all of the ideas that inspired the French Revolution, especially equality.

The leaders of Europe listened to Metternich. For decades, they followed his lead and advice in harshly suppressing any revolutionary movement. Metternich and those who agreed with him fought against the ideas of liberalism. **Liberalism** at this time was a belief in the principles of freedom and equality and the rule of laws under a constitution. A key belief of liberalism was that people had a right to revolt against governments that were unjust and limited people's freedoms. A **liberal** was anyone who believed in these principles. Liberal movements, inspired by the French Revolution, sprang up all over Europe throughout the 1800s. Liberalism became such a powerful force that the period of the 1800s in Europe is sometimes called the **Age of Liberalism**.

IN REAL LIFE

In the United States today, the term *liberal* refers to people who support government action to promote the well-being of the people of the United States. This is opposed to conservatives, who favor private action and do not believe the government should be involved. Notice how the original meaning of the word *liberal* has changed.

Wherever a liberal movement sprang up in Europe, Metternich worked to suppress it. He worked largely through the **Quadruple Alliance.** The Quadruple Alliance was made up of four countries: Great Britain, Prussia, Russia, and Metternich's Austria. These were the same four countries that had joined together to defeat Napoleon. The Quadruple Alliance was set up by the Congress of Vienna to make sure that France upheld the principles of the congress. But its major purpose was to put down any liberal uprisings.

This system of cooperation to put down liberal uprisings was called the **Metternich system**. The Metternich system worked well during the Age of Metternich. Liberal uprisings in Germany, Spain, Italy, and Portugal were put down by armies of the Quadruple Alliance.

TIP

Look at the term *Quadruple Alliance.* If you look at each word on its own, it will be easy to remember what this term means. *Quadruple* means "made up of four." *Alliance* means "a group of countries that cooperate with one another."

The Metternich system eventually faced a colossal failure. In Greece, the people rose up against the rule of the Ottoman Empire. The Greeks wanted to be independent. Metternich, a supporter of strong rule, didn't want to help the Greeks. But other nations, including members of the Quadruple Alliance, sympathized with the Greeks. They identified with the Greeks' desire to have their own nation.

European nations forced the Ottoman Empire to grant Greece its independence in 1829. This failure of the Metternich system showed that the ideas of liberalism could not be held down forever. It also showed that a new idea was taking hold. This new idea was called nationalism.

PRACTICE 149: Metternich Versus Liberalism

Decide if each statement below is true (**T**) or false (**F**). Write the correct letter on the line before each statement.

_____ **1.** Liberalism is the belief in the principles of freedom and equality, the rule of laws under a constitution, and the right to revolt.

_____ **2.** Metternich was a liberal.

Nationalism

Nationalism is the desire of a people to have an independent nation. Nationalism is also sometimes defined as a love for one's country.

Nationalists want to have their own nation, free from the rule of a larger nation or empire. But nationalism did not start out this way. Nationalism actually started as a desire to be part of larger nations.

Before the French Revolution, most French people felt loyalty to their town or region. They didn't identify with the French nation as a whole. During the French Revolution, the people of France felt united for the first time. They banded together to fight for the ideals of the revolution. They felt pride in France as a whole, not just in their own part of France.

Nationalism spread throughout Europe. When Napoleon took over other countries, the conquered peoples banded together to drive out his armies. In this way, nationalist feelings grew wherever Napoleon's armies went—and that was through most of Europe.

THINK ABOUT IT

Nationalism is still one of the most powerful forces in the world today. It often leads to armed struggle. Recent examples of nationalist movements include those in Eritrea, Chechnya, and Serbia. In all of these movements, groups of people have wanted to break away from a larger country to become independent. What other nationalist movements have you heard of? Write your answer on a separate sheet of paper.

PRACTICE 150: Nationalism

Circle the letter of the correct answer to each of the following questions.

1. What is nationalism?
   - **a.** loyalty to a ruler
   - **b.** the desire of a people to have their own nation
   - **c.** a belief that all people in a nation should be equal
   - **d.** the desire of a ruler to expand his or her territories

2. When did nationalism take hold in Europe?
   a. the late 1500s and 1600s
   b. the late 1600s and 1700s
   c. the late 1700s and 1800s
   d. the late 1800s and 1900s

3. How did Napoleon's takeover of Europe affect nationalistic feelings?
   a. It increased them.
   b. It decreased them.
   c. It had no effect on them.
   d. It had different effects in different countries.

The Unification of Italy

Today we tend to think of the world as made up of countries. But this is a rather recent development. One of the most dramatic expressions of nationalism occurred in **Italy**.

In the early 1800s, the Italian peninsula was divided into many different kingdoms. During the French Revolution, the people of Italy supported the ideas of the French Revolution. They wanted to establish a liberal government with a constitution.

After the French Revolution ended, Napoleon came to power and conquered Italy. Although the Italians resented Napoleon's rule, they were united under one ruler. This helped them see themselves as one people. Feelings of nationalism spread. They wanted a free, unified Italy.

But after Napoleon's defeat, the Congress of Vienna returned the kings of the separate states to their thrones. Many of these kings were dominated by Austria and the Metternich system. They favored absolute monarchies and opposed liberalism.

In the 1830s, a man named **Giuseppe Mazzini** called for a unified, independent Italy. Inspired by Mazzini and others, Italians revolted in 1848. The revolutionaries wanted a united Italy with a liberal government, free from foreign control. Most of them failed, put down by the Austrian army. But there was one independent liberal Italian state known as **Sardinia-Piedmont**.

The prime minister of Sardinia-Piedmont was **Count Camillo Benso di Cavour.** Cavour tried to lead revolutionaries to drive Austria out of Italy. He was partially successful. The Austrians were not driven out. But Sardinia-Piedmont grew much larger. It became the most powerful state in Italy.

But the greatest leader of Italian unification was a general named **Giuseppe Garibaldi.** Garibaldi always wore a bright red shirt into battle. His army followed his lead, and were known as the **Red Shirts.** In 1860, Garibaldi, aided by Cavour, seized southern Italy. Later that year, elections were held through most of the Italian peninsula. The people voted to unify Italy under **Victor Emmanuel II,** the king of Sardinia-Piedmont. By 1870, the Italians gained control of the remaining parts of the Italian peninsula. They declared Rome their capital. Italy had become a free, united country.

■ PRACTICE 151: The Unification of Italy

Circle the letter of the correct answer to each of the following questions.

1. Who was the first major leader of the Italian unification movement?
- **a.** Mazzini
- **b.** Cavour
- **c.** Garibaldi
- **d.** Victor Emmanuel

2. What leader of Sardinia-Piedmont tried to drive Austria out of Italy?
- **a.** Mazzini
- **b.** Cavour
- **c.** Garibaldi
- **d.** Victor Emmanuel

3. Who is considered the greatest leader of Italian unification?
- **a.** Mazzini
- **b.** Cavour
- **c.** Garibaldi
- **d.** Victor Emmanuel

The Unification of Germany

In the mid-1800s, Germany, like Italy, was a land divided. It was a patchwork of many different states. One of these states was **Prussia.** Prussia had long been the strongest German state. And it had played an important role in defeating Napoleon. Now, as nationalist feelings spread, Prussia was poised to take the lead in unifying Germany.

In 1862, **Otto von Bismarck** became the head of the king's cabinet in Prussia. This powerful man became the real ruler of Prussia. More than any other individual, Bismarck achieved the unification of Germany. Bismarck increased the power of the Prussian army. It became the best fighting force in Europe. Meanwhile, in a series of complex political moves, Bismarck increased Prussian power.

Between 1864 and 1870, Prussia went to war three times. In the Danish War, Prussia conquered Denmark. In the Seven Weeks War, Prussia defeated Austria. And in the Franco-Prussian War, Prussia crushed France.

In 1871, Bismarck met with the leaders of the other German states. Prussia's victories had given him enough power to declare the creation of the German Empire. The capital of the German Empire was, not surprisingly, the Prussian capital of Berlin. The new emperor of the German Empire was King William I, also of Prussia. But the real power was held by Bismarck in his position as chancellor. He became known as the "Iron Chancellor" for his hard, militaristic outlook.

The German Empire was dominated by Prussia. But for the first time in history, Germany was a unified nation.

■ PRACTICE 152: The Unification of Germany

Circle the letter of the correct answer to each of the following questions.

1. What German state was the most powerful?
- **a.** the German Empire
- **b.** Bismarck
- **c.** Prussia
- **d.** Emmanuel

2. What position did Bismarck hold in the German Empire?
   a. emperor
   b. king
   c. chancellor
   d. dictator

Nationalism and Liberalism

Much of the history of Europe in the 1800s can be thought of as the spread of liberalism and nationalism. By 1900, nearly every European country had a constitution and some form of democratic government. The major exception was Russia, which retained an authoritarian government.

But most of Europe had changed. This great change had started with the French Revolution and its liberal ideas. Napoleon, who came to power in its wake, had unified Europe. His domination of Europe inspired liberal and nationalistic feelings throughout the continent. With his defeat, the Congress of Vienna tried to stop the spread of liberal ideas. The Metternich system worked for a while, but ultimately nationalism and liberalism triumphed in Europe.

■ PRACTICE 153: Nationalism and Liberalism

Circle the letters of the correct answers to each of the following questions. (*Hint:* Each question has more than one correct answer.)

1. Which of the following did nearly every European country have by 1900?
   a. a constitution
   b. a monarch
   c. a form of democratic government
   d. a Metternich system

2. What two movements dominated European history in the 1800s?
   a. communism
   b. liberalism
   c. Marxism
   d. nationalism

LESSON 25: Nationalism and Expansionism in the United States

GOAL: To trace the expansion of the United States' territory and to identify the steps in this expansion

WORDS TO KNOW

Addition of 1783
Alaskan Purchase
annexation
British Cession
cession
Florida Cession
49th parallel
free states
Gadsden Purchase
Indian Removal Act
Lewis and Clark expedition
Louisiana Purchase
manifest destiny
Mexican Cession
Mexican War
Northwest Ordinance
Oregon Country Cession
Red River Cession
slave states
state
territory
Texas Annexation
Trail of Tears
treaties
Treaty of Guadalupe Hidalgo

NAMES TO KNOW

James Gadsden
Thomas Jefferson
James Polk

PLACES TO KNOW

Louisiana
Oregon Country

Manifest Destiny

By the early 1800s, the United States was a powerful nation. Its political system and the revolution that had launched it were admired in Europe and elsewhere. It had a strong industrial base and a growing network of roads, canals, and railroads.

The first European settlers in North America wanted to push the boundaries of the colonies west, into the heart of the continent. American explorers headed west, with settlers close behind. This desire to expand a nation's territory is called expansionism.

By the 1840s, the United States controlled half the continent. A new feeling began to spread throughout the country. It was called manifest destiny. **Manifest destiny** was the belief that the United States was destined to control all the land from the Atlantic Coast to the Pacific Coast.

TIP

Once again, looking at each word in a term can help you understand the term's meaning. *Manifest* means "obvious" or, sometimes, "God-given." *Destiny* means "fate." So, *manifest destiny* means "an obvious fate" or "a fate coming from God."

PRACTICE 154: Manifest Destiny

Match each definition with a term from the list below. Write the letter of the correct term on the line before each definition.

a. expansionism **b.** manifest destiny

_____ **1.** the desire to expand a nation's territory

_____ **2.** the belief that the United States was destined to rule all the land from the Atlantic Coast to the Pacific Coast

The Addition of 1783 and the Louisiana Purchase

The American Revolution ended in 1783 with the signing of the Treaty of Paris between the United States and Great Britain. This treaty granted to the United States all of the land between the Atlantic Ocean and the Mississippi River, bordered by Canada to the north (which was owned by the British) and Florida to the south (which was owned by the Spanish). This huge tract of land is sometimes called the **Addition of 1783.** It more than doubled the size of the original 13 colonies.

The United States soon grew even larger. At the time, France controlled most of central North America. The French called this land **Louisiana.** U.S. President **Thomas Jefferson** viewed Louisiana as a threat to the United States. After all, France was ruled by Napoleon, who was determined to build an empire.

Jefferson arranged to purchase Louisiana from the French. Napoleon was willing to sell the land because France needed the money to fight wars in Europe. The U.S. government paid France about $15 million for Louisiana in 1803. This transaction was called the **Louisiana Purchase.**

The Louisiana Purchase was the biggest land purchase in history. It added more than 800,000 square miles to the United States. President Jefferson sent Meriwether Lewis and William Clark to explore this new territory. Their journey is known as the **Lewis and Clark expedition.**

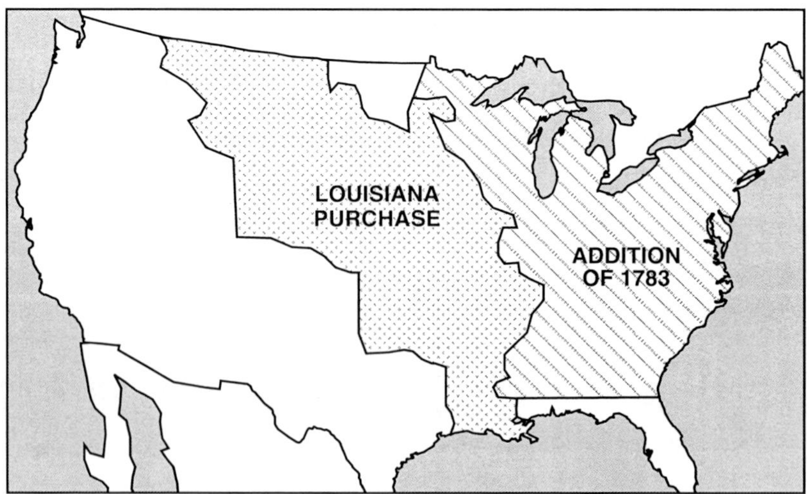

The Addition of 1783 and the Louisiana Purchase

■ PRACTICE 155: The Addition of 1783 and the Louisiana Purchase

Check each statement below that is TRUE.

☐ **1.** The Treaty of Paris granted the United States the Addition of 1783.

☐ **2.** Napoleon sold Louisiana to help the United States.

☐ **3.** The Louisiana Purchase was the biggest land purchase in history.

The British Cession and the Florida Cession

The next addition to American territory was the **British Cession** of 1818. It is also called the **Red River Cession**. A **cession** is something that is surrendered or given. The Red River Cession was part of a treaty the United States reached with Britain in 1818.

The treaty also established the **49th parallel** as the northern boundary of the United States. Today, this line forms the border between the United States and Canada.

The very next year, in 1819, the United States also received a cession from Spain. The **Florida Cession** gave Florida to the United States. At this point, the country was about half of the size it is today.

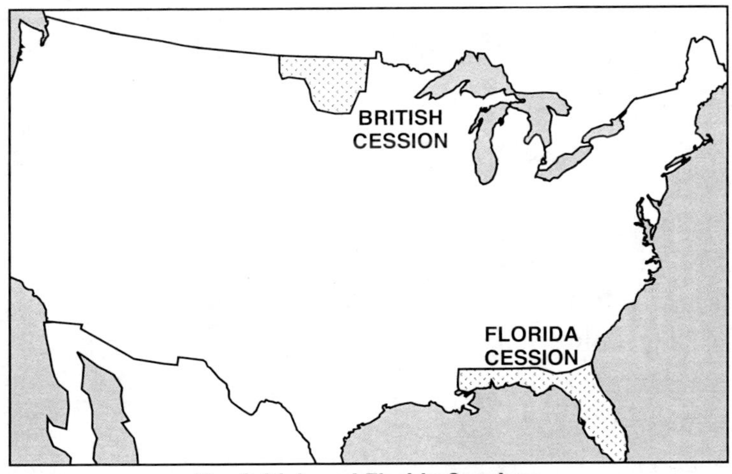

The British and Florida Cessions

■ PRACTICE 156: The British Cession and the Florida Cession

Match each description with a term from the list below. Write the letter of the correct term on the line before each description.

a. Red River Cession **b.** 1819 **c.** 1818 **d.** Spain

_____ **1.** year of the British Cession

_____ **2.** another name for the British Cession

_____ **3.** year of the Florida Cession

_____ **4.** country that the Florida Cession was acquired from

The Texas Annexation and the Mexican Cession

During the 1830s, large numbers of Americans had settled in Texas, which was then part of Mexico. (Mexico had gained its independence from Spain in 1821.) Then in 1835, these "Texicans" revolted against Mexican rule. And in 1836, they proclaimed Texas as an independent country. Texas struggled to survive as an independent nation. But after ten years, it entered the United States. The addition of the Texas Territory to the United States in 1845 is called the **Texas Annexation**. An **annexation** is an addition.

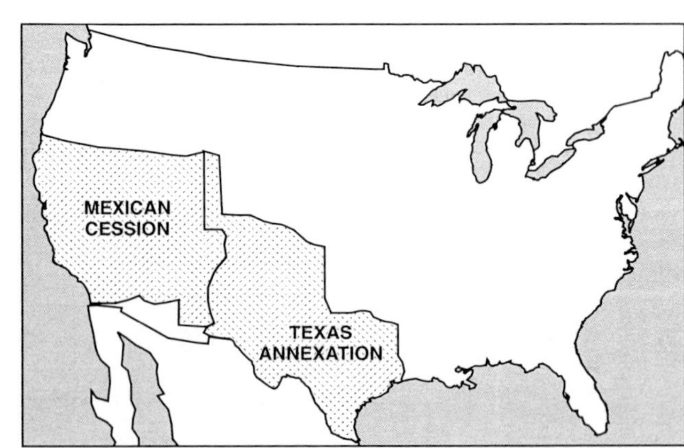

The Texas Annexation and the Mexican Cession

In 1848, the United States again added a large piece of what was once Mexico to its territory. Two years earlier, in 1846, President **James Polk** had declared war on Mexico. This conflict became known as the **Mexican War**.

The war started when President Polk sent soldiers into land that both Mexico and the United States claimed. The United States quickly defeated the weaker Mexican forces. The war was ended by the **Treaty of Guadalupe Hidalgo** in 1848. This treaty granted a huge tract of Mexican land to the United States. This land is called the **Mexican Cession.** (See the map on page 294.)

■ PRACTICE 157: The Texas Annexation and the Mexican Cession

Circle the letter of the correct answer to each of the following questions.

1. Which European country owned Texas before it became part of the United States?
   - **a.** France
   - **b.** Mexico
   - **c.** Spain
   - **d.** Portugal

2. How did the United States acquire the Mexican Cession?
   - **a.** by offering to buy it from Mexico
   - **b.** by accepting it as a gift from Mexico
   - **c.** by going to war with Mexico
   - **d.** by going to war with Spain

The Oregon Country Cession

Today, you know Oregon as a state in the northwestern United States. But in the 1840s, this region was called the Oregon Country. The Oregon Country was controlled by the British. Still, large numbers of Americans had settled there.

By this time, the idea of manifest destiny had captured the American imagination. The Americans demanded that the Oregon Country be turned over to the United States. The British did little to resist. It was of little value to them, and it was not worth fighting the United States in order to keep it. In 1846, the British gave the region to the United States in the **Oregon Country Cession.** The northern boundary of this cession was an extension of the 49th parallel, which had formed the northern boundary of Britain's 1818 cession. However, the British retained control of the large island of Vancouver off the coast of what is now the state of Washington and part of Canada.

The Oregon Country Cession

With the Oregon Country Cession, the United States for the first time stretched all the way across North America.

■ PRACTICE 158: The Oregon Country Cession

Circle the letter of the correct answer to each of the following questions.

1. From which country did the United States obtain the Oregon Country Cession?

- **a.** France
- **b.** Mexico
- **c.** Britain
- **d.** Spain

2. Which statement about the Oregon Country Cession is TRUE?

- **a.** It was the first cession obtained by the United States.
- **b.** It was obtained by the United States through warfare.
- **c.** It was the first cession that stretched the United States to the Pacific Ocean.
- **d.** It came as a result of the Mexican War.

The Gadsden Purchase, the Alaskan Purchase, and Hawaii

As you have already learned, the Mexican War was a fight between the United States and Mexico over land that both claimed was their own. The

Treaty of Guadalupe Hidalgo, which ended the Mexican War, was unclear about the exact border between the United States and Mexico. In the early 1850s, the United States representative to Mexico, **James Gadsden,** entered negotiations with the Mexican president Antonio Santa Anna to resolve this border question. Santa Anna agreed to sell the disputed area to the United States for $10 million. This became known as the **Gadsden Purchase.** With the Gadsden Purchase, the southern United States took on the familiar boundaries it has today.

Alaska was purchased in 1867 from Russia for $7.2 million. This transaction was called the **Alaskan Purchase.** The kingdom of the Hawaiian Islands was annexed in 1898 as the territory of Hawaii.

Take a moment to review the maps in this lesson. As you can see, the United States expanded quickly from east to west.

■ PRACTICE 159: The Gadsden Purchase, the Alaskan Purchase, and Hawaii

Circle the letter of the correct answer to each of the following questions.

1. Which of the following came first?
- **a.** the Alaskan Purchase
- **b.** the annexation of Hawaii
- **c.** the Gadsden Purchase
- **d.** the Louisiana Purchase

2. In which direction did the United States expand?
- **a.** west to east
- **b.** north to south
- **c.** south to north
- **d.** east to west

Territories and States

As you have read, the territory of the United States grew in three main ways: by annexation, by purchase, and by cession. All of this land eventually became parts of different states.

Most of these lands were territories before they became states. A **territory** is an area owned and governed by the United States that is eligible to become a state. A **state** is a political unit of the United States that has special powers.

In 1787, the U.S. government passed a law called the **Northwest Ordinance.** Under this law, a territory could become a state once it had a population of at least 60,000. These settlers could then petition the national government to make their territory a state. If the government approved the request, the territory had to submit a proposed state constitution. Only when this constitution was approved by the people of the territory and by the U.S. government could the government decide to accept the new state.

You might think that the United States, with its belief in manifest destiny, was always eager to accept new states. But in the mid-1800s, the admission of new states was highly controversial. Why? The answer is that at that time, states had to declare themselves as either **slave states,** where slavery was legal, or **free states,** where it was illegal. To maintain a balance of power, it was important to keep the number of slave states and free states balanced.

IN REAL LIFE

Do you know the two most recent territories to become states? They are Alaska and Hawaii; both became states in 1959. As of 2005, the United States still has territories that have not yet been accepted as states. They include Guam, part of the Virgin Islands, and Puerto Rico. Many people think that Puerto Rico should become the 51st state.

PRACTICE 160: Territories and States

Match each definition with a term from the list below. Write the letter of the correct term on the line before each definition.

a. territory **b.** state **c.** slave states **d.** free states

_____ **1.** states where slavery was illegal

_____ **2.** an area of land owned and governed by the United States that is eligible to become a state

_____ **3.** states where slavery was legal

_____ **4.** a political unit of the United States that has special powers

Treatment of Native Americans

As you have learned, the United States grew by obtaining land from Mexico, France, Britain, and Spain. But most of the land the United States obtained was already populated by Native Americans, or Indians.

Native Americans had been living in North America for at least 10,000 years. When the United States took control of their lands, it—like the European powers before it—treated the Indians harshly. In fact, the treatment of Indians as America grew west is one of the ugliest stories in American history.

The United States government made **treaties,** or agreements, with Native American peoples. Generally, these treaties promised the Indians that they would be left alone if they moved farther west, away from lands that American settlers wanted. But the United States broke treaty after treaty.

The **Indian Removal Act,** a law passed in 1830, allowed the president to move all Native Americans living east of the Mississippi River to the other side of the river. The goal was to free more land for American settlers. At the time, the Americans thought the land west of the Mississippi River was of little value.

From 1830 to about 1840, the U.S. government forced about 70,000 Native Americans on long, hard marches to the lands west of the Mississippi. These cruel marches resulted in the deaths of men, women, and children. One of the worst of these involved the Cherokee Nation of Georgia. It began in 1838. The U.S. Army rounded up Cherokee men, women, and children. The Cherokee were forced to march 1,000 miles west from their homes. They walked all through a severe winter, without enough food. About 4,000 Cherokee died on the way. This forced march came to be known as the **Trail of Tears.**

By about 1850, all of the surviving Indians who had lived in the eastern United States had been pushed onto lands beyond the Mississippi.

But Native Americans still weren't free from the pressures of westward expansion. By the 1870s, the United States no longer recognized Native American groups as independent peoples. It placed them under the control of the U.S. government. Thousands of Indians were killed, and as many pushed off their lands. By 1900, most Native Americans were confined to small reservations, far from their homelands.

PRACTICE 161: Treatment of Native Americans

Circle the letter of the correct answer to each of the following questions.

1. Which word best describes, in general, the U.S. government's treatment of Native Americans?
- **a.** kind
- **b.** neutral
- **c.** harsh
- **d.** loving

2. What was the Trail of Tears?
- **a.** the entire story of Native American treatment by the United States
- **b.** a battle with the Cherokee
- **c.** the march west that the Cherokee were forced to make
- **d.** an oral account of Native American life

3. By 1900, where did most Native Americans live?
- **a.** in their traditional homelands
- **b.** on reservations
- **c.** along the eastern seaboard
- **d.** on the Trail of Tears

LESSON 26: Slavery and Suffrage

GOAL: To discuss how slavery in the United States was abolished and how women gained the right to vote

WORDS TO KNOW

abolition movement

abolitionists

American Civil War

American Colonization Society

American Woman Suffrage Association

Emancipation Proclamation

National Woman Suffrage Association

Nineteenth Amendment

secede

Seneca Falls Convention

suffrage

suffragists

Thirteenth Amendment

women's movement

NAMES TO KNOW

Susan B. Anthony

Frederick Douglass

Abraham Lincoln

Lucretia Mott

Elizabeth Cady Stanton

Lucy Stone

PLACES TO KNOW

Liberia

North

South

Slavery in the United States

Slavery existed in America since almost the moment the Europeans discovered the continent. Between the 1500s and the 1800s, 12 million Africans were shipped to the Americas as slaves. About 600,000 enslaved Africans were shipped to North America.

By 1860, there were about four million slaves in the **South,** or the southern United States. By this time, slavery had divided the country.

Cries against slavery had been raised during the American Revolution. People wondered how a country could fight to be free while keeping so many people in bondage.

In the early 1800s, **abolitionists**—people who worked to abolish slavery—mounted a powerful campaign. Their fight to end slavery is called the **abolition movement.** One of the most eloquent abolitionists was a former slave, **Frederick Douglass.** Douglass was a brilliant public speaker, an author, and a tireless worker for abolition.

One group, the **American Colonization Society,** tried not only to free enslaved Africans, but also to return them to Africa. They helped found the colony of **Liberia** (now a country) in Africa for freed slaves.

The abolition movement slowly but surely spread throughout the **North,** or the northern United States. The North was an industrial region made up of free states. But in the South, the abolition movement was fiercely opposed. The South was an agricultural region. It saw slavery as vital to its agricultural economy.

Actually, most southerners were not slaveholders. But the rich and powerful slaveholders controlled the economy and the governments of the southern states.

Government representatives from the South wanted new states to be slave states; northern representatives wanted them to be free. These disagreements over slavery were echoed by other conflicts between the North and South.

With the election of **Abraham Lincoln** as president in 1860, the conflict reached a breaking point. Several southern states decided to **secede,** or withdraw, from the country. The **American Civil War** had begun.

As you know, the North won the Civil War. While war still raged in 1863, President Lincoln issued the **Emancipation Proclamation.** This document declared many slaves of the South to be free. In 1865, at the close of the war, the **Thirteenth Amendment** was added to the United States Constitution. It completely abolished slavery in the United States.

THINK ABOUT IT

Slavery has been part of the history of many countries from the earliest days of civilization. But only the United States had a civil war over slavery. What else might the United States have done to end slavery? Write your answer on a separate sheet of paper.

PRACTICE 162: Slavery in the United States

Check each statement below that is TRUE.

- ☐ **1.** The fight to free the slaves was called the freedom movement.
- ☐ **2.** Frederick Douglass was a famous abolitionist and a former slave.
- ☐ **3.** The Thirteenth Amendment abolished slavery.
- ☐ **4.** The Emancipation Proclamation freed all slaves in the United States.

The Growth of Women's Rights

You have learned how Native Americans and African Americans suffered during the 1800s. A third class of Americans, women, was also treated poorly.

As you know, women had been generally viewed as inferior to men for centuries. They lacked many of the basic rights that men had, including the right to own property and to participate in political affairs. But as the new ideas of the Enlightenment took hold, women began to fight for their rights. Their struggle to gain social and political power is known as the **women's movement.**

In the United States, the women's movement focused on giving women the right to vote, or **suffrage**. Those who fought for suffrage were called **suffragists.** Suffragists thought that voting was the key to advancing women's rights. If women could vote, they could use their votes to gain other rights.

Two of the most outspoken advocates of women's rights were **Lucretia Mott** and **Elizabeth Cady Stanton.** In 1848, these two brave women organized a women's rights convention in Seneca Falls, New York. The **Seneca Falls Convention** called for equal rights for women in all areas. Its declaration was modeled on the Declaration of Independence, stating: "We hold these truths to be self-evident: that all men and women are created equal. . . . " (The original Declaration did not mention women.)

Elizabeth Cady Stanton

After the Civil War, the women's movement was reenergized. Rights had been extended to former slaves who were men. It seemed reasonable to extend them to women as well. **Susan B. Anthony,** with Stanton, led the **National Woman Suffrage Association.** She made national news when she was arrested for trying to vote. Another suffragist, **Lucy Stone,** led the **American Woman Suffrage Association.** In 1890, the two groups joined.

This new organization made great progress. By 1920, 15 western states had granted women the right to vote. But it was not until 1920, with the passage of the **Nineteenth Amendment** to the Constitution, that women all over the United States finally gained the right to vote.

Susan B. Anthony

■ PRACTICE 163: The Growth of Women's Rights

Decide if each statement is true (**T**) or false (**F**). Write the letter of the correct answer on the line before each statement.

_____ **1.** The right to vote is called suffrage.

_____ **2.** Susan B. Anthony organized the Seneca Falls Convention.

_____ **3.** The Nineteenth Amendment gave women the right to vote.

UNIT 7 REVIEW

Circle the letter of the correct answer to each of the following questions.

1. Who is "the father of modern economics"?
   a. Thomas Malthus
   b. David Ricardo
   c. Karl Marx
   d. Adam Smith

2. What did the Factory Act do?
   a. set limits on working hours
   b. set limits on the age of employees
   c. both *a* and *b*
   d. outlawed unions

3. Which of the following was a principle of the Congress of Vienna?
   a. compensation
   b. balance of power
   c. a weakened France
   d. all of the above

4. What did Metternich and the Metternich system support?
   a. liberalism
   b. absolute monarchies
   c. constitutions
   d. freedom for all peoples

5. How did Napoleon's takeover of Europe affect nationalistic feelings?
   a. It increased them.
   b. It decreased them.
   c. It had no effect on them.
   d. It suppressed them.

6. Who arranged the Louisiana Purchase?
   a. Lewis and Clark
   b. James Polk
   c. Andrew Jackson
   d. Thomas Jefferson

7. Which of the following expanded American territory to the Pacific Ocean?
   a. the Mexican Cession
   b. the Louisiana Purchase
   c. the Texas Annexation
   d. the Oregon Country Cession

8. What was the Trail of Tears?
   a. the march west that eastern Native Americans were forced to make
   b. the entire story of Indian treatment by the United States
   c. a battle with Native American groups
   d. a trail through Oklahoma

9. What was the fight to free the slaves called?
   a. the freedom movement
   b. the abolition movement
   c. the Emancipation Proclamation
   d. the liberal movement

10. Who organized the Seneca Falls Convention?
   a. Elizabeth Cady Stanton
   b. Lucretia Mott
   c. Susan B. Anthony
   d. both *a* and *b*

UNIT 7 APPLICATION ACTIVITY
The Four "Isms" of Economics

In your reading, you have learned about many "isms." They include socialism, Marxism, capitalism, and communism. Each of these represents a belief system about how an economy should operate.

The four "isms" are listed in the chart below. Use the library or the Internet to help gather information about each one. Who were the great thinkers who developed each system? What are the main features of each system? Enter this information into the chart.

	Main thinkers	**Main features**
socialism		
Marxism		
capitalism		
communism		

When the chart is complete, review the main features of each system. Which "ism" agrees the most with your own beliefs? On a separate sheet of paper, write a paragraph explaining which system you agree with and why.

UNIT 8

Imperialism

LESSON 27: The Age of Imperialism and Imperialism in Africa

GOAL: To describe the major causes of the Age of Imperialism; to discuss economic, military, and political imperialism in Africa

WORDS TO KNOW

Age of Imperialism

Age of Nationalism

armed resistance

colonialism

economic imperialism

imperialism

military imperialism

peaceful resistance

political imperialism

"scramble for Africa"

NAMES TO KNOW

Leopold II

Cecil Rhodes

PLACES TO KNOW

Algeria

Belgian Congo

Cape Colony

Congo Free State

Congo River

Egypt

Rhodesia

Suez Canal

EVENTS TO KNOW

Berlin Conference

Boer War

Imperialism

In the 1800s, nationalist feelings swept Europe. Nationalism is the desire of a people to have an independent country. Nationalism became so very important that this period of European history is often called the **Age of Nationalism.** Many countries, such as Germany and Italy, became unified nations for the first time in history. Nationalistic spirit also led the United States to expand from a small area on the east coast of North America to a huge country that spanned the continent.

But nationalism is more than a people's desire to have an independent country. Nationalism is also a fierce pride in that country. This feeling is similar to patriotism, which is perhaps best defined as love for one's own country.

In the Europe of the 1800s, these feelings of pride and love of country took many forms. People celebrated national holidays, honored national flags, and sang national songs. They also fought wars to protect their nations' borders and to protect their nations' honor.

THINK ABOUT IT

Feelings of patriotism are not confined to Europe in the 1800s. They are still very much with us today. In the early 2000s, for example, the war in Iraq brought out patriotic feelings in many Americans. Patriotism is also emphasized during U.S. presidential elections. Presidential candidates use patriotic words and images to try to win favor with the voters. Do you consider yourself patriotic? Why or why not? Write your answer on a separate sheet of paper.

Another way that people expressed nationalist and patriotic feelings is through expansionism. Expansionism is the desire and attempt to expand a country's territory. The United States expanded by conquering, buying, and negotiating for additional territory. Many of the countries in Europe expanded through **colonialism,** or the establishment of colonies in other lands.

When nationalism, patriotism, expansionism, and colonialism all combine, the result is imperialism. **Imperialism** is a country's desire and attempts to dominate other nations and peoples.

In the late 1800s, many nations of Europe became imperialistic. To one degree or another, these nations tried to take over countries all around the world.

■ PRACTICE 164: Imperialism

Match each definition with a term from the list below. Write the letter of the correct term on the line before each definition.

a. nationalism **b.** patriotism **c.** expansionism **d.** imperialism

_____ **1.** a fierce pride in one's country

_____ **2.** a country's desire and attempts to dominate other nations and peoples

_____ **3.** the desire and attempt to expand a country's territory

_____ **4.** a love for one's own country

The Age of Imperialism

In the late 1800s, imperialistic policies became so widespread in Europe that this period is sometimes called the **Age of Imperialism.**

There were several reasons for the imperialistic policies of these European nations. First, feelings of nationalism and patriotism led people to think that their country was superior—the greatest one on Earth. They wanted to expand in order to express and spread their greatness.

Second, Europeans in the late 1800s thought that a country's greatness depended largely on its size. So, they followed imperialistic policies to increase the size of their countries. For example, Belgium came to control a territory in Africa that was 80 times larger than the country of Belgium itself.

A third reason for imperialism was the chance for more wealth. By controlling foreign territory and nations, the countries of Europe also controlled the natural resources of those lands, such as diamonds, gold, or timber. Often, Europeans wanted these natural resources to supply the industries in their home countries. The people of the foreign territory also became a kind of resource: They were a source of cheap labor, and a market for European exports.

Strategy was a fourth reason for imperialism. By controlling foreign ports, the countries of Europe had bases for their warships and merchant ships.

Finally, imperialism was encouraged by racism. The white peoples of Europe, as a rule, thought themselves superior to the peoples of the countries they took over.

The most successful European imperialistic countries were Belgium, Britain, France, Germany, Italy, the Netherlands, Portugal, and Spain.

PRACTICE 165: The Age of Imperialism

Circle the letter of the correct answer to each of the following questions.

1. Which of the following was a reason for European imperialistic policies?
- **a.** nationalism
- **b.** size
- **c.** wealth
- **d.** all of the above

2. Which of these European countries was imperialistic?
- **a.** the Netherlands
- **b.** Portugal
- **c.** Italy
- **d.** all of the above

Africa: Military and Economic Imperialism

Nowhere was the Age of Imperialism more dramatically demonstrated than in Africa. Put simply, European countries took over the continent in the late 1800s and early 1900s. Belgium, Britain, France, Germany, Italy, Portugal, and Spain all became major imperial powers in Africa.

Europeans had been trading with Africans since the 1400s. Over the centuries, as sailing skills and ships improved, trade increased. Much of this trade had included enslaved Africans. But in the 1800s, many of these countries outlawed slavery. The slave trade rapidly diminished.

Trade in other goods, however, continued to grow. The desire to trade in Africa was one of the main reasons for European imperialism there. Another reason was that Africa was geographically close to Europe. A third reason was that Africa was extremely rich in natural resources. Europeans wanted those natural resources for their own.

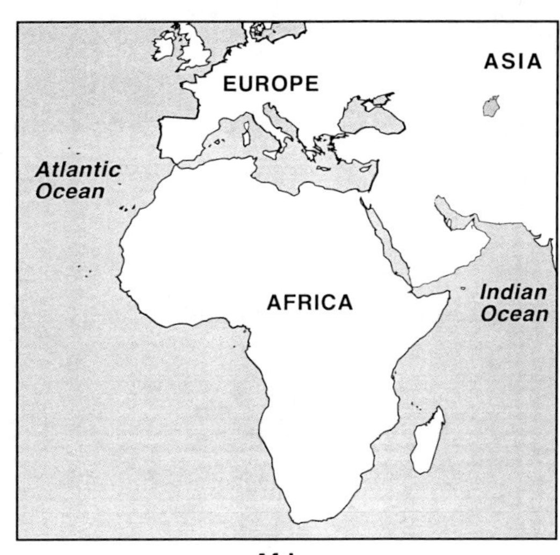

Africa

In taking over Africa, the Europeans relied on three approaches: economic imperialism, military imperialism, and political imperialism. **Economic imperialism** involves taking over countries economically. **Military imperialism** involves taking control of countries militarily. **Political imperialism** involves taking over or manipulating foreign governments.

As European trade with Africa increased, so did European economic power in the continent. As economic power increased, so did political power. When economic power failed, Europeans did not hesitate to use their superior military power, such as firearms and powerful warships, to take over.

In the 1800s, Africa was not organized into strong, large countries, as Europe was. Instead, it was a land of tribes—hundreds of them. Because these tribes were smaller than the European nations, the Europeans were more powerful. Europeans took over the continent, tribe by tribe. In order to do this, the Europeans often took advantage of traditional rivalries between tribes. They easily overcame the resistance of small tribes through economic, military, or political means. The European powers quickly came to control most of Africa.

By 1914, European countries controlled almost all of the huge African continent. In fact, in that year there were only two independent nations left: Liberia in the west and Ethiopia in the east.

■ PRACTICE 166: Africa: Military and Economic Imperialism

Match each definition with a term from the list below. Write the letter of the correct term on the line before each definition.

a. economic imperialism **c.** military imperialism
b. political imperialism **d.** 1914

_____ **1.** the year of the greatest European control of Africa

_____ **2.** the taking control of countries militarily

_____ **3.** the taking over or manipulation of foreign governments

_____ **4.** the taking over of countries economically

Economic Imperialism in Central Africa

A good example of economic imperialism is Belgium's colony in central Africa. Belgium's colony was one of the largest colonies in Africa. It was located right in the middle of the continent. For years, it was the personal property of the king of Belgium.

Belgium was the second country in Europe (after Britain) to industrialize. With this industrialization came economic strength. Throughout the 1800s, Belgium increased its economic power through foreign trade. By the late 1800s, Belgium was a major trading nation.

Much of Belgium's trade was with Africa. In 1878, the king of Belgium, **Leopold II**, directed that Belgian trading posts be set up along the **Congo River** in central Africa. Leopold was mostly interested in the rubber trees that grew in the region. In 1885, the other nations of Europe recognized the region as the personal property of Leopold. He called the colony the **Congo Free State**.

This is an example of imperialism at its worst. The Europeans, so confident of their superiority, simply took Africa as if it were uninhabited and theirs for the taking.

In the Congo "Free" State, the African peoples were anything but free. They were virtually enslaved, and were forced to gather rubber. Thousands died under the harsh treatment.

In 1908, the Belgian government took over the Congo Free State from Leopold. This was largely a result of the protests of people in Britain and the United States over Leopold's harsh treatment of the people there. The Belgian government renamed the colony the **Belgian Congo.**

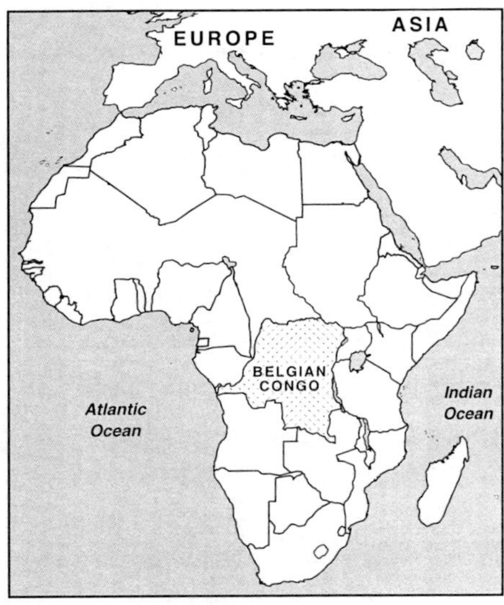

The Belgian Congo

The Belgian Congo remained Belgian property until 1960. The colony provided Belgium great wealth in the form of rubber, diamonds, gold, and other natural resources. Treatment of the Africans there improved somewhat. But for decades, they remained under the control of Belgian rulers.

■ PRACTICE 167: Economic Imperialism in Central Africa

Circle the letter of the correct answer to each of the following questions.

1. What kind of imperialism did Belgium use to take over central Africa?

- **a.** economic
- **b.** military
- **c.** political
- **d.** democratic

2. Who owned the Congo Free State?

- **a.** the Belgian government
- **b.** Leopold II
- **c.** the people of the Congo Free State
- **d.** the British government

Military and Economic Imperialism in Northern Africa

A good example of military imperialism is what took place in northern Africa. For 300 years, most of northern Africa had been controlled by the Ottoman Empire, based in Turkey. But the Ottoman Empire weakened in the 1700s and 1800s. European powers saw their chance to gain control of this valuable land.

In 1830, France invaded **Algeria,** in northern Africa. The French armies were successful, and Algeria became a part of France. But many of the people of Algeria were no happier being ruled by France than they had been under the Ottoman Empire. In 1847, many Algerians revolted against French rule. Their leader was a general and Muslim religious leader named Abd al-Qadir. But al-Qadir's forces were no match for the powerful French armies. Despite repeated revolts against French rule, the French came to control all of Algeria.

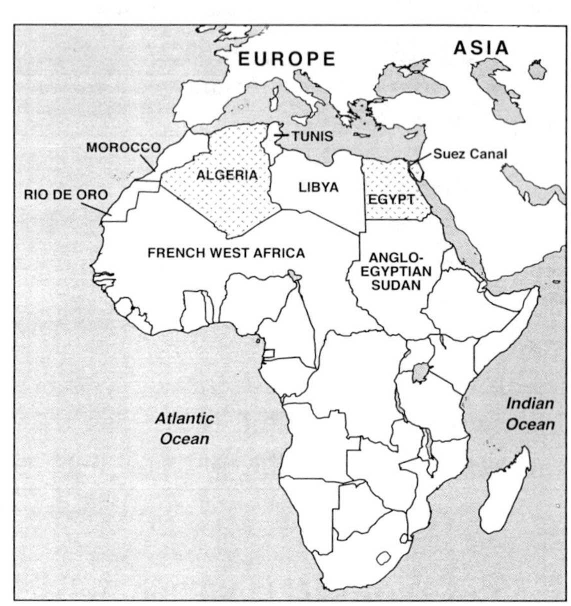

Algeria and Egypt

French control of Africa went beyond Algeria. By 1914, France controlled almost half of the continent. Most of its holdings were in the north and the west.

The British also controlled part of northern Africa. They took over **Egypt,** east of Algeria. Like the French, the British depended on military force. They also used economic imperialism.

Egypt had been controlled by the Ottoman Empire since 1517. A Turkish (Ottoman) officer named Muhammad Ali became Egypt's leader. He maintained Egypt's independence. But the rulers who followed Ali were not as successful. By the 1870s, Egypt was heavily in debt.

The British took advantage of Egypt's desperate financial situation by buying a controlling interest in the Suez Canal. The **Suez Canal** is a canal that connects the Mediterranean Sea to the Red Sea. It was important to the British because it cut a full 6,000 miles off the voyage of ships traveling between Britain and the British colony of India. Thus, Britain took control of a highly strategic part of Egypt.

The purchase of the Suez Canal gave Britain a great deal of influence in Egypt. British merchants, diplomats, and army officers were in close contact with Egypt's rulers. But many people in Egypt resented the British presence. When the Egyptians began to attack British people in Egypt, the British army invaded.

In 1882, the British defeated rebel Egyptian forces. From then on, Britain was in control of Egypt. Technically, the Egyptian government still ruled Egypt. But in reality, power was held behind the scenes by the British. This was an example of military imperialism.

THINK ABOUT IT

You have read that European nations had several reasons for following imperialistic policies: nationalistic pride, strategy, wealth, and so on. Review those pages. Then answer this question. Which of these motives seems most important in the British takeover of Egypt? Write your answer on a separate sheet of paper.

PRACTICE 168: Military and Economic Imperialism in Northern Africa

Circle the letter of the correct answer to each of the following questions.

1. Who came to control Algeria?
- **a.** Britain
- **b.** the Ottomans
- **c.** France
- **d.** Turkey

2. Why was the Suez Canal important to the British?
   a. It reduced the time it took to travel to India.
   b. It gave Britain control of Egypt.
   c. It gave Britain control of Algeria.
   d. none of the above

Military and Economic Imperialism in Southern Africa

In southern Africa, the Dutch followed imperialist policies to expand their control. The Dutch first established a trading station and fort near the Cape of Good Hope in 1652. It soon grew into a large settlement, called the **Cape Colony**.

Dutch settlers in the Cape Colony became farmers. They were called *Boers,* which is the Dutch word for *farmer.* As more and more Boers settled in southern Africa, they took over more and more land for farming. Using force, they took the land from the Africans. They forced many Africans to work as slaves.

In 1814, Britain took the Cape Colony from the Dutch by force. Within a few years, British settlers began arriving in large numbers. They made English the official language of the Cape Colony.

The Boers resented British rule. The British had freed their slaves. They set limits on the amount of land the Boers could own. To escape British rule, the Boers traveled farther inland and northward. They defeated any Africans who stood in their way and took their land.

The British were content to let the Boers go. They recognized the Boers' new lands as independent colonies. But when gold and diamonds were found on Boer land, the situation changed. British settlers streamed into Boer areas, hoping for wealth. Eventually, the Boers and the British came to blows. In the **Boer War,** the British defeated the Boers and took the Boer lands as British colonies.

The British also used force to defeat the Zulu and other African tribes in the area. In 1910, with the region firmly in British hands, Britain created the Union of South Africa, which is now the Republic of South Africa.

One of the most colorful figures of this era was a man named **Cecil Rhodes.** In the 1880s and 1890s, Rhodes was a leader of the Cape Colony. He was extremely rich. He had gained fantastic wealth by controlling diamond mines in southern Africa. Rhodes was largely responsible for the attacks on the Dutch that led to the Boer War.

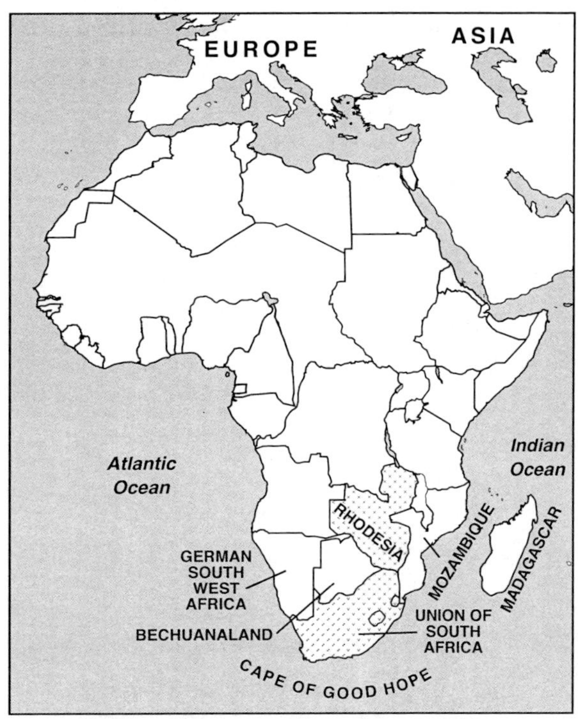

Rhodesia and the Union of South Africa

Rhodes also engineered the takeover of vast tracts of the Matabele tribe's lands. He tricked the Matabele ruler into an agreement that gave Rhodes mining rights. Rhodes secured this land in his role as the leading official of the British South Africa Company. The land was called **Rhodesia** in his honor.

Rhodesia became an independent country in 1965. Later, to symbolize its African heritage and freedom from colonial rule, the country changed its name to Zimbabwe.

IN REAL LIFE

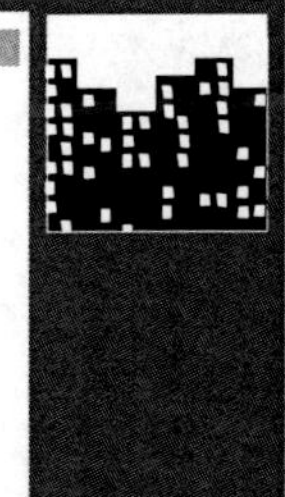

Have you ever heard someone described as a "Rhodes Scholar"? A Rhodes Scholar is an individual who has been awarded a scholarship to study at Oxford University in England. The scholarship is named for Cecil Rhodes, who attended Oxford and left the money to fund the program. You may not know any Rhodes Scholars personally, but you've heard of at least one: President Bill Clinton.

■ PRACTICE 169: Military and Economic Imperialism in Southern Africa

Circle the letter of the correct answer to each of the following questions.

1. What European nation first settled southern Africa?
   a. Britain
   b. the Netherlands
   c. Belgium
   d. France

2. Who were the Boers?
   a. British imperialists
   b. French settlers
   c. southern African tribes
   d. Dutch farmers

3. Who came to control South Africa?
   a. the Netherlands
   b. France
   c. Britain
   d. the Boers

The Berlin Conference and the "Scramble for Africa"

As you have read, France, the Netherlands, and Britain took over large parts of Africa. But they were not the only European countries to claim parts of Africa for themselves. Germany claimed a large part of eastern Africa. Italy also claimed a part of eastern Africa, as well as Libya in northern Africa. Portugal controlled large parts of southern Africa. Spain claimed several different areas of northern Africa.

These European countries competed with one another to control Africa. In 1884 and 1885, representatives of six of these nations met in Berlin, in Germany. Their meeting was called the **Berlin Conference.**

The purpose of the Berlin Conference was for the European countries to agree on the colonial boundaries in Africa. No Africans attended the conference. These six European nations were so confident of their right and ability to control Africa that they divided a whole continent among themselves—and did not consult any Africans in the process.

The Europeans' attempt to colonize Africa and keep it for themselves is called the "**scramble for Africa.**" For most of the 1800s, European settlement in Africa had been limited mostly to the coast. In the 1880s, however, they scrambled to control the entire continent. By 1914, European nations controlled all but two countries in Africa (Liberia and Ethiopia).

PRACTICE 170: The Berlin Conference and the "Scramble for Africa"

Circle the letter of the correct answer to each of the following questions.

1. How many Africans attended the Berlin Conference?
- **a.** at least one from each African state
- **b.** one from each African region
- **c.** none
- **d.** 19

2. What was the "scramble for Africa"?
- **a.** Europeans' attempts to colonize and keep Africa
- **b.** a war between the British and the Dutch in Africa
- **c.** an effort by the British to gain control of northern Africa
- **d.** Britain's purchase of the Suez Canal

African Responses to European Imperialism

When they took over Africa, European countries wanted to express their nationalistic spirit by increasing the size of their empires. They wanted Africa's abundant natural resources, such as timber, rubber, diamonds, and gold. They wanted land to make into plantations. They wanted cheap labor. To a lesser extent, they also wanted to spread their culture and their Christian religion. Occasionally, the Europeans were genuinely welcomed. Usually, however, they faced resistance, both armed and peaceful.

The Africans took to **armed resistance** many times and in many places. Occasionally, they won great battles. For example, the British were astonished by their defeat at the hands of the Zulu people in southern Africa. But the Europeans had more soldiers, better equipment, and nearly limitless wealth to pour into wars of conquest. Despite heroic African opposition, the Europeans eventually put down most armed resistance.

Africans also used **peaceful resistance.** They turned to this after their lands had been taken over. Educated Africans shared ideas about freedom, democracy, and independence. They organized strikes against colonial governments and plantations. They opened schools for African children. They formed political groups and spoke out against the injustices of colonial rule. Their success was limited, but the seeds of independence had been planted. Eventually, the Africans were able to throw off the European colonial yoke and become independent peoples once again.

THINK ABOUT IT

Imagine yourself living in an African village in the 1800s. Colonial rulers come to your village. They try to force you and your family to work for them on a plantation. They insist that your children adopt their religion. How would you feel? What would you do? Write your answers on a separate sheet of paper.

PRACTICE 171: African Responses to European Imperialism

Decide if each statement below is true (**T**) or false (**F**). Write the correct letter on the line before each statement.

_____ **1.** Africans often responded to European colonization efforts with armed resistance.

_____ **2.** Africans did not use peaceful resistance.

LESSON 28: Empire-Building in Southern Asia

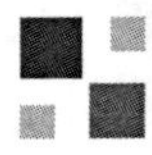

GOAL: To explain how Britain, France, and the Netherlands came to control large areas of southern Asia

WORDS TO KNOW

British India

Indian National Congress

religious imperialism

PLACES TO KNOW

Burma

Dutch East Indies

French Indochina

Indochina

Indonesia

Malay Peninsula

Netherlands Indies

Singapore

Southeast Asian Peninsula

Strait of Malacca

Strait Settlement

EVENT TO KNOW

Sepoy Rebellion

The British East India Company in India

Ever since the Portuguese explorer Vasco da Gama first reached India in 1498, Europeans had traded with India. At first, the Portuguese dominated this trade. Then the British East India Company, formed in 1600, set its sights on the lucrative trade with India. Within 100 years, this company had established thriving trading stations at Bombay, Calcutta, and Madras.

Along with the trading stations, the British built forts. When the Indian Mogul Empire began to deteriorate in the early 1700s, the British were ready to take advantage of the situation. By the mid-1700s, the British had moved deep into India.

Because there was no strong central government, local Indian rulers were free to do as they pleased. Many entered alliances with the British East India Company. The British East India Company demanded—and got—enormous powers when it entered these alliances. The Indian rulers were happy to comply as they eyed the lucrative trade opportunities. In some cases, they even appointed British traders to government positions. Through this combination of political and economic imperialism, the British East India Company made great gains in India.

Whenever these methods failed, the British turned to military imperialism. Any local ruler who refused to accept British rule was attacked. Time and again, forces of the British East India Company defeated Indian armies. In the late 1700s and early 1800s, the British East India Company virtually ruled India.

■ PRACTICE 172: The British East India Company in India

Circle the letter of the correct answer to each of the following questions.

1. What was the first European country to trade with India?
   a. Portugal
   b. Britain
   c. France
   d. Germany

2. What type of imperialism did Britain use to get control of India?
   a. economic imperialism
   b. political imperialism
   c. military imperialism
   d. all of the above

British India

In India, the British gained control largely through agreements with local princes and other rulers. In exchange for their cooperation, the British agreed to keep them in power.

But this did not sit well with many Indian people who wanted the British East India Company out of India. In 1857, a rebellion broke out. It was started by Indian soldiers who had been loyal to the British. They were called *sepoys.* The rebellion they started was called the **Sepoy Rebellion.**

The Sepoy Rebellion spread quickly. Long-term resentments against the British erupted, and violence broke out in many areas. It took the British about a year to put down the rebellion. The Sepoy Rebellion alarmed the British government. It took control of India from the British East India Company. In 1858, India came under the control of the British government and became called **British India.**

British India, now firmly under control, became very important to the British during the late 1800s. It was considered the "jewel in Britain's crown." It seemed a beautiful and an exotic land. Many British people settled there. The British enjoyed the wealth provided by India's natural resources and by the plantations they created there.

But the Indians still wanted the British out. In 1885, they established the **Indian National Congress,** a group of Indian leaders. The British allowed the Indians to establish this political body. They thought it would serve as a good safety valve for anti-British feelings, and that it would keep violence, like that of the Sepoy Rebellion, from erupting.

The British were mistaken. Soon the Indian National Congress began calling for independence. In the early 1900s, violence against the British started again with shootings and bombings. India remained under British control until after World War II, but the seeds of independence had been planted.

IN REAL LIFE

The years of British rule in India had lasting effects. One effect is in the use of English. People in different parts of India speak many different languages. India has 15 official languages, and several other languages are widely spoken. Most people do not speak enough other languages to communicate with other parts of India. Because of this, people in all these different groups use English as a common language. Although English is not an official language of India, it is the language used most in business and other communication.

■ PRACTICE 173: British India

Circle the letter of the correct answer to each of the following questions.

1. Who won the Sepoy Rebellion?
   a. the sepoys
   b. Portugal
   c. India
   d. Britain

2. Why did the British government take control of India?
   a. It wanted to put the British East India Company out of business.
   b. It wanted to give the Indians their independence.
   c. It was afraid the British East India Company was losing control of India.
   d. It thought that the British East India Company was being too strict with the Indians.

3. Why did the British allow the Indian National Congress to exist?
   a. as a safety valve to discourage rebellion
   b. to encourage Indian independence
   c. to keep violence such as the Sepoy Rebellion from erupting
   d. both *a* and *c*

Burma and Singapore

The British were not content to take over only India. They also wanted to expand their rule in the area. One region they set their sights on was **Burma,** a large nation to the east of India, near China. For years, Britain tried to expand its trade in this region. Britain's economic imperialism failed when the Burmese kingdom resisted. So, the British turned to military imperialism.

The British first attacked Burma in 1824. In 1852, a second war broke out. A third war was fought in 1885. As a result of each conflict, the British gained more territory. The end of the third war saw Britain in control of Burma. The British made it a province of India.

South and east of Burma, the island of **Singapore** lies where the Indian Ocean meets the Pacific Ocean. It is at the tip of the great peninsula that stretches out from the southeast corner of Asia. The peninsula as a whole is called the **Southeast Asian Peninsula.** The smaller peninsula that stretches out from it is called the **Malay Peninsula**. Singapore is at the tip of the Malay Peninsula.

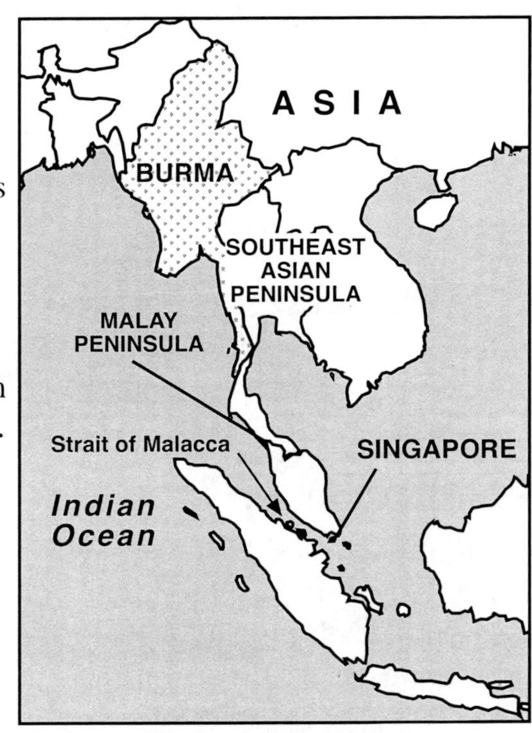

Burma and Singapore

For centuries, Singapore had been mostly uninhabited. It was a land of dense forest and swamps. Pirates hid out on the island. Few people saw value in the land itself.

The British East India Company wanted Singapore. It saw little value in the land, but great value in its location. Singapore is located at the point where the Indian Ocean and Pacific Ocean meet. The British saw it as an important port.

In 1819, the British East India Company gained control of a harbor on the island. It did so by negotiating a treaty with a ruler of what is now Malaysia, Singapore's neighbor to the north.

Within a few years, the British controlled all of Singapore. They called this area the **Strait Settlement.** Singapore borders the **Strait of Malacca,** an important sea route. Even today, the Strait of Malacca is one of the most valuable passages in the world. The British colony formed on the Strait of Malacca became a busy port and center of merchant activity. Goods from all over the region were brought to Singapore. From there, they were shipped all over the world. Singapore became a valuable part of the British Empire.

■ PRACTICE 174: Burma and Singapore

Decide if each statement below is true (**T**) or false (**F**). Write the correct letter on the line before each statement.

____ **1.** Burma was of interest to Britain because it was a strategic military base.

____ **2.** Burma is a section of India.

____ **3.** Singapore was valuable to the British because of its location.

French Indochina

The British conquered much of eastern Asia. Their long-time rivals, the French, set their sights on the great Southeast Asian Peninsula. This area was called **Indochina.**

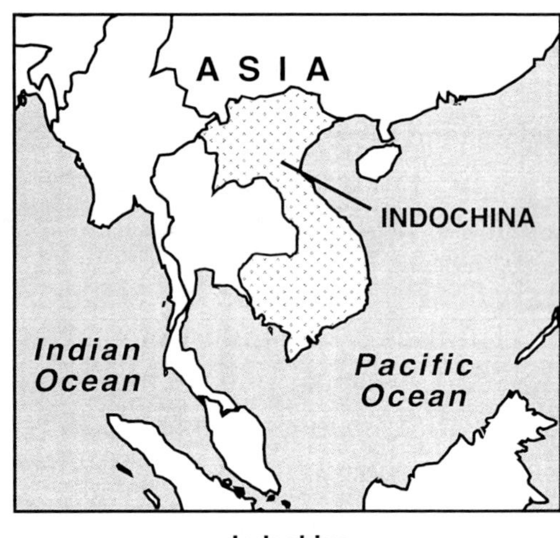

Indochina

Throughout the Age of Imperialism, Europeans used military and economic imperialism to extend their control. In Indochina, a third type of imperialism was at work: religious imperialism.

Religious imperialism is the spread of influence through the use of religion. The Europeans who spread Christianity had a heartfelt desire to do good. They thought that Christianity was the only true religion. To them, their work was not imperialistic. But to the many people they tried to convert, missionary work was just another form of imperialism.

In the early 1800s, French missionaries were extremely successful in Indochina. Thousands of people converted to Christianity. But the missionaries were not always welcome, and many were even killed. Largely to protect the French missionaries, the French sent troops to Indochina in the 1850s and 1860s.

Over the next few decades, the number of French troops in Indochina steadily increased. They came to control smaller kingdoms in the region by treaty. They defeated the larger kingdoms by military force. By 1917, the French controlled Indochina. The region became known as **French Indochina**.

IN REAL LIFE

One of the longest, most unpopular wars in history was fought in Indochina—the Vietnam War, fought in a divided Vietnam. The French kept Indochina as a colony for decades. Then, after World War II, Vietnam declared independence from France. Eventually it split in two. Communist North Vietnam sought to conquer and absorb South Vietnam. The United States became heavily involved in the war, supporting South Vietnam with both weapons and U.S. troops. After years of extraordinary bloodshed, a cease-fire agreement was signed in 1973. The war and its devastating effects can be traced back to the French domination of Indochina.

PRACTICE 175: French Indochina

Match each definition with a term from the list below. Write the letter of the correct term on the line before each definition.

a. religious imperialism **b.** French Indochina **c.** Indochina

_____ **1.** area of the Southeast Asian Peninsula

_____ **2.** spread of influence through the use of religion

_____ **3.** Indochina under French rule

The Dutch East Indies

Like Britain and France, the Netherlands also came to control large parts of Asia. Dutch presence in the region was concentrated on the islands off the coast of the Southeast Asian Peninsula.

These islands had long been known in Europe as the Indies. During the 1400s, 1500s, and 1600s, a major goal of the Europeans had been to trade with this region by sea.

In the 1600s, the Dutch took the lead in this trade. At this time, the Dutch were the greatest sea power in the world. Their ships carried half of Europe's trade goods, and they became the richest nation in Europe.

The Dutch instrument for trade in Asia was the Dutch East India Company, established in 1602. It traded in India and the East Indies. The company founded a city there, which grew into Jakarta, the capital of Indonesia. The company was an enormous success. It eventually drove rival European traders out of the area. It also colonized Ceylon (now called Sri Lanka), an island in the Indian Ocean. And the company traded extensively with Japan. The Dutch East India Company was a powerful force until about 1800.

The Indies became known as the **Dutch East Indies**, or the **Netherlands Indies.** Today most of these islands are in the country of **Indonesia.**

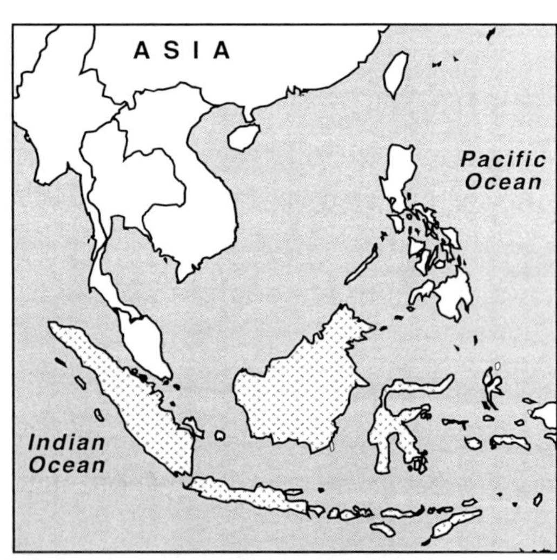

The Dutch East Indies

As a rule, the Dutch were kinder to the peoples in their colonies than other European nations were. But there were abuses nonetheless. They forced the people to grow crops for export, instead of for food. Dutch plantations replaced traditional agriculture. The Dutch grew rich from these plantations, while the natives of the islands suffered from forced labor.

TIP

As you read, be sure to refer to maps frequently. Using maps will help you picture what you are reading about. For example, you have read that the Dutch created plantations in Indonesia. By looking at the map on page 332, you can help yourself picture these plantations on the tropical islands.

Dutch abuses resulted in occasional revolts by the people in their colonies. These started soon after the Dutch colonized the region, and continued off and on for many years. A major revolt occurred in 1825, which it took the Dutch ten full years to suppress.

In the early 1900s, a sense of nationalism began to spread through the islands. Long separated by the sea, the peoples of Indonesia began to think of themselves as one. They became united in their desire for independence. Forces beyond either Dutch or Indonesian control would eventually lead to their independence.

PRACTICE 176: The Dutch East Indies

Decide if each statement below is true (**T**) or false (**F**). Write the correct letter on the line before each statement.

_____ **1.** Large parts of Asia were controlled by Britain, France, and the Netherlands.

_____ **2.** In the 1600s, the Dutch were the greatest sea power in the world.

_____ **3.** The Netherlands Indies is another name for the Dutch East Indies.

_____ **4.** The Dutch East Indies are today the islands of Indonesia.

_____ **5.** The Dutch treated natives of the region kindly.

_____ **6.** The Dutch created plantations on the islands.

LESSON 29: China and Japan Respond to European Imperialism

GOAL: To explain how foreign countries came to dominate China and how Japan became an imperialistic nation itself

WORDS TO KNOW

Boxers	**Open Door Policy**	**Treaty of Kanagawa**
industrialization	**opening of Japan**	**Treaty of Portsmouth**
Meiji Restoration	**opium**	**unequal treaties**
modernize	**sphere of influence**	

NAME TO KNOW

Commodore Matthew Perry

PLACE TO KNOW

Hong Kong

EVENTS TO KNOW

Boxer Rebellion	**Opium War**	**Russo-Japanese War**

European Contact with China

As you learned in Lesson 12, Europeans had traded with China on a limited basis for centuries. Ever since Marco Polo returned from his voyage there, the Europeans had been fascinated with China—and with Chinese goods.

China's rulers did not make trade easy. They did not feel that the West had anything to offer China. They were afraid that foreign influence would turn the peasants against the Chinese government. Despite these obstacles, the Europeans were determined to expand trade with China.

The first European nation to open maritime trade with China was Portugal, which began trade in 1543. The Portuguese also sent Christian

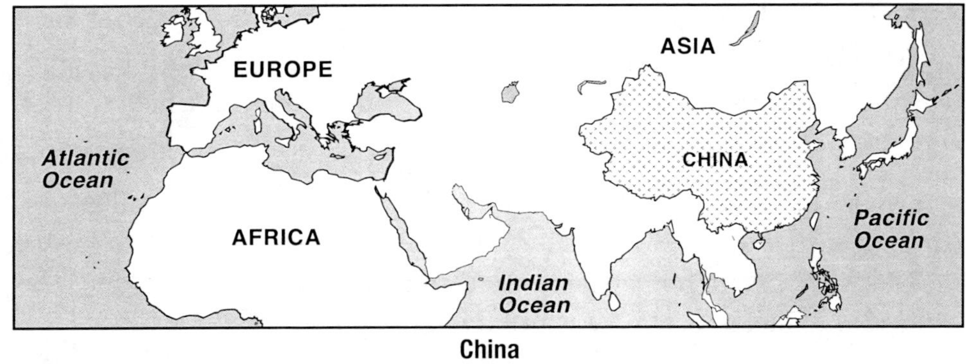

China

missionaries to China. Over time, however, many powerful Chinese began to resent the missionaries. They thought foreigners had no place in China. As a result, the Portuguese were forced to leave China in the 1700s.

The British began maritime trade with China in 1699. Like the Portuguese before them, the British faced severe restrictions in China. But they endured them in order to get tea. Tea was new to Europeans. It was very popular. Chinese tea was the best and commanded a handsome price in British markets. Over the next two centuries, British trade with China continued to grow.

■ PRACTICE 177: European Contact with China

Circle the letter of the correct answer to each of the following questions.

1. When did the British establish a sea trade with China?

- **a.** 1543
- **b.** 1699
- **c.** the 1700s
- **d.** never

2. What was the major item of British-Chinese trade?

- **a.** silk
- **b.** slaves
- **c.** tea
- **d.** arms

The Opium War and Hong Kong

By the early 1800s, Britain was conducting a brisk trade with China. The two most important Chinese goods for the British were tea, which you read about earlier, and silk.

Britain did not buy tea from China with money. Instead, it paid in cotton, which grew on Britain's colonial plantations in India. After a while, the Chinese demand for cotton leveled off. But the British demand for tea continued to increase. How was Britain to pay for all this tea?

In place of cotton, the British began to trade opium in China. **Opium** is an addictive drug. It was grown in Britain's colonies in India. The British had plenty of opium to trade.

As the British introduced more and more opium into China, many Chinese became addicted to it. The usual tragic results of drug addiction followed. So much opium was introduced to China that the Chinese did not have enough tea to pay for it. They began to pay for the drug in silver, as well.

As you might imagine, the opium trade did not sit well with the Chinese government. The drug destroyed the lives of many, many people. And the cost of the drug drained China of silver. Chinese leaders soon demanded that the opium trade be halted. The British refused. When the Chinese tried to confiscate the opium, war broke out.

This war was called the **Opium War.** It started in 1839. The Chinese were no match for the British, with their superior ships and weapons. Within three years, the British had crushed the Chinese. The treaty that ended the war in 1842 forced China to open even more of the country to British merchants. It also required China to give Britain the island of **Hong Kong.** Hong Kong remained in British hands until 1997.

The treaty that ended the Opium War was not negotiated between Britain and China. Instead, Britain dictated its terms to the Chinese. The Chinese, defeated in the war, had no choice but to sign it. It was the first of many such treaties with European countries that China would be forced to sign. In China, such treaties came to be known as **unequal treaties.**

■ PRACTICE 178: The Opium War and Hong Kong

Circle the letter of the correct answer to each of the following questions.

1. What did the British trade for tea before opium?
   - **a.** cotton
   - **b.** silver
   - **c.** silk
   - **d.** coffee

2. Who won the Opium War?
   - **a.** China
   - **b.** Hong Kong
   - **c.** Britain
   - **d.** the Netherlands

3. What happened to Hong Kong as a result of the Opium War?
   - **a.** It became an independent country.
   - **b.** It withdrew from the British Empire.
   - **c.** It signed an unequal treaty.
   - **d.** It was given to Britain until 1997.

Spheres of Influence and the Open Door Policy

At the time of the Opium War, Britain was the only country trading in China. But other countries wanted to trade there, too. These countries included Russia, France, and the United States. These countries pressed China to open trade to them.

At the time, China was weak. In the mid-1800s, a revolt of Chinese Christians had greatly weakened the Chinese government. During the rebellion, British and French citizens were attacked. The Chinese now had to fight the British and French, who had invaded in response to the attacks. Again, Britain won the war. It forced China to sign another unequal treaty.

China was now weaker than ever. Countries other than Britain that wanted to trade with China pressed their advantage. In treaty after unequal treaty, they received many rights in China.

Several nations now had a strong economic and military presence in China. To avoid conflict among themselves, these foreign countries agreed to divide China into spheres of influence. A **sphere of influence** is a region in which one foreign country has special economic and political powers. France, Germany, Britain, Japan, and Russia all had spheres of influence in China.

The United States also wanted to trade with China. In 1899, it proposed the **Open Door Policy**, to which the other nations agreed. Under the Open Door Policy, any foreign country would have the right to trade anywhere in China. (In reality, though, the spheres of influence continued.) That the United States, a foreign country, could declare how the economy of China would function is a striking indication of just how heavily dominated China was by foreign powers at the end of the 1800s.

PRACTICE 179: Spheres of Influence and the Open Door Policy

Decide if each statement below is true (**T**) or false (**F**). Write the correct letter on the line before each statement.

_____ **1.** A sphere of influence is a region in which one foreign country has special economic and political powers.

_____ **2.** The Open Door Policy was a policy proposed by the British that opened trade in certain spheres of influence.

The Boxer Rebellion

By 1900, China was heavily controlled by foreign trading powers. In the spheres of influence, foreign governments ran China's largest cities. Foreign investors built railways. This gave them more access to China's interior. Missionaries traveled the countryside. Europeans went anywhere at will. They were often disrespectful of Chinese culture and treated Chinese people poorly. Had this continued, many historians think that China would have been colonized, the way Africa and much of the rest of Asia were.

But the Chinese people resented the foreign presence in their land. Many patriotic groups plotted ways to return China to the Chinese people. One such organization was called (in English) the Society of Righteous and Harmonious Fists. The members of this society were called **Boxers.**

Chinese Soldiers in the Early 1900s

In 1900, the Boxers began to attack foreigners throughout China. They also attacked anything that was foreign, or foreign-influenced. They attacked Chinese who had converted to Christianity. They attacked anyone who cooperated with any foreign power. They burned down foreign schools, churches, and residences. Hundreds of people were killed. These attacks became known as the **Boxer Rebellion.**

In 1901, forces from several powers combined to crush the Boxer Rebellion. The foreign nations forced China to execute leaders of the rebellion and to pay Europeans hundreds of millions of dollars in damages. It was another unequal treaty.

With the end of the Boxer Rebellion, China was completely dominated by foreign powers. But the uprising had helped inspire nationalistic feelings in the Chinese people. Eventually, they would express these feelings in another revolution.

PRACTICE 180: The Boxer Rebellion

Decide if each statement below is true (**T**) or false (**F**). Write the correct letter on the line before each statement.

_____ **1.** The Boxers were members of a Chinese patriotic group, the Society of Righteous and Harmonious Fists.

_____ **2.** The Boxers defended the right of foreigners to travel and live in China.

_____ **3.** The Boxers were ultimately defeated by the European powers in China.

The End of Japanese Isolation

For centuries, the island nation of Japan had isolated itself from other countries. This began to change in the mid-1500s with the arrival of Portuguese traders.

The Portuguese traders brought change to Japan. They introduced firearms, which could defeat the samurai warriors. Moreover, the traders were followed by missionaries. Their conversion of hundreds of thousands of Japanese to Christianity was seen as religious imperialism. The rulers of Japan viewed the spread of Christianity as corrupting Japanese culture and threatening their rule.

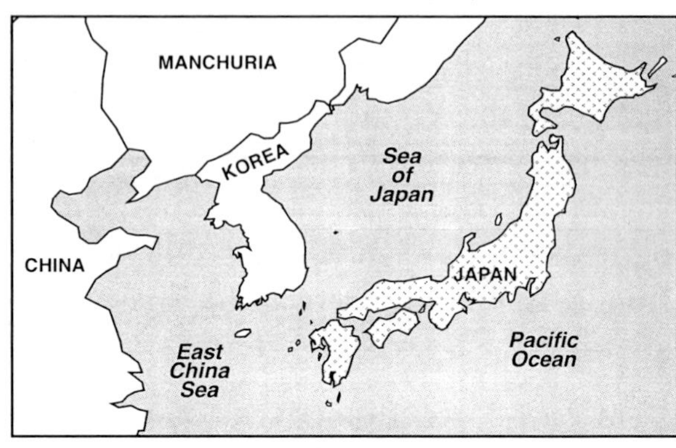

Japan

When the Dutch followed the Portuguese to Japan, the Japanese became alarmed. Despite the wealth that trade brought, the Japanese rulers decided to stop foreign influence.

In about 1640, the leaders of Japan closed the country to all foreigners. This is known as the closing of Japan. Under this new policy, traders and missionaries were no longer allowed to set foot in Japan. Even shipwrecked sailors who struggled to the Japanese shore were often killed. Japan remained "closed" for about 200 years.

The poor treatment of shipwrecked sailors proved to be the beginning of the end of Japanese isolationism. In those days, shipwrecks were quite common. A surprisingly large number of castaways ended up on Japanese soil. Many of them were Americans.

News of the poor treatment of American sailors reached the United States. President Millard Fillmore decided to do something about it. In 1853, he sent a naval force under **Commodore Matthew Perry** to Japan. Perry's orders were to negotiate a treaty with Japan that would guarantee good treatment for American sailors. He also was sent to seek open American trade with Japan.

Perry presented the requests of the United States to Japan. He then left to give the Japanese time to consider the requests. When he returned a year later, in 1854, Japan agreed to the **Treaty of Kanagawa.** This treaty opened Japan to American traders and pledged Japanese aid to American sailors. Soon thereafter, the Japanese signed similar treaties with other countries, including the Netherlands, Britain, and France. Japan's decision after 200 years to open its country again to foreigners is called the **opening of Japan.**

Commodore Matthew Perry

■ PRACTICE 181: The End of Japanese Isolation

Circle the letter of the correct answer to each of the following questions.

1. Why was Japan closed in about 1640?
- **a.** to learn foreign languages and belief systems
- **b.** to prepare for war with the United States
- **c.** to end foreign influence in Japan
- **d.** to allow the Japanese to grow rich through trade

2. Why was Japan opened in the mid-1800s?
- **a.** to end a civil war within its own lands
- **b.** to begin trading with foreign countries
- **c.** to lower the number of shipwrecks
- **d.** to spread Japanese religious practices throughout the world

Japanese Modernization and Expansionism

The opening of Japan in 1854 created a sharp controversy within the country. Many Japanese wanted their society and government to stay the way they had been for centuries. Others wanted the country to **modernize,** or adopt new ideas and technologies that they were learning about from their renewed foreign contacts.

Eventually, the two sides fought over the issue. In the 1860s, Japanese samurai clashed in a civil war. In 1868, those who favored modernization won. They restored the emperor to the throne, replacing the shoguns who had ruled Japan for so long. The restoration of the emperor is called the **Meiji Restoration**.

TIP

Meiji means "enlightened." Supporters of the emperor and of modern ideas thought themselves "enlightened" to the possibilities of modernizing Japan.

Under the Meiji emperor, Japan underwent rapid modernization. The social-class system was abolished. A centralized government was created. A new constitution was written.

But the most dramatic change in Japan during the late 1800s was industrialization. **Industrialization** means changing from an economy based on agriculture to one based on industry. The Japanese government spent huge sums buying foreign machinery and expertise. Then private investment in modern industry was encouraged. By 1900, Japan had all the makings of an industrial country.

Japan was the first Asian country to industrialize. With industrialization came new economic—and military—power. Japan set its sights on Manchuria, a region northeast of China. Russia had stationed a huge army in Manchuria during the Boxer Rebellion. Japan demanded that the Russians leave Manchuria. The Russians refused.

In 1904, Japan attacked the Russian fleet, beginning the **Russo-Japanese War**. The Japanese defeated the Russians in sea and land battles. But the war was costly. In 1905, the Japanese asked the United States to oversee peace talks. Japan and Russia agreed to sign the **Treaty of Portsmouth**.

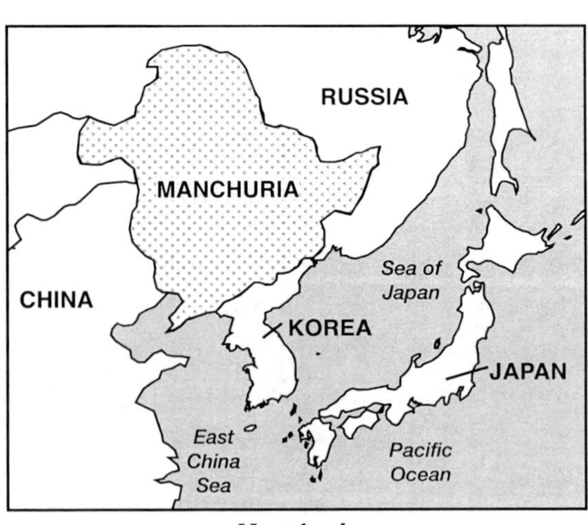

Manchuria

The Treaty of Portsmouth gave Japan control of Manchuria. Five years later, Japan annexed Korea—another region that Japan and Russia had contested. Japan had begun to build an empire.

PRACTICE 182: Japanese Modernization and Expansionism

Circle the letter of the correct answer to each of the following questions.

1. Who won the 1860s civil war in Japan?
   - **a.** those who favored modernization
   - **b.** those who opposed modernization
   - **c.** the samurai
   - **d.** Manchuria

2. Who ruled Japan before the Meiji Restoration?
   - **a.** the common people
   - **b.** the emperor
   - **c.** the missionaries
   - **d.** the shoguns

3. When did Japan become the first nation in Asia to industrialize?
   - **a.** in the early 1800s
   - **b.** after the Meiji Restoration
   - **c.** after the Russo-Japanese War
   - **d.** after 1900

4. What was the issue behind the Russo-Japanese War?
   - **a.** the opening of Japan
   - **b.** whether Japan should industrialize
   - **c.** control over Manchuria
   - **d.** the Treaty of Portsmouth

LESSON 30: Imperialism Around the World

GOAL: To discuss the extent of European empires during the Age of Imperialism; to explain how the United States acquired overseas territories

WORDS TO KNOW

British Empire

empire

Europeanization

global

"Remember the *Maine*!"

Rough Riders

U.S.S. *Maine*

NAME TO KNOW

Theodore Roosevelt

PLACES TO KNOW

Australia

Guam

Havana

Philippines

Puerto Rico

EVENTS TO KNOW

Battle of Manila Bay

Spanish-American War

Empires

In the late 1800s and early 1900s, Belgium, France, Britain, Germany, Italy, the Netherlands, Portugal, and Spain established large empires. An **empire** is a government that unites many different nations under the rule of one nation or ruler.

Perhaps the most famous European empire was the **British Empire.** It included nearly half of North America, holdings in South America, large holdings in Africa and Asia, and all of Australia. **Australia** had been unknown to the Europeans until the 1600s, toward the end of the Age of Exploration. In 1770 a British sailor, Captain James Cook, explored the eastern coast of Australia and claimed the land for Britain. The earliest British settlers of Australia were actually prisoners, sent to a British prison colony there.

Captain James Cook

The British Empire included territories in the Northern, Southern, Eastern, and Western hemispheres. To this day, for many people, the word "empire" means the British Empire.

TIP

There was a saying, "The sun never sets on the British Empire." Can you see where this saying came from? Because the British Empire stretched all the way around the world, the sun was always shining on some part of it.

PRACTICE 183: Empires

Circle the letter of the correct answer to each of the following questions.

1. Which continents did the British Empire include?
   - **a.** Africa
   - **b.** the Americas and Australia
   - **c.** Asia
   - **d.** all of the above

2. Which hemispheres did the British Empire include?
   - **a.** the Northern Hemisphere
   - **b.** the Eastern and Western Hemispheres
   - **c.** the Southern Hemisphere
   - **d.** all of the above

U.S. Imperialism

Throughout the 1800s, the United States also grew in power. American ships and traders sailed all around the globe. The United States, like other nations, sought trading privileges and spheres of influence. In this they were successful, but they did not colonize and engage in empire-building like the Europeans. Rather, they concentrated on expanding their territory in North America.

But in 1898, the Americans fought the **Spanish-American War.** This war developed from U.S. disagreements with Spain about Cuba. Cuba was a Spanish colony. Spain ruled Cuba harshly, and the people of Cuba wanted to be independent. Although Spanish rule was oppressive, American newspaper accounts greatly exaggerated Spanish brutality.

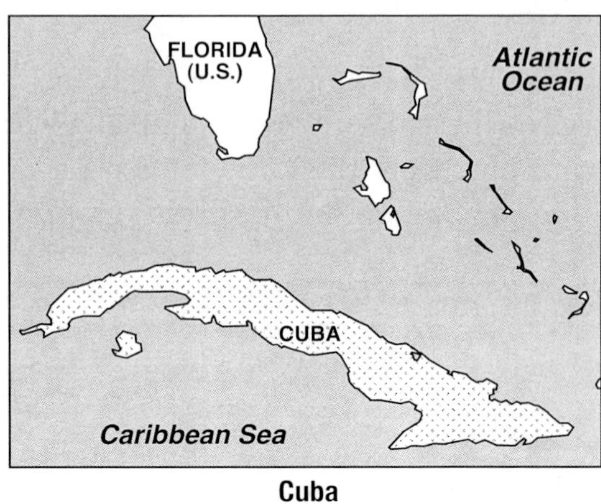

Cuba

This raised American anger against Spain. More and more Americans wanted to intervene and help the Cuban people.

In January 1898, the American battleship **U.S.S. *Maine*** sailed into the Cuban port city of **Havana.** The *Maine's* mission was to protect Americans from the riots that had broken out against Spanish rule. On February 25, the *Maine* exploded and sank. The Americans claimed the Spanish blew it up. To this day, though, the cause of the explosion remains a mystery. Some historians think it was the Cubans who actually destroyed the *Maine,* in an effort to goad the United States into war with Spain. Others think the explosion was an accident.

Regardless, the loss of the *Maine* infuriated Americans. **"Remember the *Maine*!"** became a war cry. U.S. President William McKinley at once demanded immediate independence for Cuba. Spain refused, and the United States declared war.

The war lasted only a few months. In the **Battle of Manila Bay,** U.S. ships destroyed the Spanish fleet in the **Philippines.** The Philippines, a group of islands in the South Pacific, was another Spanish colony. The United States won this battle without losing one American life.

Meanwhile, another group of American ships surrounded Cuba. On the island itself, U.S. forces attacked the city of Santiago de Cuba. Here, **Theodore Roosevelt,** later a U.S. president, led his **Rough Riders** into battle. They charged up a small mountain called Kettle Hill, helping to secure an important American victory. Many people think they went up San Juan Hill, but that is incorrect.

Overwhelmed by the Americans, the Spanish surrendered. The treaty that ended the war was the Treaty of Paris. Under this treaty, Cuba was given its independence. The United States took control of the Pacific islands of the Philippines and **Guam,** and the Caribbean island of **Puerto Rico.**

The Spanish-American War marked the birth of the United States as an imperialistic world power. Before, U.S. expansion had concentrated on North America. Now, the United States was proving its might overseas.

IN REAL LIFE

As of 2005, Puerto Rico was still a U.S. territory, not a state. To some people, Puerto Rico seems "foreign" because it was once under Spanish rule. But so were many southwestern states, including Texas, New Mexico, Arizona, and southern California.

PRACTICE 184: U.S. Imperialism

Circle the letter of the correct answer to each of the following questions.

1. When was the Spanish-American War?

a. 1897
b. 1898
c. 1899
d. 1906

2. What territory did the United States gain as a result of the war?

a. Puerto Rico
b. the Philippines
c. Guam
d. all of the above

The Features of Imperialism

When European countries took over other nations, it was because they wanted things for themselves. They wanted to express their nationalistic spirit by increasing the size of their empires. They wanted other nations' natural resources, such as timber, rubber, diamonds, and gold. They wanted land to make into plantations. They wanted cheap labor. And, to a lesser extent, they wanted to spread their culture and their Christian religion.

As a rule, the Europeans gave little or no thought to the needs and desires of the other nations' peoples. They viewed other nations merely as a source of wealth. The colonies were run by and for the Europeans. Such disregard for other nations' viewpoints was one major feature of European imperialism.

A second feature of European rule was harsh treatment of other peoples. The Europeans treated the original inhabitants of the colonies as second-class citizens. They were paid poorly, if at all, for back-breaking work. They were rarely given justice in courts. They were beaten, brutalized, and humiliated.

A third feature was forced labor. Throughout the colonies, native peoples were forced to work for Europeans—tending plantations, mining, constructing roads, erecting buildings, or working as servants.

A fourth feature was the destruction of traditional economies. For centuries, peoples in lands colonized by the Europeans had grown food crops to feed themselves. The Europeans replaced food crops with cash crops grown for export. Europeans also enforced the production of raw materials, such as rubber and minerals, for export.

A fifth feature was the destruction of cultures. The Europeans altered systems of government and cultural practices that had worked well for centuries. Missionaries worked to replace traditional religions. Even native languages were, in many places, replaced by European languages.

But imperialism also brought some benefits to the colonies. Sometimes the new agricultural systems increased people's standard of living. Colonized nations gained knowledge of new technology—railroads, telegraphs, and so on. Many people received first-rate educations in Europe. European rule was also able to stop local wars that had raged for years. Europeans introduced modern health and sanitation measures to their colonies. And many Europeans worked hard to help the native people of the colonies.

THINK ABOUT IT

Many Europeans believed that it was their duty to "civilize" the peoples of their colonies. They changed centuries-old traditions by introducing new governments, economies, health and sanitation practices, schools, and cultural standards to these colonies. They believed that these changes were good and necessary. This idea of bringing change to other countries and cultures "for their own good" is still an issue in the world today. How do you feel about this way of thinking? Is it ever right for one group to force new ways on another group? What if the new ways are intended to stop human rights abuses and violence? Write your answers on a separate sheet of paper.

PRACTICE 185: The Features of Imperialism

Decide if each statement below is true (**T**) or false (**F**). Write the correct letter on the line before each statement.

_____ **1.** Two features of European imperialism were disregard for other nations' viewpoints and destruction of traditional economies.

_____ **2.** For some colonies, there were also benefits to European control.

Europeanization

As you have learned, European nations stretched their influence around the world during the late 1800s and early 1900s. The effects of this **global,** or worldwide, imperialism have been felt ever since.

Perhaps the single greatest and longest-lasting effect of European imperialism was the Europeanization of the world. **Europeanization** is a term some historians use to describe the global influence of European language, culture, ideas, and technology. Today, European languages, especially English, are spoken all over the world. European ideas and technologies are found nearly everywhere. Christianity, spread by European missionaries, is the largest religion in the world.

In short, the way your world is today is largely a result of what you have been reading about: the global reach of the Europeans in the Age of Imperialism.

■ PRACTICE 186: Europeanization

Circle the letter of the correct answer to each of the following questions.

1. What is Europeanization?
   - **a.** the global influence of European culture
   - **b.** the global influence of European technology
   - **c.** the global influence of European languages
   - **d.** all of the above

2. What is "global" imperialism?
   - **a.** circular imperialism
   - **b.** worldwide imperialism
   - **c.** Asian imperialism
   - **d.** none of the above

UNIT 8 REVIEW

Circle the letter of the correct answer to each of the following questions.

1. Which of the following is a major imperialistic country of Europe?
   - **a.** Britain
   - **b.** Germany
   - **c.** Belgium
   - **d.** all of the above

2. What was the purpose of the Berlin Conference?
   a. to divide Africa among European nations
   b. to bring an end to the Boer War
   c. to slow the colonization of Africa
   d. to grant independence to African countries

3. What was the result of the Sepoy Rebellion in India?
   a. The British East India Company signed a treaty with the Indians.
   b. The British government took control of India.
   c. The Indians won their independence.
   d. France invaded to help the Indians.

4. Which statement about Indochina is TRUE?
   a. Religious imperialism was used in Indochina.
   b. Indochina was never colonized.
   c. Indochina is located in southwest Asia.
   d. Indochina was colonized by the Vietnamese.

5. What product of India did the British use to trade in China?
   a. wheat
   b. cotton
   c. coffee
   d. silk

6. Who proposed the Open Door Policy?
   a. Britain
   b. the United States
   c. China
   d. Japan

7. What was the Russo-Japanese War fought over?
   a. the opening of Japan
   b. whether Japan should industrialize
   c. control over Korea
   d. control over Manchuria

8. What territory did the United States gain as a result of the Spanish-American War?
   a. Puerto Rico
   b. the Philippines
   c. Guam
   d. all of the above

9. What was the U.S.S. *Maine*?
   a. a written account of the Spanish-American War
   b. territory acquired by the United States in the Spanish-American War
   c. an American battleship that exploded just before the Spanish-American War
   d. an American battleship that won the battle of Manila Bay

10. As a rule, what did European colonists do to traditional economies?
   a. left them alone
   b. respected them
   c. changed them slightly
   d. changed them drastically

UNIT 8 APPLICATION ACTIVITY
The Pros and Cons of Colonization

During the Age of Imperialism, European nations colonized one foreign land after another. And they did so with little thought for the people who lived in these lands.

Was European imperialism a great injustice to the native peoples of colonized lands? Or did colonization actually benefit them?

Choose one area that was colonized. Do some research. Try to pinpoint specific changes that took place as a result of colonization. Then imagine that you are a native of that colony. In the chart on page 353, list four "pros" and four "cons" of colonization for you and your family. For example, did the European power build more schools in the colony? This might be a positive change, or a "pro." Did the European power take jobs away from the native people? This would be a negative change, or a "con."

- Name of colony: ______________________________

- European nation that colonized this land: ______________________

Pros	Cons
1. ______________________ ______________________	**1.** ______________________ ______________________
2. ______________________ ______________________	**2.** ______________________ ______________________
3. ______________________ ______________________	**3.** ______________________ ______________________
4. ______________________ ______________________	**4.** ______________________ ______________________

Now, look at your completed chart. Which side do you think is more convincing—the pros or the cons? Would you support colonization or protest it? On a separate sheet of paper, explain which side you would support and why.

APPENDIXES

A. Names to Know

Akbar—the greatest of the Mogul emperors

Anthony, Susan B.—a leading U.S. suffragist

Arkwright, Richard—the inventor of the water frame

Ashikaga Takauji—the first shogun of the Ashikaga shogunate in Japan

Atahualpa—the last ruler of the Incas, captured and killed by Pizarro

Aurangzeb—a cruel Mogul emperor who helped bring about the fall of the Mogul Empire and opened the way for greater British influence

Babur the Tiger—the founder of the Mogul Empire

Bell, Alexander Graham—the inventor of the telephone

Boccaccio, Giovanni—an Italian writer, one of the first humanists

Bolívar, Simón—the greatest leader of the revolutions of South America

Bonaparte, Napoleon—the general who seized control of France from the Directory

Brahe, Tycho—a Danish astronomer famous for making and recording observations

Brahms, Johannes—a great German composer of the Romantic Movement

Brown, Moses—Samuel Slater's partner

Cabot, John—an Italian explorer who sailed for England and explored North America

Calvin, John—a Reformation leader who helped bring Protestantism to France and other countries in Western Europe

Cartier, Jacques—a French explorer who explored Canada

Cartwright, Edmund—the inventor of the steam-powered loom

Catherine the Great—Russia's "enlightened monarch" of the Age of Reason

Cavour, Count Camillo Benso di—the leader of Sardinia-Piedmont and of the Italian unification movement

Chopin, Frédéric—a great Polish composer of the Romantic Movement

Christina, Queen—Sweden's "enlightened monarch" of the Age of Reason

Columbus, Christopher—an Italian explorer who was the first European to reach the Americas

Copernicus, Nicolaus—a Polish astronomer who put forth the idea of the heliocentric system

Cortés, Hernando—a Spanish conquistador who conquered the Aztec Empire

Crompton, Samuel—the inventor of the spinning mule

Cugnot, Nicholas—the inventor of the powered tractor

da Gama, Vasco—a Portuguese explorer who was the first European to sail to Asia

da Verrazano, Giovanni—an Italian explorer who sailed for France and searched for the Northwest Passage

da Vinci, Leonardo—a great Italian artist and thinker

Darby, Abraham—the developer of improved iron-making methods

Darby, Abraham II—the developer of improved iron-making methods

de La Salle, Robert—a French explorer who traveled the Mississippi River and claimed the surrounding land for France

de San Martín, José—a leader of revolutions in South America

de Soto, Hernando—a Spanish explorer who traveled across much of North America

Deere, John—an inventor of the steel plow

Descartes, René—a leading French thinker of the Age of Reason

Dias, Bartholomeu—a Portuguese explorer who was the first to sail around the tip of Africa

Diderot, Denis—a leading French thinker of the Age of Reason who assembled an important encyclopedia

Donatello—a great Italian Renaissance sculptor

Douglass, Frederick—a former slave and leading abolitionist

Drake, Sir Francis—an English explorer who searched for the Northwest Passage from the western coast of North America

Frederick the Great—Prussia's "enlightened monarch" of the Age of Reason

Frobisher, Martin—an English explorer who searched for the Northwest Passage

Gadsden, James—a U.S. representative to Mexico who arranged the Gadsden Purchase

Galen—a Greek physician whose word was accepted as fact during the Middle Ages

Galileo—an Italian astronomer, sometimes called "the father of experimental science"

Garibaldi, Giuseppe—a general and leader of the Italian unification movement

Giotto—a great Italian Renaissance painter; the first humanist painter

Gutenberg, Johannes—a German who developed the methods of modern printing

Hargreaves, James—the inventor of the spinning jenny

Hastings, Warren—the first British East India Company governor general of India

Henry the Navigator—the Portuguese director of several African coastal explorations

Hidalgo y Costilla, Miguel—a priest who fought for Mexican independence

Isabella I—the Spanish queen who supported Columbus

Jefferson, Thomas—the U.S. president who wrote the Declaration of Independence and arranged the Louisiana Purchase

Joseph II—an "enlightened monarch" of the Age of Reason

Kangxi—the Qing emperor of China from 1661 to 1722

Keats, John—a British poet of the Romantic Movement

Kepler, Johannes—a German astronomer who developed laws of planetary motion

Leopold II—a king of Belgium who made the Congo his personal property

Lincoln, Abraham—the president of the United States during the Civil War

Locke, John—a leading British thinker of the Age of Reason

Lorenzo the Magnificent—the most famous and powerful member of the Italian Medici family

Louis XVI—a king of France during the French Revolution

Lowell, Francis—one of the leaders of the Industrial Revolution in America

Luther, Martin—a German monk who became the leader of the Reformation

Magellan, Ferdinand—a Portuguese explorer whose expedition was the first to circumnavigate the world

Malthus, Thomas —an important British economist of the 1700s

Marx, Karl—a German social critic who put forth new ideas about society, government, and the economy

Mazzini, Giuseppe—a leader of the Italian unification movement

McCormick, Cyrus—the inventor of the reaper

Medici, Cosimo de'—the great leader of the Medici family in Italy, called "the father of his country"

Medici, Giovanni de'—the first great, wealthy member of the Medici family

Medicis—a famous, powerful Italian ruling family who did much to support the thinkers of the Renaissance

Michelangelo—a great Italian Renaissance sculptor and painter

Minamoto—the family from which Japan's first shogun came

Minamoto Yoritomo—Japan's first shogun

Montesquieu—a leading French thinker of the Age of Reason

Montezuma II—the Aztec ruler held hostage by Cortés

More, Sir Thomas—the British author of *Utopia*; an early supporter of ideal communities

Morelos y Pavón, José María—a priest who fought for Mexican independence

Morse, Samuel F. B.—the inventor of the first reliable telegraph

Mott, Lucretia—a leading U.S. suffragist

Nanak—the founder of the Sikh religion

Núñez de Balboa, Vasco—a Spanish explorer who was the first European to discover the Pacific

Nurhachi—the chief who united the many tribes of Manchuria

Owen, Robert—a major supporter of ideal communities

Pedro—the leader of Brazil who declared it independent from Portugal

Perry, Matthew—an American naval commodore who led the opening of Japan

Petrarch—an Italian poet, one of the first humanists

Pizarro, Francisco—a Spanish conquistador who conquered the Inca Empire

Polk, James—the U.S. president who started the Mexican War

Ponce de León, Juan—a Spanish explorer who searched for the Fountain of Youth in Florida

Ptolemy—a Greek thinker who recorded the ideas of Greek astronomy

Raphael—a great Italian Renaissance painter

Rhodes, Cecil—a wealthy colonial leader in southern Africa

Ricardo, David—an important British economist of the 1700s

Robespierre, Maximilien—a notorious leader of the French Revolution

Roosevelt, Theodore—a soldier of the Spanish-American War and later a U.S. president

Rousseau, Jean-Jacques—a leading French thinker and writer of the Age of Reason

Sebastián del Cano, Juan—a sailor with Magellan who took over after Magellan's death

Shah Jahan—a great emperor of the Mogul Empire who built the Taj Mahal

Shakespeare, William—English playwright during the Renaissance whose plays are still performed today

Shelley, Percy Bysshe—a British poet of the Romantic Movement

Slater, Samuel—a British man who brought knowledge of textile machinery from Britain to the United States

Smith, Adam—an important British economist of the 1700s; known as "the father of modern economics"

Stanton, Elizabeth Cady—a leading U.S. suffragist

Stone, Lucy—a leading U.S. suffragist

Tokugawa Ieyasu—the first shogun of the Tokugawa shogunate in Japan

Toussaint-Louverture—the leader of the battle for Haitian independence

Tull, Jethro—the inventor of the agricultural drill

van Beethoven, Ludwig—a great German composer of the Romantic Movement

Vesalius, Andreas—a Flemish anatomist who described the human body based on detailed, firsthand observations

Vespucci, Amerigo—an Italian navigator who sailed for Portugal and helped explore South America

Victor Emmanuel II—a king of Sardinia-Piedmont and then of a unified Italy

Voltaire—a leading French thinker and writer of the Age of Reason

von Bismarck, Otto—the leader of Prussia and then of the German Empire

von Metternich, Prince Klemens—the leader of the Congress of Vienna

Washington, George—the leader of American troops during the American Revolution, later first U.S. president

Watt, James—an inventor who radically improved the steam engine

Whitney, Eli—the inventor of the cotton gin

Wordsworth, William—a British poet of the Romantic Movement

B. Places to Know

Algeria—a country in northern Africa

America—the name given to the New World to honor Amerigo Vespucci

Amsterdam—the capital of the Netherlands

Argentina—a South American country

Australia—a continent taken over by the British

Beijing—a city that was established as the capital of China during the Ming dynasty

Belgian Congo—a Belgian colony in central Africa

Belgium—the first country to industrialize after Britain

Bolivia—a South American country

Bombay—an Indian city that became a major British trading port

Brazil—a South American country

Burma—a large nation in Southeast Asia

Calcutta—an Indian city that became a major British trading port

Calicut, India—the Asian port reached by Vasco da Gama

Cape Colony—a Dutch colony in southern Africa

Cape of Good Hope—the name for the tip of Africa

Cape Town—a Dutch settlement in southern Africa

Ceuta—the first European toehold in Africa

Colombia—a South American country

Congo Free State—King Leopold's personal colony in Africa

Congo River—a central African river

Costa Rica—a Central American country; formerly part of the United Provinces of Central America

Cuba—a major island off the coast of North America in the Caribbean Sea

Dutch East Indies—Indonesia under Dutch rule

Ecuador—a South American country

Edo—the new capital of Japan, established during the Tokugawa shogunate

Egypt—a country in northern Africa

El Salvador—a Central American country; formerly part of the United Provinces of Central America

France—a European country

French Indochina—Indochina under French rule

Germany—a European country

Golden Temple—the most holy site of Sikhism

Gran Colombia—a Latin American country organized by Simón Bolívar

Guam—an island in the Pacific Ocean won by the United States in the Spanish-American War

Guangzhou—the location of the British trading station in China

Guatemala—a Central American country; formerly part of the United Provinces of Central America

Haiti—a country on the island of Hispaniola in the West Indies

Havana—a major port city in Cuba

Hispaniola—a major island off the coast of North America

Honduras—a Central American country; formerly part of the United Provinces of Central America

Hong Kong—an island off China

India—an Asian nation that attracted traders from the Netherlands and Britain

Indies—what Europeans called the eastern parts of Asia (India, China, Japan, and the islands of the southwest Pacific)

Indochina—an area of the Southeast Asian Peninsula

Indonesia—a region of islands between Southeast Asia and Australia

Isabella—the first European colony in America, founded by Columbus

Italy—a country of Europe on a peninsula jutting into the Mediterranean

Jamestown—the first permanent English settlement in the New World

Latin America—Central and South America

Liberia—an African colony founded by the American Colonization Society

Lima—a city in Peru founded by Pizarro

Louisiana—a huge area of central North America, sold to the United States by France

Lowell, Massachusetts—a planned industrial city in the United States

Macao—the location of the Portuguese trading station in China

Madras—an Indian city that became a major British trading port

Malay Peninsula—a peninsula that extends from the Southeast Asian Peninsula

Manchester—a British textile city

Manchuria—a region to the northeast of China

Merrimack River—a New England river that powered many textile mills

Mexico—a Latin American country

Nagasaki—the location of the Dutch trading station in Japan

Netherlands Indies—another name for the Dutch East Indies

New World—the Americas

Nicaragua—a Central American country; formerly part of the United Provinces of Central America

North—the northern United States, made up of mostly free states

Oregon Country—land in western North America

Peru—a country in South America where much of the Inca Empire was formerly located

Philippines—a group of islands in the South Pacific

Prussia—a leading German state

Puerto Rico—an island in the Caribbean Sea won by the United States in the Spanish-American War

Rhodesia—a colony and country named for Cecil Rhodes; later called Zimbabwe

Saint Domingue—a French colony on Hispaniola

San Salvador—the island where Columbus first landed in the New World

Sardinia—an Italian island in the Mediterranean Sea

Singapore—an island at the tip of the Malay Peninsula

South—the southern United States, made up of slave states

Southeast Asian Peninsula—a large peninsula in Southeast Asia

Strait of Malacca—an important sea route bordered by Singapore

Strait Settlement—Singapore as a British colony

Suez Canal—a canal between the Mediterranean Sea and the Red Sea

Taj Mahal—a famous building in India built by Shah Jahan

Tenochtitlán—a great city that was the capital of the Aztec Empire

Tokyo—capital of Japan, formerly known as Edo

United Provinces of Central America—an organization of countries that broke away from Mexico

Venezuela—a South American country

West Indies—the islands that separate the Atlantic Ocean from the Caribbean Sea

C. Events to Know

Battle of Manila Bay—an important naval battle of the Spanish-American War

Battle of Plassey—the 1757 battle that firmly established British control of India

Berlin Conference—a meeting at which European leaders divided Africa among themselves

Boer War—a war between the Boers and the British in southern Africa

Boxer Rebellion—an uprising of the Boxers against foreigners

Opium War—a war between Britain and China over the British opium trade in China

Russo-Japanese War—a war between Russia and Japan over Manchuria

Sepoy Rebellion—a revolt against the British East India Company in India

Spanish-American War—a war between the United States and Spain over Cuba

Waterloo—the battle at which Napoleon was finally defeated

GLOSSARY

abolition movement (a-buh-LI-shun MOOV-munt) the fight to abolish slavery

abolitionists (a-buh-LI-shun-ists) people who worked to abolish slavery

absolute monarchy (ab-suh-LOOT MO-nur-kee) a monarchy that holds absolute power

Addition of 1783 (uh-DI-shun UV sev-un-teen-AY-tee-three) land obtained by the United States through the Treaty of Paris

Admiral of the Ocean Sea (AD-muh-rul UV THUH OH-shun SEE) the title awarded Columbus by Queen Isabella

Age of Exploration (AYJ UV ek-spluh-RAY-shun) the period from about 1400 to 1600, when Europeans started to explore overseas

Age of Imperialism (AYJ UV im-PIR-ee-uh-li-zum) a period in 1800s Europe, when nations sought to dominate other nations and acquire their territory

Age of Invasions (AYJ UV in-VAY-zhunz) a period of Indian history from about 500 to about 1500

Age of Liberalism (AYJ UV LI-buh-ruh-li-zum) a period of European history in the 1800s, when liberal ideas spread

Age of Metternich (AYJ UV ME-tur-nik) a period of European history from 1815 to 1845, when Metternich and his ideas had great power

---

PRONUNCIATION KEY

CAPITAL LETTERS show the stressed syllables.

a	as in m**a**t	f	as in **f**it
ay	as in d**ay**, s**ay**	g	as in **g**o
ch	as in **ch**ew	i	as in s**i**t
e	as in b**e**d	j	as in **j**ob, **g**em
ee	as in **e**ven, **ea**sy, n**ee**d	k	as in **c**ool, **k**ey

Age of Nationalism (AYJ UV NASH-uh-nuh-li-zum) a period of nationalistic feelings and national unifications in 1800s Europe

Age of Rationalism (AYJ UV RASH-uh-nuh-li-zum) another name for the Age of Reason

Age of Reason (AYJ UV REE-zun) a period of European history that lasted from the 1600s to the late 1700s, when philosophers used logic to observe and describe the world

Agricultural Age (a-gri-KUL-chuh-rul AYJ) the second great era of human history, brought about by the First Agricultural Revolution

agriculture (A-gri-kul-chur) the growing of food, or farming

Alaskan Purchase (uh-LAS-kun PUR-chus) the purchase of Alaska from Russia by the United States

American Civil War (uh-MER-uh-kun SI-vul WOR) a war fought between the northern and southern parts of the United States, 1861–1865

American Colonization Society (uh-MER-uh-kun ka-luh-nuh-ZAY-shun suh-SY-uh-tee) a group that worked to return freed slaves to Africa

American Revolution (uh-MER-uh-kun re-vuh-LOO-shun) the revolution of American colonists against British rule

American Woman Suffrage Association (uh-MER-uh-kun WU-mun SUH-frij uh-soh-see-AY-shun) a group that worked to get women the right to vote.

PRONUNCIATION KEY

CAPITAL LETTERS show the stressed syllables.

ng as in runni**ng**

o as in c**o**t, f**a**ther

oh as in g**o**, n**o**te

oo as in t**oo**

sh as in **sh**y

th as in **th**in

u as in b**u**t, s**o**me

uh as in **a**bout, tak**e**n, lem**o**n, penc**i**l

ur as in t**er**m

y as in l**i**ne, fl**y**

zh as in vi**s**ion, mea**s**ure

Anglicanism (an-GLUH-cun-izm) a version of Protestantism that is the official church of England

annexation (a-nek-SAY-shun) an addition of territory

armed resistance (ARMD ri-ZIS-tunts) one way Africans resisted European imperialism

Ashikaga shogunate (a-shee-KA-ga SHOH-guh-nut) the period of Japanese history when shoguns came from the Ashikaga family

Aztec Empire (AZ-tek EM-pyr) a great Central American Indian empire conquered by de Soto

balance of powers (BA-luns UV POW-urs) the idea that the powers of the different branches of government should be balanced

Bastille (ba-STEEL) a prison and fort in Paris stormed by French revolutionaries

Battles of Lexington and Concord (BA-tulz UV LEK-sing-tun AND KON-kord) the first battles of the American Revolution

Book of Songs (BUHK UV SONGS) a book of poetry by Petrarch

Boston Tea Party (BOS-tun TEE PAR-tee) an American protest of the Tea Act

bourgeoisie (burzh-wa-ZEE) rich owners of the means of production and those who support them

Boxers (BOK-surs) patriotic Chinese who revolted against foreign rule

---

PRONUNCIATION KEY

CAPITAL LETTERS show the stressed syllables.

a	as in m**a**t	f	as in **f**it
ay	as in d**ay**, s**ay**	g	as in **g**o
ch	as in **ch**ew	i	as in s**i**t
e	as in b**e**d	j	as in **j**ob, **g**em
ee	as in **e**ven, **ea**sy, n**ee**d	k	as in **c**ool, **k**ey

Britain (BRI-tun) an island nation to the west of continental Europe, once the center of a global empire

British Cession (BRI-tish SE-shun) land obtained by the United States from Britain in 1818

British East India Company (BRI-tish EEST IN-dee-uh KUM-puh-nee) an English company that traded with India

British Empire (BRI-tish EM-pyr) an empire created by the British during the Age of Imperialism

British India (BRI-tish IN-dee-uh) India under the rule of the British government

Bushido (BU-shi-doh) the strict code of bravery and honor by which samurai lived

capital (KA-puh-tul) money invested in the means of production

capitalism (KA-puh-tul-iz-um) an economy in which the means of production are privately owned and the desire for profit drives the economy

capitalists (KA-puh-tul-ists) people who control money and the means of production in a capitalist society

caravel (KAR-uh-vul) sailing ship developed in Portugal that was easier to sail than earlier ships

castes (KASTS) rigid class divisions in Hindu society

PRONUNCIATION KEY

CAPITAL LETTERS show the stressed syllables.

ng as in runni**ng**

o as in c**o**t, f**a**ther

oh as in g**o**, n**o**te

oo as in t**oo**

sh as in **sh**y

th as in **th**in

u as in b**u**t, s**o**me

uh as in **a**bout, tak**e**n, lem**o**n, penc**il**

ur as in t**er**m

y as in l**i**ne, fl**y**

zh as in vi**s**ion, mea**s**ure

ceiling of the Sistine Chapel (SEE-ling UV THUH SIS-teen CHA-pul) a great painting by Michelangelo on the ceiling of the Vatican's Sistine Chapel

cession (SE-shun) something surrendered or given

child labor (CHYLD LAY-bur) the employment of children

circumnavigate (sur-kum-NA-vuh-gayt) to sail all the way around

circumnavigation (sur-kum-na-vuh-GAY-shun) a complete sailing around

closing of Japan (KLOHZ-ing UV juh-PAN) the Japanese decision to prohibit foreigners from coming to Japan

coal (KOHL) a mineral burned to power steam engines and used in making iron

Code Napoleon (KOHD nuh-POH-lee-un) the system of civil law created by Napoleon

cog (KOG) a strong ship built in northern Europe

colonialism (kuh-LOH-nee-uh-li-zum) the establishment of colonies in other lands

colonists (KA-luh-nists) people who live in colonies

colonization (ka-luh-nuh-ZAY-shun) the practice of establishing colonies

colony (KA-luh-nee) a settlement established by a foreign country

Columbian Exchange (kuh-LUM-bee-un iks-CHAYNJ) the movement of

PRONUNCIATION KEY

CAPITAL LETTERS show the stressed syllables.

a as in m**a**t

ay as in d**ay**, s**ay**

ch as in **ch**ew

e as in b**e**d

ee as in **e**ven, **ea**sy, n**ee**d

f as in **f**it

g as in **g**o

i as in s**i**t

j as in **j**ob, **g**em

k as in **c**ool, **k**ey

individuals, peoples, cultures, ideas, tools, goods, plants, animals, diseases, and other things between the Americas and Europe

Committee of Public Safety (kuh-MI-tee UV PUH-blik SAYF-tee) a Committee of the National Convention that came to control the French government

Communications Revolution (kuh-myoo-nuh-KAY-shunz re-vuh-LOO-shun) great improvements in communication made during the 1800s

communism (KOM-yuh-ni-zum) a classless society in which everyone owns the means of production

The Communist Manifesto (THUH KOM-yuh-nist ma-nuh-FES-toh) Karl Marx's great literary work

compensation (kom-pun-SAY-shun) payments to make up for a loss to an individual or nation

Congress of Vienna (KON-grus UV vee-E-nuh) a meeting of European leaders in 1814 and 1815 to restore order to Europe

conquistadors (kon-KEES-tuh-dorz) Spanish conquerors of the New World

Constitution (kon-stuh-TOO-shun) the plan of government of the United States

Consulate (KON-suh-lut) the government formed by Napoleon

Continental System (kon-tun-EN-tul SIS-tum) the Napoleonic system that forbade countries on the European continent to trade with Britain

---

PRONUNCIATION KEY

CAPITAL LETTERS show the stressed syllables.

ng as in runni**ng**
o as in c**o**t, f**a**ther
oh as in g**o**, n**o**te
oo as in t**oo**
sh as in **sh**y
th as in **th**in
u as in b**u**t, s**o**me
uh as in **a**bout, tak**e**n, lem**o**n, penc**il**
ur as in t**er**m
y as in l**i**ne, fl**y**
zh as in vi**s**ion, mea**s**ure

Copernican Revolution (kuh-PUR-ni-kun re-vuh-LOO-shun) the great change from the belief in the geocentric system to the heliocentric system

Copernican system (kuh-PUR-ni-kun SIS-tum) another name for the heliocentric system

cottage industry (KO-tij IN-dus-tree) another name for the domestic system

cotton (KO-tun) the crop from which most cloth is made

cotton gin (KO-tun JIN) a machine that separates cotton fiber from the seeds; one of the two most important inventions of the Industrial Revolution

coup d'état (koo day-TA) a takeover of a government

courtiers (KOHR-tee-urz) members of courts

courts (KOHRTS) groups of people associated with rulers

crop rotation (KROP roh-TAY-shun) changing the crops grown in each field each growing season

cultural exchange (KUL-chuh-rul iks-CHAYNJ) the exchange of ideas between peoples of different cultures

daimyo (DY-mee-oh) a powerful landholding lord in Japanese feudalism

Dark Ages (DARK AYJ-uz) another term for the Middle Ages, referring to the lack of learning of most people of the time

---

PRONUNCIATION KEY

CAPITAL LETTERS show the stressed syllables.

a	as in m**a**t	f	as in **f**it
ay	as in d**ay**, s**ay**	g	as in **g**o
ch	as in **ch**ew	i	as in s**i**t
e	as in b**e**d	j	as in **j**ob, **g**em
ee	as in **e**ven, **ea**sy, n**ee**d	k	as in **c**ool, **k**ey

David (DAY-vud) a sculpture by Michelangelo; also a sculpture by Donatello

The Decameron (THUH duh-KAM-ur-on) a book of stories by Boccaccio

decentralized (dee-SEN-truh-lyzd) not located at one central place

Declaration of Independence (de-kluh-RAY-shun UV in-duh-PEN-duns) the American statement of independence from Britain

Declaration of the Rights of Man and of the Citizen (de-kluh-RAY-shun UV THUH RYTS UV MAN AND UV THUH SI-tuh-zun) the document adopted by the National Assembly in France

deism (DEE-i-zum) a theory that states that God created the universe and then left it alone to operate by universal laws

deists (DEE-ists) believers in deism

demand (di-MAND) the desire for goods

dictatorship of the proletariat (dik-TAY-tur-ship UV THUH proh-luh-TER-ee-ut) the stage in Marxism when the proletariat uses force to keep the power they have seized

Directory (duh-REK-tuh-ree) the governmental body that replaced the National Convention in France

discoverers (dis-KUH-vur-urz) a term for sailors who explored during the Age of Exploration

---

PRONUNCIATION KEY

CAPITAL LETTERS show the stressed syllables.

ng as in runni**ng**

o as in c**o**t, f**a**ther

oh as in g**o**, n**o**te

oo as in t**oo**

sh as in **sh**y

th as in **th**in

u as in b**u**t, s**o**me

uh as in **a**bout, tak**e**n, lem**o**n, penc**il**

ur as in t**er**m

y as in l**i**ne, fl**y**

zh as in vi**s**ion, mea**s**ure

divine right (duh-VYN RYT) the idea that monarchs get their authority from God

domains (doh-MAYNS) daimyo-ruled regions into which Japan was divided during the Tokugawa shogunate

domestic system (duh-MES-tik SIS-tum) a manufacturing system in which work is done in workers' homes

drill (DRIL) a seed-planting machine

Dutch (DUCH) the people of the Netherlands

Dutch East India Company (DUCH EEST IN-dee-uh KUM-puh-nee) a Dutch company that traded with India and eastern Asia

Dutch West India Company (DUCH WEST IN-dee-uh KUM-puh-nee) a Dutch company that traded with the New World and western Africa

dynasty (DY-nuh-stee) a series of rulers from the same family or group of people

East Indiaman (EEST IN-dee-uh-man) a large, armed trading ship

economic imperialism (e-kuh-NO-mik im-PIR-ee-uh-li-zum) the taking over of countries economically

economist (i-KO-nuh-mist) someone who studies and writes about the economy

ellipse (i-LIPS) an oval; the path planets follow in their orbits

---

PRONUNCIATION KEY

CAPITAL LETTERS show the stressed syllables.

a	as in m**a**t	f	as in **f**it
ay	as in d**ay**, s**ay**	g	as in **g**o
ch	as in **ch**ew	i	as in s**i**t
e	as in b**e**d	j	as in **j**ob, **g**em
ee	as in **e**ven, **ea**sy, n**ee**d	k	as in **c**ool, **k**ey

Emancipation Proclamation (i-man-suh-PAY-shun pro-kluh-MAY-shun) the declaration that freed the slaves during the U.S. Civil War

Emperor of France (EM-pur-ur UV FRANTS) the title given to Napoleon in 1804

empire (EM-pyr) a government that unites many different nations under the rule of one nation or ruler

enclosure movement (in-KLO-zhur MOOV-munt) a British movement toward larger farms

"enlightened" monarchs (in-LY-tund MO-nurks) rulers of the Age of Reason who paid attention to leading ideas of the time

Enlightenment (in-LY-tun-munt) another name for the Age of Reason

estates (is-TAYTS) classes of French people

Estates-General (is-TAYTS-JEN-rul) the governmental body called to meet by Louis XVI

ethnocentrism (eth-noh-SEN-tri-zum) the belief that one's own culture is the best

European balance of power (yur-uh-PEE-un BA-luns UV POW-ur) a principle of the Congress of Vienna that called for balance in economic, political, and military power in European nations

Europeanization (yur-uh-PEE-uh-nuh-ZAY-shun) the global influence of European language, culture, ideas, and technology

---

PRONUNCIATION KEY

CAPITAL LETTERS show the stressed syllables.

ng as in runni**ng**
o as in c**o**t, f**a**ther
oh as in g**o**, n**o**te
oo as in t**oo**
sh as in **sh**y
th as in **th**in
u as in b**u**t, s**o**me
uh as in **a**bout, tak**e**n, lem**o**n, penc**i**l
ur as in t**er**m
y as in l**i**ne, fl**y**
zh as in vi**s**ion, mea**s**ure

excommunicate (ek-skuh-MYOO-nuh-kayt) to cut someone off, such as from the Roman Catholic Church

expansionism (ik-SPAN-shuh-ni-zum) the desire and attempt to expand a country's territory and/or influence

experiments (ik-SPER-uh-munts) activities designed to test a scientific idea or theory

explorers (ik-SPLOR-urz) a term for sailors who explored during the Age of Exploration

Factory Act (FAK-tuh-ree AKT) an 1819 British law that limited working hours for children

factory system (FAK-tuh-ree SIS-tum) production done in factories with workers who earn wages

feudalism (FYOO-dul-i-zum) the system of government in Europe during most of the Middle Ages

firearms (FYR-arms) weapons introduced to Japan by European traders

First Agricultural Revolution (FURST a-gri-KUL-chuh-rul re-vuh-LOO-shun) the great change from a wandering lifestyle to a settled lifestyle based on farming

First Continental Congress (FURST kan-tun-EN-tul KON-grus) the meeting of American colonists to demand fair treatment by Britain

First Estate (FURST is-TAYT) a class of French people made up of religious officials

---

PRONUNCIATION KEY

CAPITAL LETTERS show the stressed syllables.

a	as in m**a**t	f	as in **f**it
ay	as in d**ay**, s**ay**	g	as in **g**o
ch	as in **ch**ew	i	as in s**i**t
e	as in b**e**d	j	as in **j**ob, **g**em
ee	as in **e**ven, **ea**sy, n**ee**d	k	as in **c**ool, **k**ey

First Global Age (FURST GLOH-bul AYJ) a time when people from many parts of the globe interacted

"the first humanists" (THUH FURST HYOO-muh-nists) a term that refers to Petrarch and Boccaccio

Florida Cession (FLOR-uh-duh SE-shun) land obtained by the United States from Spain

flying shuttle (FLY-ing SHUH-tul) an early machine that could weave automatically

foot binding (FUHT BYND-ing) the practice of crippling women, common in urban areas during the Qing dynasty

forecastle (FOHR-ka-sul) the front castle of a ship

Fountain of Youth (FOWN-tun UV YOOTH) a mythical pool whose waters restore youth

49th parallel (FOR-tee-ninth PAR-uh-lel) the parallel that marked the northern boundary of the United States

fourth voyage (FORTH VOY-ij) Columbus's fourth trip, during which he hoped to find a sea passage through the Americas to Asia

frame and plank construction (FRAYM AND PLANK kun-STRUK-shun) an efficient method of constructing strong, light ships

free enterprise system (FREE EN-tur-pryz SIS-tum) an economy where everyone is free to make choices and profits

---

PRONUNCIATION KEY

CAPITAL LETTERS show the stressed syllables.

ng as in runni**ng**

o as in c**o**t, f**a**ther

oh as in g**o**, n**o**te

oo as in t**oo**

sh as in **sh**y

th as in **th**in

u as in b**u**t, s**o**me

uh as in **a**bout, tak**e**n, lem**o**n, penc**i**l

ur as in t**er**m

y as in l**i**ne, fl**y**

zh as in vi**s**ion, mea**s**ure

free states (FREE STAYTS) U.S. states where slavery was illegal

French and Indian War (FRENCH AND IN-dee-un WOR) a war between the French and the British in North America

French Revolution (FRENCH re-vuh-LOO-shun) a revolution in France that took place between 1789 and 1799

full-rigged ship (FUL-RIGD SHIP) a type of ship used by explorers during the Age of Exploration

Gadsden Purchase (GADZ-dun PUR-chus) the purchase of land by the United States from Mexico

galleon (GA-lee-un) a large, armed trading ship

geocentric system (jee-oh-SEN-trik SIS-tum) the idea that Earth is at the center of the universe

global (GLOH-bul) worldwide

Great Peace of the Tokugawas (GRAYT PEES UV THUH to-ku-GA-wuhz) a term that refers to the lack of internal conflict in Japan during the Tokugawa shogunate

Great Wall of China (GRAYT WAL UV CHY-nuh) a huge wall built in northern China to keep out invaders from the north

gurus (GOO-rooz) teachers of the Sikh religion

hand loom (HAND LOOM) a framework on which threads are woven together to make cloth

---

PRONUNCIATION KEY

CAPITAL LETTERS show the stressed syllables.

a as in m**a**t

ay as in d**ay**, s**ay**

ch as in **ch**ew

e as in b**e**d

ee as in **e**ven, **ea**sy, n**ee**d

f as in **f**it

g as in **g**o

i as in s**i**t

j as in **j**ob, **g**em

k as in **c**ool, **k**ey

hara-kiri (har-i-KIR-ee) another name for *seppuku*

heliocentric system (hee-lee-oh-SEN-trik SIS-tum) the idea that Earth and the other planets orbit the Sun

Hinduism (HIN-doo-i-zum) a set of spiritual beliefs held by many people in India

humanism (HYOO-muh-ni-zum) thinking and work that concentrates on human life in the human world; intellectual core of the Renaissance that contrasted with the focus on theology during the Middle Ages

the Hundred Days (THUH HUN-drud DAYS) the period of Napoleon's rule from his return from Elba to his defeat at Waterloo

Hunting and Gathering Age (HUNT-ing AND GA-thuh-ring AYJ) the first great era of human history

ideal communities (y-DEEL kuh-MYOO-nuh-teez) small communities founded on socialist ideas

imperialism (im-PIR-ee-uh-li-zum) a country's desire and attempts to dominate and control other nations and peoples

Inca Empire (ING-kuh EM-pyr) a great South American Indian empire conquered by Pizarro

Indian National Congress (IN-dee-un NA-shuh-nul KON-grus) a group of Indian leaders opposed to British rule

---

PRONUNCIATION KEY

CAPITAL LETTERS show the stressed syllables.

ng	as in runni**ng**	u	as in b**u**t, s**o**me
o	as in c**o**t, f**a**ther	uh	as in **a**bout, tak**e**n, lem**o**n, penc**i**l
oh	as in g**o**, n**o**te	ur	as in t**er**m
oo	as in t**oo**	y	as in l**i**ne, fl**y**
sh	as in **sh**y	zh	as in vi**s**ion, mea**s**ure
th	as in **th**in		

Indian Removal Act (IN-dee-un ri-MOO-vul AKT) the law that gave the U.S. president the authority to move Indians to the west of the Mississippi River

Indians (IN-dee-unz) Native Americans; a name given them by Columbus

industrial (in-DUS-tree-ul) having to do with industry

Industrial Age (in-DUS-tree-ul AYJ) the third great era of human history, brought about by the Industrial Revolution

industrial cities (in-DUS-tree-ul SI-teez) cities built around industries

Industrial Revolution (in-DUS-tree-ul re-vuh-LOO-shun) the great change within industry in the 1700s and 1800s

industrialization (in-dus-tree-uh-luh-ZAY-shun) the process of changing from an economy based on agriculture to one based on industry

industrialized (in-DUS-tree-uh-lyzd) a term used to describe a country whose industry is widespread and important

industry (IN-dus-tree) the production of goods

Inquisition (in-kwuh-ZI-shun) an arm of the Roman Catholic Church set up to investigate people who contradicted church teachings

iron (y-urn) a versatile metal used for many tools and machines of the Industrial Revolution

Islam (is-LOM) a religion founded in Arabia that believes in one God, Allah

---

PRONUNCIATION KEY

CAPITAL LETTERS show the stressed syllables.

a	as in m**a**t	f	as in **f**it
ay	as in d**ay**, s**ay**	g	as in **g**o
ch	as in **ch**ew	i	as in s**i**t
e	as in b**e**d	j	as in **j**ob, **g**em
ee	as in **e**ven, **ea**sy, n**ee**d	k	as in **c**ool, **k**ey

Italian Renaissance (uh-TAL-yun re-nuh-SONTS) the early part of the Renaissance, when ideas such as humanism were taking hold in Italy

Japanese feudalism (ja-puh-NEEZ FYOO-dul-i-zum) a system of government in which power is held by the daimyos, a shogun, and a figurehead emperor

laissez-faire (le-say-FAYR) the idea that the government should not interfere in the economy; that the government should "let it be"

The Last Supper (THUH LAST SUH-pur) a famous painting by Leonardo da Vinci

lateen sail (luh-TEEN SAYL) an efficient triangular sail

law of competition (LO UV kam-puh-TI-shun) a natural law of economics

law of supply and demand (LO UV suh-PLY AND di-MAND) a natural law of economics

laws of planetary motion (LOZ UV PLA-nuh-ter-ee MOH-shun) rules put forth by Kepler about the orbits of planets

legitimacy (li-JI-tuh-muh-see) a principle of the Congress of Vienna that said the rightful rulers of Europe were nobles and ruling families

Lewis and Clark expedition (LEW-is AND KLARK EKS-puh-di-shun) 1801 expedition to explore the new lands of the Louisiana Purchase

liberal (LI-brul) someone who believes in the principles of liberalism

---

PRONUNCIATION KEY

CAPITAL LETTERS show the stressed syllables.

ng	as in runni**ng**	u	as in b**u**t, s**o**me
o	as in c**o**t, f**a**ther	uh	as in **a**bout, tak**e**n, lem**o**n, penc**il**
oh	as in g**o**, n**o**te	ur	as in t**er**m
oo	as in t**oo**	y	as in l**i**ne, fl**y**
sh	as in **sh**y	zh	as in vi**s**ion, mea**s**ure
th	as in **th**in		

liberalism (LI-bruh-li-zum) the belief in the principles of freedom and equality and the rule of laws under a constitution

"the Liberator" (THUH LI-buh-RAY-tur) the name given to honor Simón Bolívar of South America

Louisiana Purchase (loo-ee-zee-A-nuh PUR-chus) the American purchase of Louisiana from France

Lowell Girls (LOH-ul GURLZ) female workers in the Lowell mills

Luddites (LUH-dyts) British workers who rioted in many industrial cities

Manchus (MAN-chooz) the people of Manchuria united under Nurhachi

manifest destiny (MA-nuh-fest DES-tuh-nee) the belief that the United States was destined to own all the land between the Atlantic Coast and the Pacific Coast

manorialism (MA-nor-ee-ul-i-zum) the economic system, based on the manor, of the Middle Ages

Marathas (muh-RA-tuhz) a Hindu group that retook most of central and western India after Aurangzeb's death

Marxism (MARK-si-zum) Marx's ideas

Marxists (MARK-sists) believers in Marxism

means of production (MEENS UV pruh-DUK-shun) the tools, equipment, and investment money used to produce goods

---

PRONUNCIATION KEY

CAPITAL LETTERS show the stressed syllables.

a	as in m**a**t	f	as in **f**it
ay	as in d**ay**, s**ay**	g	as in **g**o
ch	as in **ch**ew	i	as in s**i**t
e	as in b**e**d	j	as in **j**ob, **g**em
ee	as in **e**ven, **ea**sy, n**ee**d	k	as in **c**ool, **k**ey

mechanical universe (mi-KA-ni-kul YOO-nuh-vurs) the idea that the universe operates like a clock, according to universal laws

mechanization (me-kuh-nuh-ZAY-shun) the use of automated machinery to increase production

Meiji Restoration (MAY-jee res-tuh-RAY-shun) the restoration of the emperor in Japan in 1868

mercantilism (MUR-kun-tul-li-zum) the idea of having colonies exist solely for the benefit of the home country

Metternich system (ME-tur-nik SIS-tum) the cooperation of European governments to put down liberal uprisings

Mexican Cession (MEK-si-kun SE-shun) land obtained by the United States as a result of the Mexican War

Mexican War (MEK-si-kun WOR) a war between the United States and Mexico, 1846–1848

middle class (MI-dul KLAS) a class of traders and merchants who were richer than peasants but poorer than nobles

migration (my-GRAY-shun) the movement of people

military imperialism (MI-luh-ter-ee im-PIR-ee-uh-li-zum) the taking control of countries militarily

mills (MILZ) textile factories

PRONUNCIATION KEY

CAPITAL LETTERS show the stressed syllables.

ng	as in runni**ng**	u	as in b**u**t, s**o**me
o	as in c**o**t, f**a**ther	uh	as in **a**bout, tak**e**n, lem**o**n, penc**i**l
oh	as in g**o**, n**o**te	ur	as in t**er**m
oo	as in t**oo**	y	as in l**i**ne, fl**y**
sh	as in **sh**y	zh	as in vi**s**ion, mea**s**ure
th	as in **th**in		

Minamoto shogunate (mi-na-MOH-toh SHOH-guh-nut) the period during which Minamotos controlled the Japanese shogunate

Ming dynasty (MING DY-nuh-stee) a dynasty of Chinese rulers that lasted from 1368 to 1644

missionaries (MI-shuh-ner-eez) Christians trying to spread their faith

missions (MI-shunz) Spanish churches established to spread Christianity

modernize (MO-dur-nyz) to adopt new ideas and technologies

Mogul Empire (MOH-gul EM-pyr) an empire created by Babur the Tiger that ruled India when European trade was established there

Moguls (MOH-gulz) descendants of the Mongols who ruled in India

Mona Lisa (MOH-nuh LEE-suh) a famous painting by Leonardo da Vinci

Morse Code (MORS KOHD) a series of dots and dashes used to send messages over telegraph lines

Mundus Novus (MUN-dus NOH-vus) Amerigo Vespucci's written account of his voyages

Napoleonic Era (nuh-POH-lee-O-nik ER-uh) a period of French and European history during which Napoleon ruled France

Napoleonic Wars (nuh-POH-lee-O-nik WORZ) wars between France, led by Napoleon, and other European powers from 1803 to 1815

National Assembly (NA-shuh-nul uh-SEM-blee) the governmental body created to replace the Estates-General in France

---

PRONUNCIATION KEY

CAPITAL LETTERS show the stressed syllables.

a	as in m**a**t	f	as in **f**it
ay	as in d**ay**, s**ay**	g	as in **g**o
ch	as in **ch**ew	i	as in s**i**t
e	as in b**e**d	j	as in **j**ob, **g**em
ee	as in **e**ven, **ea**sy, n**ee**d	k	as in **c**ool, **k**ey

National Convention (NA-shuh-nul kun-VEN-shun) the governmental body that declared France a republic

National Woman Suffrage Association (NA-shuh-nul wuh-mun SUH-frij uh-soh-see-AY-shun) a group that worked to get women the right to vote

nationalism (NA-shuh-nuh-li-zum) the desire of a people to have an independent country

natural laws of economics (NA-chuh-rul LOZ UV e-kuh-NO-miks) ideas that economies operate in permanent and unchangeable ways

Niña (NEE-nyuh) one of the three ships on Columbus's first voyage

Nineteenth Amendment (nyn-TEENTH uh-MEND-munt) the amendment to the U.S. Constitution that granted women the right to vote

Ninety-five Theses (NYN-tee-fyv THEE-seez) a document in which Martin Luther denounced the corruption of the Roman Catholic Church

Northwest Ordinance (north-WEST OR-dun-unts) the law that describes how territories become states

Northwest Passage (north-WEST PA-sij) a hoped-for sea passage from the Atlantic Ocean through the New World to the Pacific Ocean

notebooks (NOHT-buhks) refers to the notebooks kept by Leonardo da Vinci in which he recorded and sketched many of his ideas

PRONUNCIATION KEY

CAPITAL LETTERS show the stressed syllables.

ng as in runni**ng**

o as in c**o**t, f**a**ther

oh as in g**o**, n**o**te

oo as in t**oo**

sh as in **sh**y

th as in **th**in

u as in b**u**t, s**o**me

uh as in **a**bout, tak**e**n, lem**o**n, penc**il**

ur as in t**er**m

y as in l**i**ne, fl**y**

zh as in vi**s**ion, mea**s**ure

observation (ob-sur-VAY-shun) the careful, objective looking at a subject; a characteristic of modern science

Open Door Policy (OH-pun DOHR PO-luh-see) a policy proposed by the United States that opened all areas of China to trade with all nations

opening of Japan (OH-pun-ing UV juh-PAN) Japan's decision to again open the country to foreigners

opium (OH-pee-um) an addictive drug traded by the British in China

Oregon Country Cession (OR-i-gun KUN-tree SE-shun) land obtained by the United States from Britain

Ottoman Empire (O-tuh-mun EM-pyr) (1299–1923) empire centered in Turkey that at one time stretched from the Persian Gulf to the Balkans

peaceful resistance (PEES-ful ri-ZIS-tunts) one way Africans resisted European imperialism

philosopher (fuh-LO-suh-fur) someone who thinks and writes about important ideas of human existence

Pinta (PIN-tuh) one of the three ships on Columbus's first voyage

plantations (plan-TAY-shunz) large European farms in the New World

political imperialism (puh-LI-ti-kul im-PIR-ee-uh-li-zum) the taking over or manipulation of foreign governments

porcelain (POHR-suh-lun) an important Chinese trade good made of ceramic

---

PRONUNCIATION KEY

CAPITAL LETTERS show the stressed syllables.

a	as in m**a**t	f	as in **f**it
ay	as in d**ay**, s**ay**	g	as in **g**o
ch	as in **ch**ew	i	as in s**i**t
e	as in b**e**d	j	as in **j**ob, **g**em
ee	as in **e**ven, **ea**sy, n**ee**d	k	as in **c**ool, **k**ey

proletariat (proh-luh-TER-ee-ut) working-class people

Protestant ethic (PRO-tus-tunt E-thik) a way of life based on Protestant beliefs and teachings

Protestants (PRO-tus-tunts) people who follow the Christian religious ideas first put forth during the Reformation

Ptolemaic system (ta-luh-MAY-ik SIS-tum) another name for the geocentric system

Puritans (PYUR-uh-tunz) English Protestants who denied the authority of the Anglican Church

Qing dynasty (CHING DY-nuh-stee) a Manchu dynasty in China that lasted from 1644 to 1911

Quadruple Alliance (kwa-DROO-pul uh-LY-unts) the alliance of Great Britain, Prussia, Russia, and Austria

Quetzalcoatl (ket-sul-kuh-WO-tul) an Aztec god

queue (KYOO) a hairstyle Manchus forced Chinese men to wear during the Qing dynasty

racism (RAY-si-zum) a prejudice against people of other races

rational will (RA-shuh-nul WIL) the ability of people to think and act rationally, according to reason; a basic belief of thinkers of the Age of Reason

reaper (REE-pur) a harvesting machine

PRONUNCIATION KEY

CAPITAL LETTERS show the stressed syllables.

ng as in runni**ng**
o as in c**o**t, f**a**ther
oh as in g**o**, n**o**te
oo as in t**oo**
sh as in **sh**y
th as in **th**in
u as in b**u**t, s**o**me
uh as in **a**bout, tak**e**n, lem**o**n, penc**il**
ur as in t**er**m
y as in l**i**ne, fl**y**
zh as in vi**si**on, mea**s**ure

reason (REE-zun) the human ability to think rationally

recorded (ri-KORD-ed) refers to writing down an observation; characteristic of modern science

Red River Cession (RED RI-vur SE-shun) the British Cession

Red Shirts (RED SHURTS) Garibaldi's soldiers

reform movement (ri-FORM MOOV-munt) an attempt to change existing conditions

Reformation (re-fur-MAY-shun) the great religious revolution of the 1500s that challenged the Roman Catholic Church and led to the development of Protestantism

Reign of Terror (RAYN UV TER-ur) the term for the harsh rule of the Committee of Public Safety during the French Revolution

religious imperialism (ri-LI-jus im-PIR-ee-uh-li-zum) the spread of influence through the use of religion

"Remember the *Maine*!" (ri-MEM-bur THUH MAYN) an American war cry of the Spanish-American War

Renaissance (re-nuh-SONTS) the era of European history after the Middle Ages, marked by great advancements in the arts and scholarship

revolution (re-vuh-LOO-shun) the overthrow of an established government

---

PRONUNCIATION KEY

CAPITAL LETTERS show the stressed syllables.

a	as in m**a**t	f	as in **f**it
ay	as in d**ay**, s**ay**	g	as in **g**o
ch	as in **ch**ew	i	as in s**i**t
e	as in b**e**d	j	as in **j**ob, **g**em
ee	as in **e**ven, **ea**sy, n**ee**d	k	as in **c**ool, **k**ey

revolution of the proletariat (re-vuh-LOO-shun UV THUH proh-luh-TER-ee-ut) the takeover of the means of production and of the government by the working class

roller-spinning machine (ROH-lur-spin-ing muh-SHEEN) an early mechanized spinning machine invented by Lewis Paul

Roman Catholic Church (ROH-min KATH-lik CHURCH) the Christian church that had its seat in Rome; the only Christian church before the Reformation

Romantic Movement (roh-MAN-tik MOOV-munt) a literary and an artistic movement that emphasized feelings and the beauty of life

Romanticism (roh-MAN-tuh-si-zum) another name for the Romantic Movement

Rough Riders (RUF RY-durz) Theodore Roosevelt's soldiers in the Spanish-American War

rudder (RUH-dur) a device used to steer ships

sale of indulgences (SAYL UV in-DUL-juns-ez) a practice of the Roman Catholic Church in which people could purchase indulgences, or pardons, from their sins

samurai (SA-muh-ry) warriors and the warrior class of feudal Japan

Santa Maria (SAN-tuh muh-REE-uh) one of the three ships on Columbus's first voyage

---

PRONUNCIATION KEY

CAPITAL LETTERS show the stressed syllables.

ng as in runni**ng**

o as in c**o**t, f**a**ther

oh as in g**o**, n**o**te

oo as in t**oo**

sh as in **sh**y

th as in **th**in

u as in b**u**t, s**o**me

uh as in **a**bout, tak**e**n, lem**o**n, penc**i**l

ur as in t**er**m

y as in l**i**ne, fl**y**

zh as in vi**s**ion, mea**s**ure

The School of Athens (SKOOL UV A-thunz) a famous painting by Raphael

science (SY-unts) a way of gaining knowledge by making observations, identifying and recording facts, and organizing these facts into a system

"scramble for Africa" (SKRAM-bul FOR A-fri-kuh) Europeans' attempts to control Africa

scurvy (SKUR-vee) a disease that killed many sailors during the Age of Exploration

sea dogs (SEE DOGZ) English sea captains who raided Portuguese and Spanish ships

sea route (SEE ROOT) a path followed by ships at sea

secede (si-SEED) to withdraw

Second Agricultural Revolution (SE-kund a-gri-KUL-chuh-rul re-vuh-LOO-shun) a period of important changes in agriculture in the 1700s

Second Estate (SE-kund is-TAYT) a class of French people made up of nobles

second voyage (SE-kund VOY-ij) Columbus's second trip, during which he founded the settlement of Isabella

Seneca Falls Convention (SE-ni-kuh FOLS kun-VEN-shun) a U.S. women's movement convention of 1848

PRONUNCIATION KEY

CAPITAL LETTERS show the stressed syllables.

a	as in m**a**t	f	as in **f**it
ay	as in d**ay**, s**ay**	g	as in **g**o
ch	as in **ch**ew	i	as in s**i**t
e	as in b**e**d	j	as in **j**ob, **g**em
ee	as in **e**ven, **ea**sy, n**ee**d	k	as in **c**ool, **k**ey

separation of powers (se-puh-RAY-shun UV POW-urs) the idea that the powers of government should be divided among different branches

seppuku (se-POO-koo) ritual suicide of the samurai

shogun (SHOH-gun) a general of Japan

shogunate (SHOH-guh-nut) Japanese government under the shogun

Sikhism (SEE-ki-zum) a new religion founded by Nanak that blended elements of Islam and Hinduism

slave states (SLAYV STAYTS) U.S. states where slavery was legal

slave trade (SLAYV TRAYD) the term for the European trade in African slaves

smelting (SMELT-ing) the process of separating iron from other materials in rock

social changes (SOH-shul CHAYNJ-ez) major changes in the way people live in society

socialism (SOH-shuh-li-zum) a political and an economic idea that governments, rather than private citizens, should run the means of production

socialists (SOH-shuh-lists) believers in socialism

South Sea (SOWTH SEE) Spain's original name for the Pacific Ocean

sphere of influence (SFEER UV IN-floo-unts) a region in which one foreign country has special economic and political powers

---

PRONUNCIATION KEY

CAPITAL LETTERS show the stressed syllables.

ng as in runni**ng**
o as in c**o**t, f**a**ther
oh as in g**o**, n**o**te
oo as in t**oo**
sh as in **sh**y
th as in **th**in
u as in b**u**t, s**o**me
uh as in **a**bout, tak**e**n, lem**o**n, penc**i**l
ur as in t**er**m
y as in l**i**ne, fl**y**
zh as in vi**s**ion, mea**s**ure

spinning (SPIN-ing) the process of turning raw fiber into thread and yarn

spinning jenny (SPIN-ing JEN-ee) a spinning machine invented by James Hargreaves

spinning mule (SPIN-ing MYOOL) an efficient spinning machine invented by Samuel Crompton

spinning wheel (SPIN-ing WHEEL) a foot-powered machine that spins raw material, such as cotton or wool, into thread

state (STAYT) a political unit of the United States that has special powers

steam engine (STEEM EN-jun) a machine powered by the steam from boiling water; one of the two most important inventions of the Industrial Revolution

steam-powered loom (STEEM-POW-urd LOOM) a weaving machine powered by a steam engine; invented by Edmund Cartwright

sterncastle (STERN KA-sul) the back castle of a ship

Strait of Magellan (STRAYT UV muh-JE-lun) the strait through which Magellan sailed from the Atlantic Ocean to the Pacific Ocean

strikes (STRYKS) refusals of workers to work until their demands are met

suffrage (SUH-frij) the right to vote

suffragists (SUF-ri-jists) people who fought for women's suffrage

telegraph (TE-luh-graf) a communication device that sends coded electrical signals over wires

---

PRONUNCIATION KEY

CAPITAL LETTERS show the stressed syllables.

a	as in m**a**t	f	as in **f**it
ay	as in d**ay**, s**ay**	g	as in **g**o
ch	as in **ch**ew	i	as in s**i**t
e	as in b**e**d	j	as in **j**ob, **g**em
ee	as in **e**ven, **ea**sy, n**ee**d	k	as in **c**ool, **k**ey

Ten Hours Act (TEN OWRZ AKT) an 1847 British law that limited the work day to ten hours

tenement houses (TE-nuh-munt HOW-sez) unsafe, poorly maintained apartment buildings

territory (TER-uh-tohr-ee) an area of land owned and governed by the United States that is eligible to become a state

Texas Annexation (TEK-sus a-nek-SAY-shun) the addition of Texas to the United States

textile industry (TEK-styl IN-dus-tree) the industry that makes cloth and clothing; the Industrial Revolution began in Britain in the textile industry

theology (thee-O-luh-jee) the study of God; primary pursuit of scholars during the Middle Ages

Third Estate (THURD is-TAYT) a class of French people made up of middle-class merchants, government officials, and peasants

third voyage (THURD VOY-ij) Columbus's third trip, during which he landed in South America

Thirteenth Amendment (thur-TEENTH uh-MEND-munt) the amendment to the U.S. Constitution that abolished slavery

Tokugawa shogunate (TOH-ku-GA-wuh SHOH-guh-nut) the period of Japanese history when shoguns came from the Tokugawa family

trade (TRAYD) the buying and selling of goods

PRONUNCIATION KEY

CAPITAL LETTERS show the stressed syllables.

ng	as in runni**ng**	u	as in b**u**t, s**o**me
o	as in c**o**t, f**a**ther	uh	as in **a**bout, tak**e**n, lem**o**n, penc**il**
oh	as in g**o**, n**o**te	ur	as in t**er**m
oo	as in t**oo**	y	as in l**i**ne, fl**y**
sh	as in **sh**y	zh	as in vi**s**ion, mea**s**ure
th	as in **th**in		

trade routes (TRAYD ROOTS) land or sea paths followed by traders

trading nations of Europe (TRAYD-ing NAY-shuns UV YUR-up) Spain, France, England, Portugal, and the Netherlands

trading station (TRAYD-ing STAY-shun) a small compound of buildings where traders lived, goods were stored, and trades took place

Trail of Tears (TRAYL UV TEERS) the forced march of the Cherokee people to the west of the Mississippi River

Transportation Revolution (trans-pur-TAY-shun re-vuh-LOO-shun) great advances made in transportation in the late 1700s and early 1800s

treaties (TREE-teez) formal agreements between two or more groups or nations

Treaty of Guadalupe Hidalgo (TREE-tee UV gwa-dul-OOP hi-DAL-goh) the treaty that ended the Mexican War and created the Mexican Cession

Treaty of Kanagawa (TREE-tee UV ka-NA-ga-wa) a United States-Japanese treaty that opened Japan, ending 200 years of isolation

Treaty of Paris (TREE-tee UV PAR-us) the 1783 treaty that recognized American independence, ending the American Revolution; the 1898 treaty that ended the Spanish-American War

Treaty of Portsmouth (TREE-tee UV POHRTS-muth) a treaty that ended the Russo-Japanese War

triangular trade (tri-ANG-yoo-lur TRAYD) trade among Europe, Africa, and the Americas; refers to the exchange of cheap goods from Europe, slaves from Africa, and products from the New World

---

PRONUNCIATION KEY

CAPITAL LETTERS show the stressed syllables.

a	as in m**a**t	f	as in **f**it
ay	as in d**ay**, s**ay**	g	as in **g**o
ch	as in **ch**ew	i	as in s**i**t
e	as in b**e**d	j	as in **j**ob, **g**em
ee	as in **e**ven, **ea**sy, n**ee**d	k	as in **c**ool, **k**ey

U.S.S. *Maine* (YOO ES ES MAYN) an American battleship sunk in the harbor of Havana, Cuba

unequal treaties (un-EE-kwul TREE-tees) a Chinese term for the treaties China was forced to sign with foreign governments

unions (YOON-yuns) workers' organizations

universal laws (yoo-nuh-VUR-sul LOZ) rules that govern nature and people; a basic belief of thinkers of the Age of Reason

urban working class (UR-bun WURK-ing KLAS) a new social class brought about by the Industrial Revolution

urbanization (ur-buh-nuh-ZAY-shun) the growth of towns and cities

utopian socialists (yoo-TOH-pee-un SOH-shuh-lists) supporters of ideal communities

viceroys (VYS-rohys) Spanish governors in the New World

water frame (WO-tur FRAYM) an efficient spinning machine invented by Richard Arkwright

weakened France (WEEK-und FRANTS) a principle of the Congress of Vienna that aimed to keep rulers of France from becoming powerful enough to be a threat to other nations in Europe

weaving (WEEV-ing) the process of combining threads to make cloth

women's movement (WI-muns MOOV-munt) the struggle of women for political and social power

---

PRONUNCIATION KEY

CAPITAL LETTERS show the stressed syllables.

ng	as in runni**ng**	u	as in b**u**t, s**o**me
o	as in c**o**t, f**a**ther	uh	as in **a**bout, tak**e**n, lem**o**n, penc**i**l
oh	as in g**o**, n**o**te	ur	as in t**er**m
oo	as in t**oo**	y	as in l**i**ne, fl**y**
sh	as in **sh**y	zh	as in vi**s**ion, mea**s**ure
th	as in **th**in		

INDEX